Elections and

Democracy

in Central

America

Elections and

Democracy

in Central

America

Edited by John A. Booth and Mitchell A. Seligson

The
University
of North
Carolina
Press
Chapel Hill
and London

© 1989 The University of North Carolina Press

All rights reserved

Manufactured in the United States of America

The paper in this book meets the guidelines for permanence and durability of the Committee on Production Guidelines for Book Longevity of the Council on Library Resources.

93 92 91 90 89 5 4 3 2 1

Library of Congress Cataloging-in-Publication Data

Elections and democracy in Central America.

   Includes index.
   1. Elections—Central America. I. Booth, John A.
II. Seligson, Mitchell A.
JL1418.E44   1989   324.9728′053   88-28089
ISBN 0-8078-1843-7 (alk. paper)
ISBN 0-8078-4249-4 (pbk.: alk. paper)

To Margaret Booth Dunnington

and Louis A. Seligson

Contents

Elections and

Democracy

in Central

America

Introduction

From Uncertainty to Uncertainty

The Institutionalization of
Elections in Central America

Mitchell A. Seligson

"The process of establishing a democracy is a process of institutionalizing uncertainty. . . ."—Adam Przeworski, "Some Problems in the Study of the Transition to Democracy"

For at least the past five centuries, Central Americans have lived in a highly uncertain world. The basic necessities of life, food, clothing, and shelter, so long taken for granted by the great majority of their North American neighbors, have never been assured to Central Americans. While journalistic accounts stress the poverty of the region as it stands today, and blame it for some, if not all, of the current civil strife, impoverishment has been an almost constant feature of life in Central America throughout its recorded history.

Indeed, although most agree that the Spanish conquest and colonization exploited the region unmercifully and, more important, produced a series of pandemics that decimated the native population, poverty and starvation were prominent in the isthmus long before the arrival of the Spaniards. Hence, although the debates among archaeologists have yet to be definitively resolved, the disappearance of the Mayan civilization in Guatemala *prior* to the arrival of the Spanish colonizers is generally linked to the failure of the fragile ecology of the land to support its growing population. In short, the uncertainty of survival is not a novel condition in Central America.

But if survival has been characterized by extreme uncertainty in Central America, politics has been highly predictable, indeed, almost totally certain in one regard. For centuries, there was never much doubt as to who would rule these mini-states: soldiers, strongmen, and foreign armies. Rarely did popular sentiment play an important role. While it is true that since Independence in the nineteenth century elections were held from time to time, literacy, property, and gender restrictions excluded most citizens from the electoral process through the 1940s.

Even when the electorates were expanded, elections were canceled and citizens told that it was in the "national interest" to postpone the "disruptive process" until a more propitious moment arrived. When elections did occur, votes were bought or coerced, ballot boxes were stuffed, and vote totals fudged. On numerous occasions elections were interrupted at the counting stage or the winners were deposed in favor of the army's preferred candidates. On the whole, then, the elections themselves, such as they were, proved little, since the election process was not truly over until the soldiers, strongmen, and foreign armies had their final say. The rule of naked force proved to be the only element of political certainty.

The 1970s and 1980s have seen a new, higher level of uncertainty in the region. Never in its history has Central America undergone such widespread revolution, civil war, and foreign military intervention. The Nicaraguan Revolution and ensuing contra counterrevolution, the protracted civil war in El Salvador, and the brutal guerrilla struggle in Guatemala have caused unprecedented numbers of deaths and injuries in the civil population and created a massive refugee problem. The problem of the physical uncertainty of life has never been greater.

In this environment, the recent emergence of free, open, and competitive elections throughout the region promises to introduce an element of political uncertainty into the region, but one that is likely to be welcomed by the great majority of the population. If we accept Przeworski's often quoted definition of democracy cited in the epigraph of this chapter, democracy implies uncertainty about the outcome of each electoral episode.

For elections to be meaningful, their outcome cannot be predetermined: challengers must have the potential to beat incumbents. Institutionalization of uncertainty implies that victor and loser accept this uncertainty as a fundamental rule of the game. So long as they do not, an election becomes merely one mechanism, not *the* mechanism, for acquiring the right to rule. In that sense, then, the elections that have been occurring in Central America in the 1980s do not equate with the establishment of democracy, even though one cannot have a democratic system without elections. What the elections have the potential of doing is institutionalizing political uncertainty, a necessary but clearly not sufficient condition for democracy.

Recent elections in Central America have been fundamentally different from the great majority of those that have preceded them. With the exception of Costa Rica, a nation that fought a short, albeit bloody, civil war in the 1940s over the integrity of the electoral process, free, open, competitive, and internationally observed elections are an almost completely new phenomenon in the region. Even their harshest critics admit that these elections have been supported with great enthusiasm by the voters. But this should come as no surprise; citizens who chronically have been deprived of the right to express their political preference are understandably enthusiastic about the opportunity to do so now.

The key question that these elections leave unanswered is what long-term impact they will have on democratization in Central America. The analysis of that question is the subject of this volume. The collection is the outgrowth of a panel organized by the editors of the volume at the 1986 Congress of the Latin American Studies Association, held in Boston. The panel brought together a group of scholars who had been working in Central America long before the Sandinista Revolution and the civil war in El Salvador made the isthmus a key center of geopolitical attention for the United States government. Each of the presenters on the panel had been studying Central American politics for nearly twenty years, and some longer. While the length of their experience does not necessarily make them wiser than newcomers, it does give them a sense of perspective possibly lacking among scholars who began studying the region only after Central America became front-page news. It was with a certain sense of wry amusement that the panelists looked out upon a standing-room-only audience at the panel; these same scholars had grown accustomed to presenting papers on Central America only a decade before to audiences that were sometimes smaller than the number of panelists.

Each of the authors was asked to address the central question of the implications for democracy of the recent elections in Central America. This was a difficult task because it required the scholars to predict the impact of recent, short-term events (that is, elections) on long-term processes (that is, democratization). It was especially difficult for the Central American region for, with the exception of Costa Rica, experience with democracy had been so limited. It was further complicated by the heavy pressures of international actors and by the vagaries of the wars raging in the region.

In order to assist the authors in addressing common themes, John A. Booth prepared a framework for analysis that appears as chapter 1 of this volume. In that essay, Booth reviews various definitions of democracy, both classical and modern, and concludes that a broad definition in which democracy is seen as "popular participation in rule" is the most appropriate for understanding the Central American cases. By taking this perspective, he focuses on elections as a subset of a larger process of democratization: elections may help lead to popular participation in rule, but they do not define it. There was widespread agreement among the authors on this point. This was, however, perhaps the only area in which they agreed. Since several of the authors are expert in more than one country in the region, there was an overlapping of expertise but often a disagreement among them as to the implications of the recent elections for the process of democratization in general and in particular countries.

The authors do not arrive at a consensus in this volume and the reader should not expect to find one. This lack of consensus should come as no surprise to anyone familiar with the literature on Central America, or, for that matter, the literature on democracy. The rapidity of change in the region, along with the heavy dose of international involvement, has given rise to widely differing analyses, and there are contending ideological models for democracy in conflict in Central America. Unfortunately, many recent publications on the region have been more polemical than substantive. The contributions in this volume concentrate on substance.

In spite of their frequent disagreements over interpretation, each of the authors addresses some or all of six questions Booth poses in his introductory essay. He derives these questions from his review of the definitions of democracy, and, taken as a group, the questions enable the authors to assess the probable impact of elections on democracy. Booth's six questions, discussed in detail in chapter 1, are as follows:

1. What is the effect of the election(s) on the range of political participation?

2. What is the effect of the election(s) on the breadth of participation?

3. What is the effect of the election(s) on the depth of participation?

4. Did the election(s) occur in an environment conducive to the free exercise of full participatory rights, and was the conduct of the election(s) fair?

5. Did the election(s) consolidate or help consolidate a stable regime under democratic rules?

6. Did the election(s) contribute toward a political culture of support for participation and democratic rules?

Readers of these chapters might draw different conclusions from those presented in the papers. The questions themselves, however, should be useful for those interested in a systematic framework of analysis.

Chapter 2 looks at Honduras, often viewed as the geopolitical axis of Central America. Mark B. Rosenberg examines the shaky foundations of the transition from military to civilian rule and raises serious questions about the commitment to the institutionalization of uncertainty among some of those who have been elected to high office. José Z. García in chapter 3 then examines the history of recent elections in El Salvador and suggests a number of conditions that need to be met for the process of democratization to succeed. In chapter 4 Robert H. Trudeau emphasizes the history of state repression in Guatemala and the continued importance of the military in almost all aspects of political life. In chapter 5 Susanne Jonas contrasts the Guatemalan and Nicaraguan cases and sees Nicaragua further along the road to democratization than Guatemala. Mitchell A. Seligson and Miguel Gómez B. in chapter 6 argue that Costa Rica, Central America's only well-established democracy, has already achieved the goals implied by Booth's six questions and suggest that the central question in the Costa Rican case is forecasting the stability of democratic rule in the context of a severe economic downturn. While synthesis of these country-based studies, in the context of the fundamental disagreements expressed, is not possible, John Peeler reviews the chapters with reference to the six questions as they apply to the prospects for democracy in each of the countries treated in the volume.

Events move very quickly in Central America. At the time of the writing of this introduction new hope for peace has emerged as the "Esquipulas II" agreement signed in Guatemala in August 1987 is being implemented. Although the main focus in the agreement is the ending of regional hostilities, a key element is the call for democratization, defined as the promotion of a process of pluralist and participatory democracy along with the establishment of free and democratic elections in each of the countries. A regional truce might bring to an end the civil strife that has afflicted the area throughout this decade. It will not, however, guarantee democracy in any of the countries. Democratization is a long-term process, especially in a region that has had so little experience with it. Nonetheless, as this volume demonstrates in considerable detail, electoral democracy has rapidly emerged throughout the region. Perhaps the search for regional peace will end up producing regional democracy as well.

References

Przeworski, Adam. 1986. Some Problems in the Study of the Transition to Democracy. In *Transitions from Authoritarian Rule: Comparative Perspectives*, edited by Guillermo O'Donnell, Philippe C. Schmitter, and Laurence Whitehead. Baltimore: Johns Hopkins University Press.

1 Elections and Democracy in Central America

A Framework for Analysis

John A. Booth

Many observers regarded Marco Vinicio Cerezo Arévalo's assumption of the presidency of Guatemala in January 1986 as a signal moment in the history of Central America because it meant that, for the first time in memory, all five isthmian nations had elected governments. This remarkable "outbreak" of elected regimes in the region was part of a larger process underway throughout the hemisphere, as many South American states had also replaced military with elected civilian governments in the last decade (Drake and Silva, 1986; Malloy and Seligson, 1987; *Contemporary Marxism,* 1986).

Political scientists have long ignored the elections of Central America, except those of Costa Rica, because they have so often been either fraudulently manipulated or, if properly carried out, later overturned by military coups. It is widely assumed that elections may promote democracy, but for decades dictatorial regimes in Nicaragua, Guatemala, and El Salvador have periodically held elections that merely reinforced or justified authoritarian rule. Indeed three of the most brutal regimes in Central American history came to power through elections: those of Nicaragua's Anastasio Somoza Debayle (1967–79), Guatemala's Romeo Lucas García (1978–82), and El Salvador's Gen. Carlos Humberto Romero (1977–79).

Given the region's checkered electoral past, Central American elections in the 1980s have attracted considerable and sometimes almost astonished international attention. Many nations and nongovernmental organizations, for example, sent delegations to witness the elections in El Salvador in 1982 and 1984, Nicaragua in 1984, and Guatemala in 1985. Several nations and various international political party organizations contributed financial support and technical advice to Central American election agencies and parties.

Among countries outside the region, the United States has taken the liveliest interest in recent Central American elections. The Reagan administration has encouraged and supported—using diplomatic, financial, and political means—the holding of elections and the transition from military to civilian regimes in Honduras, El Salvador, and Guatemala. President Reagan has also taken some credit for what he calls the "democratization" of Central America and has sought to take advantage of this process of return to civilian rule to win support in the U.S. Congress for his Central American policies (U.S. Department of State, 1987:12–17). The Reagan administration has also worked hard to block and discredit the Nicaraguan election of 1984 (LASA, 1984:28–32).

The remarkable coincidence of so many elected regimes in Central America and the United States' active promotion of some of these elections and opposition to others—all in the name of democracy—requires that Central American elections be the subject of serious scholarly study. Opinions diverge widely among policymakers, political theorists, and students of politics, however, about the essence of democracy and the role of elections in democratic governance. Key issues we must consider, then, are what constitutes political democracy and what elections have to do with democracy.

The Problem of Defining Democracy

One problem with the relationship of elections to democracy is a chronic imprecision of terminology. Political scientists either sloppily or conflictingly define and use the term "democracy" almost as frequently as politicians distort its meaning for political purposes. It is instructive to examine three common misuses of the word before attempting to define it more precisely.

First, the term "democracy" often carries immense ideological freight. In common political parlance the word has become so broad as to be virtually meaningless. Politicians, ideologues, the media, and scholars apply it to political systems as diverse as the United States, Mexico, the Soviet Union, and El Salvador. Democracy has become a word like those used by Humpty Dumpty—employed to mean precisely what the speaker of the moment intends it to mean, no more and no less.

Second, many persons tend to equate democracy with elections alone. In this very narrow approach, the label "democratic" is applied to any political system in which citizens may take part in electing their leaders. In this understanding, democracy is akin to a state of political grace that may be attained solely by holding elections. Overlooked in this approach are the key facts of political power and the ability of citizens to influence decisions. Central America has such a long history of militaries overthrowing elected regimes and dictators manipulating elections that no one should give credence to such a simpleminded equation.

Two personal experiences help illustrate how vexing these problems can be to one trying to understand or explain the real political world of contemporary Central America. I served on election observation delegations to the national elections of Nicaragua (1984) and Guatemala (1985). By my estimation, those of the observer teams, and the assessments of other election observers, both the Nicaraguan and Guatemalan elections were technically and administratively very similar and virtually without significant fraud (LASA, 1984; Booth et al., 1985). Nevertheless, President Reagan described the election in Nicaragua as a "Soviet-style sham" (New York Times, 20 July 1984), while the U.S. Department of State described the election in Guatemala as the "final step in the reestablishment of democracy there" (U.S. Department of State, 1985:2). Thus, the U.S. government, pursuing different policy ends in each circumstance, displayed astounding disregard for both fact and the electoral context of each case in order to describe apparently very similar events in radically different ways. Such political distortions by the influential and powerful badly obscure the meaning of these particular elections and their possible contribution to democracy in Central America.

In a similarly confounding way, the 1982 and 1984 Salvadoran elections are always described by the U.S. government as very "democratic," even though others regard them as deeply flawed (Herman and Brodhead, 1984:93–153). To further confuse things, some observers contend that Nicaragua's 1984 election consolidated democracy there, while Guatemala's 1985 and El Salvador's 1982 and 1984 elections were merely manipulated from outside to permit the United States to send military aid to their governments (Herman and Brodhead, 1984; Jonas, 1986:i–v; Petras, 1986:1–15; Rabine, 1986:59–64). Indeed, in the Salvadoran and Guatemalan cases, some critics contend that their recent elections actually solidified antidemocratic rule and undermined progress toward democracy. This contention cannot be easily disregarded, given the number of Central American dictatorships that have come to power or retained power through elections.

The virtual equation of democracy with elections is a posture that has become common in post–World War II political science in the United States. Schumpeter (1943), Berelson (1954), and Dahl (1956), among others, have argued that allegedly inherent tendencies of mass publics to be authoritarian, irrational, antidemocratic, intolerant of civil liberties, and ill informed about political issues require that mass participation in decision making be confined mainly to leadership choice in elections that are carefully managed by plural, competing elites. Thus, for many contemporary pluralist-elitist theorists, elections constitute the central element of democracy; they are the main and preferred vehicle for the participation of mass publics in politics.

Third, some would equate democracy with particular types of regime or constitutional arrangements, especially ones in which some emphasis is placed on the people. This equation occurs at two levels.

In the vernacular of the nationalist, one's own system is "democratic." In the United States, for example, most of us view our own liberal, republican, constitutional regime with its periodic public election of leaders as the world's best example of democracy. Supporters of the revolutionary socialist government of Cuba, in contrast, with equal fervor regard their own unelected government as democratic because it promotes popular participation in some decision making and administration and works toward distributive equity among the people.

Some contemporary political theorists describe particular types of regimes or particular constitutions as "democracies," although they are sometimes more precise than the man on the street. But because it is the nature of political theorists to disagree with one another, they have produced not one but a plethora of contending typologies and models of democracy. Macpherson (1977, 1966) traces liberalism through various stages of historical evolution— protective (or Lockean) democracy, developmental democracy, and equilibrium (pluralist) democracy—and contrasts them with utopian, participatory, Communist, and Third World variants. Cohen (1982) identifies individualist and socialist democracies, but describes Communism as nondemocratic. Przeworski (1985) describes social democracy as a liberal constitutional regime that would reform rather than replace capitalism, as would revolutionary socialism.

Lijphart (1984, 1977) has studied both consociational democracies in plural societies and constitutional, electoral governments. In the latter category he identifies two ideal types of democracy: majoritarian (parliamentary, fused executive and legislative authority, two-party dominance) and consensus (presidential, separation of powers, bicameral legislatures, multiparty). He finds, however, that real systems range across four actual types, two of which combine certain elements of each ideal type. Yates (1982) describes the modern U.S. system as a bureaucratic democracy, a bureaucratized twentieth-century outgrowth of the pluralist system created by the framers of the U.S. Constitution. O'Donnell et al. (1986) examine transitions from authoritarian rule to liberal, constitutional regimes in Europe and Latin America. Diamond et al. (1988) explore democracy in the Third World, focusing on sociocultural, economic, and political factors that may foster liberal, pluralist, constitutional regimes. All of these studies treat democracy in general within the pluralist-elitist approach that has constituted the mainstream of U.S. political science in recent decades and is perhaps best epitomized in Dahl's *Polyarchy* (1971).

Classical Definitions

This pluralist-elitist conception of democracy has been sharply criticized as too narrow by Bachrach (1966), Pateman (1970), and others, who charge that it distorts the original meaning of the term democracy. "Classical" democratic theorists,[1] who have had a clearer vision of democracy than most of the approaches just mentioned, may offer us a way out of this definitional thicket.

Theorists over three millennia have identified the main characteristics of democratic governance. The key elements may be discerned quickly in the root of the word itself: *demos* means the people, *kratein* means rule—rule by the people. Until obfuscation by the pluralist-elitist revisionists in the wake of World War II, the essential characteristic of democracy had generally been defined as the participation in rule of a society by its general populace. One convenient formulation of this idea treats democracy as *participation by the mass of people in a community in its governance (making and carrying out decisions)*. Political participation lies at the heart of democracy (Pateman, 1970:1–44). Such participation generally has been viewed as requiring equality of the right to participate for all sane, noncriminal adults.

Aristotle, for example, defined democracy as that constitution in which those who are both poor and free form a sovereign majority and therefore exercise some decision-making power in ruling and in judging in disputes (Aristotle, 1962:74–81). Thomas Jefferson described the version of democracy that he most preferred as a "government by its citizens in mass, acting directly and personally, according to rules established by the majority" (Jefferson, 1935a:83). John Stuart Mill described the "ideally best form of government" as one in which every citizen is "at least occasionally, called on to take an actual part in the government by the personal discharge of some public function, local or general" (Mill, 1958:42).

The classical theorists of democracy strongly emphasized the educative effect produced in the citizenry by participation. Mill, for example, argued that "among the foremost benefits of free government is that education of the intelligence and of the sentiments which is carried down to the very lowest ranks of the people when they are called on to take a part in acts which directly affect the great interests of their country" (Mill, 1958:128). The political ability and civic values of the individual citizen are believed to develop through participation in politics. Similarly, the political culture of the society becomes more amenable to democracy and more attentive to the collective good as citizens participate in public affairs.

The classical approach to defining democracy has several implications. First, democracy involves public participation in decision making and administration, and this participation can vary in amount and quality. Democracy, therefore, is *not a constant*—not a condition defined by the possession of certain traits, be they holding elections or having a particular sort of constitution or having a regime of the correct ideology. Rather, democracy is a *variable*. There may be more or less democracy, depending upon the amount and quality of public participation in decision making and rule in any particular system.

Because democracy is variable, it is theoretically (and at least partly practically) possible to measure how much or how little of it there is in a particular society at a given moment. This can be done by measuring and evaluating the amount and quality of political participation going on. One useful approach to evaluating the amount and nature of democracy has been formulated by Carl Cohen (1971:8–37), who identifies three dimensions of democracy. The first is the *breadth of democracy*, or the fraction of the citizenry participating in making and carrying out decisions. Breadth may vary according to the type of participation, from wide in the case of voting, for example, to rather narrow (few participating) in holding public office in most representative systems.

The second dimension is the *range* of democracy, the array of issues and decisions over which the public exercises decisions (for example, leader selection, areas subject to legislation, dispute resolution). Classical liberal polities have relatively small ranges of participation because much economic decision making is reserved for the private sector. Socialist regimes, in contrast, have a much wider range of economic activity subject to public decisions because the economy is subject to public ownership and regulation.

Cohen's third dimension is the *depth* of democracy, or the potential for efficacy and the autonomy of popular participation. Participation is deep when it truly has the potential to influence public decisions, and when it is autonomous (that is, not manipulated or controlled by others than those participating). The person or group taking part need not be efficacious (achieve his/their goals) to have deep participation, but merely have had the potential to have prevailed. One need not win in every contest or achieve every political goal, but one must have a chance to influence policy.

One critical problem of democracy is the size of the community being governed. A small community (such as a Swiss commune, a New England town, or a Central American cooperative) may be effectively ruled by direct popular action (Aristotle, 1962; Mill, 1958:213–14), but the larger the community, the more unwieldy direct participation becomes. Larger systems require representative government in order to function efficiently (Madison, 1961a:81–84, 1961b:100; Jefferson, 1935a:83; Mill, 1958:212–28). Jefferson argued that where it was impossible because of size for all to take part in governance, in order to conserve the most democracy "the powers of government, being divided, should be exercised each by representatives" (Jefferson, 1935a:83). There is a necessary loss in the breadth of democracy, however, when a small number of representatives and administrative specialists make and carry out decisions on behalf of the mass of citizens. There is a necessary loss in the depth of democracy when citizens must delegate to leaders the determination of public decisions instead of making decisions as a whole. Depth of democracy is also sacrificed when political parties and other elites mediate between specialized institutions of representative government and the mass of citizens by selecting candidates for public office and setting the agendas and terms of public debate.

For the purposes of discussion in this chapter, democracy is treated in the broader, classical sense of popular participation in rule, rather than the narrower, electoral focus associated with the position of the pluralist-elitists.

Rights and Democracy

Certain rights are essential to democracy. First, the most obvious and important, regardless of the type of political system in question, is the right to participate in public decisions. Citizens must have the effective freedom to participate in leadership choice (elections), policy decisions, and the implementation of decisions. Second, it follows that the principal condition under which the rights of one individual to participate in rule might be limited should be only to protect the fundamental right of other citizens to so participate.[2] Third, a constitution, an agreed-upon contract among citizens specifying the rules for political intercourse, is of fundamental importance to protect citizens' rights. To promote democracy, a constitution must establish the right to participate and protect that right for both majorities and minorities (whether major subgroups within the community or winners and losers on particular decisions) from encroachment by each other.

In practical terms, essential democratic rights would include the right to speak freely and to publish political opinion, the right to oppose incumbents in office and to remain safe and free, the right to associate and assemble freely for political ends, the right to petition the government, and the right to seek and win redress from abuses of authority by incumbents in power.

Regime Consolidation

The political culture of elites and masses can be critical factors conditioning democracy: the greater the proportion of a citizenry supporting and participating in public affairs, supporting key civil liberties, and agreeing on the same participatory regime (rules governing participation), the better sustained will be democracy. This same proposition is particularly true for sociopolitical elites: the greater the proportion of a society's top political, social, and economic leaders supporting citizen participation, civil liberties, and a participatory polity, the stronger and more stable will be democracy.

Peeler (1985) correctly notes that the emergence of Latin America's three long-standing liberal democracies (Colombia, Venezuela, and Costa Rica) depended upon the consolidation of a "regime," an agreement among key elites to abide by a particular set of political rules.[3] Particularly in situations of great economic inequality or in times of societal stress, elite commitment to and support for popular participation and for a participatory regime (the constitutional rules of the game) are essential. This is so because elites' control of key economic, institutional, and coercive resources would in times of stress or disagreement tempt them to restrict or suspend the participatory rights of majorities or of other minorities. To so restrict or suspend such participation, of course, would diminish both democracy and stability.

A special sort of election, which may be called "democratizing,"[4] can help consolidate a stable and lasting "regime" or constitutional system. Such a regime is a pattern of systematic expectations among groups—key elite and mass factions—that interact within a particular set of consensual political rules, both constitutional and informal. As Karl (1986:10) points out, "An enduring political democracy must rest upon a consensus which does not require that contending forces have similar programs or visions of society. Such consensus is founded on a historic compromise among major political actors and social forces." In or around a democratizing election such a regime is forged, largely among important minorities (key political and economic elites) in the polity, when they agree to accommodate each other. The forging of a regime among political and economic elites requires them to embrace and thereafter play by a set of rules of the game that includes respect for legitimate competitors' rights, acceptance of a certain amount of mass involvement in politics, a definition of the role of the state, and agreement upon means for resolution of conflict. The specific type of electoral system adopted may affect the prospects for the stability of the regime (Nohlen, 1987:17–41).

Because a truly democratizing election itself is only one small aspect of the forging of a regime, Karl (1986:9) stresses that "elections themselves do not constitute democracy," and may actually impede the creation of a regime if unfairly manipulated or if imposed by forces from outside a society. Arguing along similar lines, Herman and Brodhead (1984:5) see externally manipulated elections as barriers to democratization. They define "demonstration elections" as "organized and staged by a foreign power primarily to pacify its own restive home population, reassuring it that ongoing interventionary processes are legitimate and appreciated by their foreign objects." Their demonstration election concept can be extended to include elections held not under the aegis of an external power, but staged by a government for its own symbolic purposes (Booth, 1986:38–40). Both externally and internally managed demonstration elections would typically lack freedoms to organize, to campaign and speak freely, and to vote without coercion. An election may also liberalize without democratizing. That is, an authoritarian regime may relax its usual repression during an election for the purpose of legitimizing itself or refurbishing its image, but without truly adopting lasting participatory norms (Middlebrook, 1986; Drake and Silva, 1986; Dillon Soares, 1986; Cornelius, 1986).

Political Culture

The extent to which elections build or consolidate a political culture favorable toward popular participation in rule is also central to their importance for democracy. In a polity in which tyranny has suppressed popular and elite familiary with participation in politics, a fair and free election can encourage public commitment to participation in leadership choice, mobilize interests, inform opinion, and educate the public. A series of fair and free elections can, over time, nurture cultural commitment (among both key political and economic elites and among masses) to participation, civil liberties, and an electoral regime, as evidence from Costa Rica, Venezuela, and Colombia demonstrates (Peeler, 1985). Citizens' commitment to democratic practice and civil liberties can grow through civic education and political experience (Booth and Seligson, 1984:106–8). The greater the proportion of a nation's citizens committed to democratic practices and values, the less likely they would be to resort to undemocratic political means or to accept the blandishments of antidemocratic ideologues. Political culture evolves gradually, however, and will not change merely because of a single election (Paz, 1985:20).

Elections and Democracy

Against this theoretical background, we may begin to assess more systematically the importance of elections for democracy. The previous discussion can be summarized as a series of six questions that may help us to assess the contribution of elections to democratic governance.

1. *What is the effect of the election(s) on the range of political participation?*
Elections in modern nation states afford a rather circumscribed range of opportunities for popular participation. An election provides a relatively brief and occasional opportunity to discuss politics, campaign, electioneer, and vote. Despite the sporadic nature of electoral activity, some partisan participation—militancy within a party, proselytizing, and so forth—may well continue after the election has ended among the minority of any populace that engages in partisan activism, particularly if there are prospects for future fair elections. Especially where elections and partisan activity have been barred or where elections have been fraudulently manipulated, the holding of an open election campaign and fair balloting offers a marked expansion of the range of political

participation available to citizens. Moreover, taking part in choosing a leader, ruling party, or representative can provide a significant opportunity for protecting one's self-interest or for promoting one's political goals.

Despite their potential to increase the array of participatory opportunities, however, elections and partisan activity constitute but a fraction of the political activity of any nation. The actual making of policy decisions, the execution of those decisions, and the adjudication of disputes constitute vast arenas of ongoing public activity. In most countries, elections, party activity, and voting—even if highly efficacious—influence these arenas only tangentially if at all. In some nations, the use of citizen initiative and referendum elections for making public decisions offers the public greater opportunities to decide policy matters directly (Magleby, 1984; Barber, 1974), but such practices are relatively rare in Latin America.

2. *What is the effect of the election(s) on the breadth of participation?*

The breadth of participation (fraction of the citizenry participating) in elections is typically greatest for the actual casting of the ballot: voting in national elections by up to three-quarters of those eligible is common in many countries. Participation is customarily much narrower for campaigning and partisan activism (usually less than a quarter of the populace). Because citizens who have been forced to participate in consistently manipulated or fraudulent elections often become politically inactive, the introduction of open campaigns and fair elections can encourage a large increase in electoral participation and therefore broaden democracy.

It should be noted, however, that many other forms of political participation—voluntary group activity, contacting public officials, discussing public affairs—may involve more of the populace more of the time than most forms of electoral participation. Citizen involvement in such other, nonelectoral activities may not be significantly altered by the presence or absence of elections; they appear to go on in many types of regimes. It should also be noted that, with few exceptions, citizen participation in formal governmental arenas tends to be consistently higher among those who are more prosperous and better educated. Overall, then, elections and campaigns may broaden citizen political participation substantially, but only within certain arenas, only for certain social strata, and typically only for limited periods.

3. *What is the effect of the election(s) on the depth of participation?*

The depth of participation involves its quality, the extent to which it has real potential for influence, and the autonomy of participation. In an open campaign and free election, the outcome would depend upon the actual distribution of votes cast, and neither parties nor individual voters would be subject to coercion during the campaign or balloting. In such an open electoral environment, the mobilization of support by parties could educate citizens on issues and permit them to join the coalition that appears to offer the most advantageous package of policies.

However, electoral participation is shallow in most elections in modern nation states for several reasons. First, the choice open to the voter is typically very small (for example, between Party A and Party B, or Candidate X and Candidate Y), and the issues to be decided or choices to be made have almost always been framed beforehand by elites. Such limitations are particularly true in proportional representation systems (the norm in Latin America), in which candidates are typically selected by national party elites rather than by voters in primaries. Second, elections usually convey limited information to candidates because secret ballots do not reveal how any individual voted or why. Therefore, a conscientious winning candidate might study election results with care, yet discern only with difficulty any trace of a mandate to guide postelection behavior. On the other hand, participation as a party activist or officeholder may bring a citizen closer to shaping these decisions. Such participation would thus convey deeper influence than the average voter would ever exercise, but normally only a minority of even activists actually authoritatively shape decisions.

4. *Did the election(s) occur in an environment conducive to the free exercise of full participatory rights, and was the conduct of the election(s) fair?*

Such questions about the setting, procedures, and technical conduct of elections are the sort of issues typically examined by careful election observers to determine the quality of particular elections. By most contemporary standards, the central issue at stake is fundamental fairness, measured mainly in terms of equality of opportunity, so that each citizen's vote weighs equally with those of all others (García Laguardia, 1986:8–9).[5] Ideally under this principle of "one person, one vote," the context of the election and its procedures and implementation should afford the following conditions to each citizen:

—free and equal opportunity to receive information about issues, parties, and candidates;

—free and equal opportunity to speak on political issues;

—free and equal opportunity to register to vote;

—free and equal opportunity to vote;

—ballot secrecy, including the right to deposit secretly a null or blank ballot;

—freedom from intimidation or coercion as to how to vote;

—equal weight of the counted vote.

The obtaining of these conditions for individual citizens requires other structural and contextual conditions for the polity as a whole:

—freedom for parties to organize, electioneer, campaign, and distribute propaganda;

—absence of unfair advantage for particular minorities, especially for incumbents;

—mechanisms to adjudicate and redress grievances among contenders;

—fair and free systems of registration and election administration and an honest count of the votes;

—losers' respect for the winners' right to rule; respect for the right of losers and other minorities to continued participation.

The evaluation of such conditions by observers and participants is a fairly straightforward matter in an open electoral environment. There has arisen in Central America and Latin America overall a small legal-scholarly-technical industry that studies, advises on, and promotes fair elections, including the Association of Electoral Organizations of Central America and the Caribbean and the Inter-American Center for Electoral Advice and Promotion, a subsidiary of the Inter-American Court of Human Rights. Many human rights and special interest organizations monitor and observe elections in Central America.

5. *Did the election(s) consolidate or help consolidate a stable regime under democratic rules?*

The establishment of an electoral, constitutional regime can be judged only superficially by the criteria mentioned in the previous section. Such procedural standards are necessary but not sufficient conditions for democratization. While the absence of open and fair campaigning and a free and fairly counted election would surely signal that a procedurally democratic regime was lacking, the mere presence of such conditions might not mean movement toward democracy. As noted above, authoritarian regimes can—without relinquishing a tight grip on power, accommodating other political forces, or accepting democratic norms—liberalize election procedures. External pressures can temporarily coerce warring elite factions into temporary and unstable cooperation around democratic procedural norms.

A sufficient condition for the consolidation of a regime may be reached by the establishment of a consensus among key elites to (1) accommodate each other in the political game, (2) continue playing within democratic procedural norms, and (3) accept popular participation in politics. Unfortunately for our purposes here, such an interelite consensus may not be easy to identify in practical terms, especially at the time in which a particular election is held. Unless forged through an overt pact at a particular historical moment, those involved may not be fully conscious of the emergence of consensus on those criteria, so that evidence about consensus on a new regime may be available only through hindsight.

Sometimes regime-defining consensus is established through an overt pact by negotiations among rival elites. Colombia's historic National Front pact of 1957 between warring Liberals and Conservatives was such an overt agreement. Liberal-Conservative negotiations led to a national referendum on the accord and national presidential-congressional elections. The new regime had strong support from powerful national economic interests from the beginning because the bourgeoisie was well represented among the parties' leaders. The consolidation of Venezuela's democratic regime took longer and was more tenuous. After sectarian conflict undermined an interlude of civilian rule in the late 1940s, Venezuela's three major parties reached an accord in the late 1950s to play by liberal democratic rules if the dictator Pérez Jiménez could be toppled. Support for the liberal regime by the national bourgeoisie developed slowly in Venezuela, and forbearance from intervention by the armed forces was tenuous at first.

6. *Did the election(s) contribute toward a political culture of support for participation and democratic rules?*

The growth of elite and popular support for participatory politics and democratic rules and liberties is likely to be fitful and to require the passage of many years, if not decades. Indeed, some commentators argue that Latin American political culture begins from historical roots in Catholic Spain and has been so shaped by centuries of political history that the region's culture is generally antithetical to democratic beliefs. Others have argued that these traditions have recently led major Latin American elite and middle-sector groups to forge antidemocratic alliances with military authoritarians in defense of their class interests (Wiarda, 1974; O'Donnell, 1979). Despite such pessimistic readings, there is a democratic tradition in Latin American culture (Paz, 1985). Moreover, survey research has uncovered strong commitment to democratic values and practices in countries as diverse as liberal-democratic Costa Rica and authoritarian Mexico.[6]

Democratic values and support for civil liberties develop among populations through participation. A series of fair and free elections could increase popular confidence in elections per se, in participatory norms, and in a regime. It is also true, however, that other types of political participation, particularly those that are more continuous or relevant to ongoing and immediately important activities in the everyday lives of citizens, may be more likely than electoral participation to build participatory norms and support for civil liberties. It has been forcefully argued by Pateman (1970:45–111), for example, that workplace and community participation offer greater potential for building democratic political culture than do sporadic voting, campaigning, and party activism.

Elections and Democracy in Central America

Based on the foregoing, one should obviously not conclude that the mere election of civilian governments in Central American nations means that democratization is sweeping the isthmus. On the other hand, if democracy means participation in rule, the holding of elections in Central America could well mean that there is more democracy, albeit perhaps not a great deal more.

In order to understand the contribution of elections to democracy in Central America, one must examine each nation in the region individually. It is not sufficient merely to look at each case at this particular historical moment; one must evaluate overall trends in popular participation. It is necessary to go beyond the particular technical aspects of elections and election systems to the developing sociopolitical contexts within which they have been held. One must consider over time how, if at all, elections may contribute to the development of political culture among elites and masses, as well as to regime formation.

Costa Rica

All observers agree that Costa Rica is a classical liberal, representative, constitutional polity with a high degree of electoral honesty. The contemporary Costa Rican political system has its roots in a colonial system marked by (for Central America) relative economic equality and an absence of both mineral wealth and an indigenous populace with which to exploit it. Costa Ricans developed an egalitarian social culture that was reinforced by the need of agricultural elites to co-opt workers as the modern coffee export economy developed in the nineteenth and twentieth centuries. Concessions to workers that gradually extended political rights and a low level of civil conflict contributed to the emergence of a prototypical liberal regime in the early twentieth century (Booth, 1988).

After growing economic and political unrest and intraelite conflict shattered that regime in the 1940s, an attempt by the incumbent government to fraudulently manipulate the 1948 election led to a brief civil war led by José Figueres and the National Liberation Movement. The insurgents defeated the regime and armed forces, and the National Liberation junta ruled for a year by decree.

In 1949 an elected constituent assembly rewrote the Costa Rican constitution; it abolished the armed forces, established a fourth branch of government to guarantee electoral honesty, curtailed executive power with extensive checks and balances, restricted the Communist party, weakened labor unions as well as certain privileges of the coffee bourgeoisie, and rejected many of the National Liberation Movement's own pet projects. The junta then relinquished power to the real winner of the 1948 election, politically consecrating the principle of electoral honesty. The National Liberation Movement constituted itself into a political party (the PLN), contested and won the 1953 election, then relinquished power after losing in 1958.

The regime consolidated in the 1948–58 period has been characterized by the mutual accommodation and alternation in power of the social democratic PLN and its more conservative opponents, the preservation of a mixed economy and social welfare policies that have modestly attenuated the effects of poverty for many Costa Ricans, extensive civil liberties, and governmental promotion of certain types of popular participation through the formation of community development, health, nutrition, and economic cooperative organizations.

Honest elections in a climate of extensive political freedom for individuals, parties, most voluntary associations, and the press have been the jewels in Costa Rica's crown for three decades. There clearly exist both an elite and a mass consensus about the regime that have weathered unscathed some difficult periods of economic strife, as Seligson and Gómez reveal in their contribution to this work.[7]

It appears likely that several decades of honest, competitive elections, a good human and civil rights climate, and social democratic policies have combined to nurture the commitment of most Costa Ricans to participatory rules and fundamental civil liberties. In comparative terms, the breadth of Costa Rican political participation appears extensive and the range of participation is moderate (due to the mixed economy and government mobilization of interest groups), but overall the depth of participation is rather modest.

Recent trends of growing external pressures have raised some alarm about the future evolution of the Costa Rican regime. Because of Reagan administration policies and Costa Rica's own, as well as its post-1981 debt crisis, the country has been heavily pressured to curtail its social welfare policies and reduce the participation of the state in the economy. Such policies have modestly reduced the range of political participation (that is, areas of national life subject to influence by public pressure) by expanding the Costa Rican private sector at the cost of the public sector. Despite expectations to the contrary, curtailment of social welfare policies since 1982 apparently has not seriously eroded support for the regime. Successful U.S. pressure to increase the size and strength of Costa Rica's security forces in cooperation with American policies against Nicaragua has aroused fears of possible military intervention in politics. External pressures that have undercut constitutional norms and international neutrality, the presence of large numbers of anti-Sandinista rebels, increased paramilitary activity, and increased antileftist propaganda in Costa Rica have all contributed to some erosion of the government's respect for human rights in recent years (*Mesoamerica*, 1987:1; *El Día*, 1987:13; Miami *Herald*, 1985:14A).

El Salvador

Centuries of profound economic inequality and racist exploitation of Indian and mestizo poor by a socioeconomic elite descended from the conquerors have bequeathed densely populated, modern El Salvador severe problems of economic and social inequity. Popular demands for redress of various problems have periodically surfaced, but have been regularly and often violently repressed by the national bourgeoisie and the government. A brief reformist experiment in 1931 was quickly overthrown by the dictatorial General Hernández Martínez. When labor, peasant, and student groups assayed an abortive revolt in 1932, the dictator massacred thirty thousand people, mostly innocent peasants, and thus snuffed out for decades any inclination toward popular participation.

Hernández Martínez ruled tyrannically until the 1940s, when he was replaced by a more modern regime of military officers who ruled through their own party, fraudulently manipulated elections, and repressed opposition. Economic policies of the 1960s and 1970s led to industrialization and urbanization and the growth of demands for change from labor and middle-class groups. Growing labor and opposition party pressures placed increasing strains on the military regime in the 1970s as an armed insurgency developed. The government of General Carlos Humberto Romero (1977–79) mobilized anti-Communist paramilitary forces and death squads within the armed forces to terrorize the populace out of opposition, but this strategy merely further inflamed and multiplied opponents.

In 1979 reformist military, party, and business elements collaborated in the October 15 coup that toppled Romero; their goal was to bring about reform before the opposition could erupt into rebellion, as had just happened in neighboring Nicaragua. This reformism was strongly supported by the Carter administration, which provided economic assistance and restored military aid to the Salvadoran government. Rightist elements, however, took over the Junta, blocked its reforms, and accelerated repression. This drove moderates off the Junta and unified the opposition—many parties, unions, peasant leagues, and other forces—into a political coalition, the Revolutionary Democratic Front (FDR). The FDR joined forces in late 1980 with five Marxist guerrilla groups known as the Farabundo Martí Liberation Front (FMLN) in a revolutionary challenge to the Junta. Armed rebellion gained force rapidly, and rebels had soon captured significant areas of Salvadoran territory that the U.S.-financed but inept armed forces could not recapture.

By 1982 it appeared to an alarmed Reagan administration that continued human rights atrocities by the military and far right endangered the by then extensive U.S. military and economic aid going to El Salvador. Pressure was thus exerted on the Junta to call elections for a constituent assembly. The 1982 campaign for election to that body took place in a climate of extreme human rights violations and intimidation of citizens, parties, and the press. Observers concurred that there were many procedural irregularities (e.g., Baloyra, 1982: 169–75; Herman and Brodhead, 1984:119–34), but some disagreed about whether the count itself was distorted.

The resultant assembly was dominated by parties of the right, which blocked most significant economic reforms proposed for the new constitution. U.S. aid continued to flow to the armed forces in a feverish, and ultimately successful, effort to strengthen the government's military posture. Christian Democrat José Napoleón Duarte won presidential elections held in 1984. These elections, again conducted under U.S. pressure and with U.S. technical assistance, were reported to have been procedurally better than those of 1982, but the human rights climate remained abysmal, and intimidation of participants, restrictions on the press, and campaigning remained serious problems.

Did a new regime committed to democratic rules, mutual accommodation of major elite elements, and mass participation emerge from the 1982 and 1984 elections? As Baloyra (1982:167–84) and García in his contribution here demonstrate, the answer is no. A very uneasy and unstable government involving the Christian Democrats, radical right, bourgeoisie, and armed forces was arranged with benefit of strong external pressure by the United States. From 1982 to 1984 the radical right, led by the ARENA party, dominated the Assembly; in 1984 the Christian Democrats won the presidency, to the great chagrin of the right. The situation of stalemated mutual tolerance between these highly antagonistic forces developed and persisted under the necessity of helping persuade the U.S. Congress to continue economic support for the government and the military in its struggle against the rebel FMLN-FDR. Most observers believe that this marriage of convenience would fly apart the instant U.S. pressure for continued mutual tolerance among its elements was removed. García, however, in his chapter seems optimistic that a new and potentially stable government can gradually be developed by the Christian Democrats.

In my opinion, however, the challenge of consolidating a regime with mutual elite accommodation among the radical right, the bourgeoisie, the PDC, and the armed factions of right and left is enormous. Moreover, it seems even less likely that all these groups would tolerate popular participation. Economic problems and the 1986 earthquake have apparently eroded the political support for the Christian Democrats and brought a renewal of some labor conflict and other protests. The return to El Salvador of FDR political leaders under the terms of the 1987 Guatemalan peace accord has spawned renewed rightist terror and introduced great new uncertainties into the polity.

Have Salvadoran elections since 1982 contributed to the emergence or reinforcement of a political culture of democracy? It seems extremely unlikely, given the continuous abuse of human rights by public authorities and the inability of the Duarte government to control the armed forces or restore any semblance of the rule of law. Peaceful, legal political participation in the 1960s and 1970s contributed to the mobilization and rebellion of the late 1970s and early 1980s. Frustrated elites and masses turned to confrontational and violent means against a recalcitrant regime, which lashed back with vicious intemperance. Procedurally flawed elections conducted under external pressure have largely failed to address most of the grievances that led to popular mobilization to begin with. If some Salvadorans may have miraculously learned values of democratic fair play in that chaotic and murderous environment, no doubt just as many learned the culture of intimidation and terror, while hundreds of thousands of others fled abroad to escape the political madness of El Salvador.

The overall breadth of political participation in El Salvador is very limited for the bulk of the populace, recent elections notwithstanding. Mobilization of popular demands through unions, peasant leagues, and parties involved a large part of the population in the late 1970s and early 1980s. The use of terror by the state and far right to curtail such demands has had two effects: to convert many of those demanding reforms into revolutionaries collaborating with the FMLN-FDR and to alienate many Salvadorans from participation in politics because of simple fear or disgust at the daily brutality of the nation's politics. Ultimately the civil conflict, in many ways a struggle over who may participate and under what terms, has made participation more narrow and shallow for most Salvadorans. It has also led thousands of others to intensify and deepen their participation by violent means.

Guatemala

Guatemala, the northernmost and most populous Central American state, is roughly half Indian. Guatemala's socioeconomic history has been marked by exploitation of the indigenous populace's labor to benefit the creole and mestizo politico-economic elite. The national political culture early developed profoundly racist traits and a penchant for brutality in the political arena. From Independence into the mid-twentieth century, Guatemala had several long and brutal dictatorships.

In 1944 a movement based in the middle sectors and labor succeeded in toppling the Ubico regime. The 1944–54 "democratic revolution" saw the installation of a constitutionally elected civilian regime, considerable mobilization of working-class and Indian groups into the political arena, and both a broadening and deepening of political participation. But the elected government lacked vital consensual accommodation of many key economic and political actors. When President Jacobo Arbenz's government sought to expand the public sector through agrarian reform that would have redistributed land held by national and foreign owners, the armed forces permitted, and the

Guatemalan bourgeoisie applauded, a CIA-backed revolt by Guatemalan exiles. The 1954 National Liberation Movement (MLN) shattered the democratizing experiment as the new Castillo Armas regime and army moved to curtail the political participation encouraged by the revolution. Thousands of labor, party, and Indian leaders were killed, imprisoned, or driven into exile.

In the late 1950s the armed forces wrested political power away from the MLN and began to rule Guatemala outright. An abortive reformist coup from within the army in 1960 eventually led to the establishment of Guatemala's first Marxist guerrilla insurgency. A fairly elected civilian government from 1966 to 1970 provided a figurehead for rapid escalation of military control over the polity, a violent counterinsurgency program, and intensive use of state terror against perceived "subversives." During the 1970s the armed forces–dominated regime aggressively promoted industrialization and economic growth in collaboration with the national bourgeoisie. During that era "death squads" run by the regime killed thousands of labor unionists, students, development workers, and political party activists. The reign of terror decimated the leadership cadres of most parties and heavily suppressed political participation. Voting in Guatemala's fraudulently manipulated elections dropped to very low levels.

Under the regime of General Romeo Lucas García (1978–82), state terror reached horrific new heights when economic difficulties and the effects of the 1976 earthquake spawned economic unrest and labor mobilization, and reorganized insurgents began to step up their struggle. Younger army officers overthrew Lucas when he manipulated the results of the 1982 presidential election; they installed General Efraín Ríos Montt to begin a process of tightly managed reform. Under Ríos the army conducted a brutal counterinsurgency campaign in the Indian highlands that took tens of thousands of civilian lives but did little damage to the Guatemalan National Revolutionary Union (UNRG) insurgent coalition.

Ríos's failure to progress toward return of power to civilians led to his ouster in 1983 by the same younger officers, who replaced him with General Oscar Humberto Mejía Victores. As the Guatemalan economy declined rapidly, and with the example of the Argentine military regime, which was embarrassed by trials for its human rights abuses after the Malvinas war, General Mejía moved to preempt such problems for the Guatemalan armed forces by returning formal power to civilians.

The armed forces conducted relatively clean elections (albeit in a highly repressive climate) for a constituent assembly that rewrote the constitution. The assembly then convened and held the 1985 national election for congress and the presidency. Observers judged the 1985 election to have been procedurally fair and accurately counted, but conducted in an atmosphere of crushing fear of political repression that badly impeded communication. The Christian Democratic government of Vinicio Cerezo today rules with the advice and counsel of the military, which was exempted from prosecution for its past human rights abuses by the outgoing Mejía government and which retains virtually absolute control over military affairs.

Recent evidence reveals that as of early 1987 in Guatemala City and other major cities parties, unions, private associations, and development workers—once targets of fierce repression—enjoyed considerable latitude for participation, expression of their opinions, and organization.[8] Politically motivated human rights abuses had declined markedly, but no official human rights organizations had been formed nor had any effort been made to prosecute human rights violators. The massive military presence and control over the population and the counterinsurgency war against the URNG continued in rural areas, severely depressing opportunities for participation.

Has Guatemala "taken the final step to democracy," as the State Department rhapsodized in 1985? Political participation has increased in breadth and range under the new civilian government, but evidence as to its depth, efficacy, and staying power remains to be seen. No lasting consensus on a regime has yet been forged, although there is evidence that key elements of the national capitalist class, some political parties, and some military elements are committed to the civilian representative government for the time being. Labor and peasant organizations are mobilizing rapidly in the freer climate and intend to test the range of their freedom. All observers agree that the tolerance of the armed forces for such participation is the key to the survival of the civilian government. Most Guatemalan political activists and professionals and some business leaders appear to prefer participatory rules and increased political freedom to the three-decade reign of terror, but public experience with and commitment to such rules and participation will likely grow only very slowly, and then only if the civilian government and more open political environment persist.

Jonas's contribution advances one very important interpretation of the Guatemalan situation. She argues that, though driven by deep contradictions in Guatemalan society, the new regime is unlikely to promote true democratization and the development of a system that will promote the interests of the majority of Guatemalans. The new civilian government will permit the armed forces and bourgeoisie increased legitimacy and will attract badly needed economic aid. Even President Cerezo does not believe that a new regime has been consolidated; he refers to his own administration as one of "transition." Given the popular expectations and demands for economic reform that appear to be developing in Guatemala today, severe strains could soon be placed on the commitment to civilian government of that pivotal institution in the Guatemalan polity—the armed forces.

There is clearly broader and wider-ranging popular political participation in Guatemala today than there has been in decades. One effect of the 1987 Central American peace accord was a brief dialogue between the URNG and government and to bring some exiled politicians back to the country to chance the new political opening. We may nevertheless not know for many years whether the 1985 election truly contributed to a process of democratization, or merely to a liberalization of the old regime.

Honduras

Honduras has shared several traits with most of its Central American neighbors—high levels of internal conflict, dictatorship, and dependence on export agriculture—conditions aggravated by its weak resource base and generally poor soils. Honduran national elites failed to consolidate and integrate the nation politically and economically to the degree of neighboring states, and Honduras remained the poorest Central American nation even as it developed a flourishing banana industry under foreign ownership in the twentieth century. An ancient feud between liberal and conservative elements was marked by great turbulence in the nineteenth century, followed by Liberal party preeminence between the 1890s and 1932, and then by National party dominion until 1949. The Liberals were resurgent in the 1950s, but in 1956–57 the military stepped in to resolve a political crisis. In 1963 a military coup led by Colonel Oswaldo López Arellano and backed by the National party seized power, intending to stay in control.

Modernization and industrial development characterized the 1960s, raising demands for change among the emergent middle sector. Honduras's disastrous 1969 war with El Salvador aggravated unrest. Although López's early years in power were marked by conservative policies, in the early 1970s he assumed a developmentalist posture and implemented a number of populist policies, including a sweeping agrarian reform law. The officer corps replaced López with Colonel Juan Melgar Castro in 1975, and then in 1978 replaced Castro with Colonel Policarpo Paz García. Each successive military president was more development oriented and placed less emphasis on social reform and populism. Despite efforts to promote economic development, Honduran economic problems grew, and economic and party leaders became progressively more critical of military rule.

The Nicaraguan Revolution and burgeoning domestic discontent eventually convinced top military leaders to return power to civilians. General Paz convened constituent assembly elections in 1980; while the constitution was being rewritten, a presidential election was held in 1981. Liberal Roberto Suazo Córdoba won that relatively clean and fair election and assumed the presidency in 1982. Liberal José Azcona Hoyo succeeded Suazo after another clean and fair election in 1986.

Had Honduras experienced a regime-consolidating and truly democratizing election in 1981? As Rosenberg points out in his contribution to this work, evidence so far suggests that major political elites still lack commitment to accommodating each other and playing by democratic rules. President Suazo himself provoked a constitutional crisis in 1986 by attempting to impose a successor on his party and the country by manipulating the Congress and electoral system. National party leaders still speak wistfully of the López Arellano military regime and what they remember as days of "real national progress" during the 1970s. National party leaders often seem far more interested in narrow and short-run sectarian advantage than in accommodating each other for the sake of maintaining constitutional processes. In the ultimate irony, the Honduran armed forces and the United States may have kept the constitutional processes from being overturned in the 1986 crisis.

Honduran mass political culture could well be developing increased commitment to electoral and participatory rules under the Honduran civilian regimes of the 1980s, but this would probably also be partly due to the extensive peasant and labor organization present in the country. There can be no doubt that the elections since 1980 have provided renewed opportunities for political participation that had been repressed in the previous decade. However, the period has also seen a marked rise in political terror by public security forces. Although the death toll from political repression in Honduras since 1980 probably numbers only in the low hundreds, in comparison to the tens of thousands in El Salvador and Guatemala, it could well have had a chilling effect on participation.

Nicaragua

Nicaragua has suffered more civil war and foreign intervention in its affairs than almost any country in the hemisphere. The nineteenth and early twentieth centuries saw frequent conflict between the Liberal and Conservative parties, aggravated periodically by outside interference. Though small in population and relatively rich in land and other natural resources, Nicaragua, with its great lake and river system, has always attracted foreign meddling. American filibusterer William Walker exploited Nicaraguan Liberals' desires to take over the Conservative-dominated government and a struggle for control of Vanderbilt's trans-isthmian transit company. He invaded in 1855 and seized control of Nicaragua for himself. His ouster by Central American conservatives in the National War of 1857 established a three-decade period of Conservative party rule.

In the 1890s the Liberals returned to power under the leadership of nationalistic, development-oriented Benjamín Zelaya. When Zelaya sought foreign suitors to build a canal in Nicaragua to compete with the U.S.-owned Panama Canal, the United States in 1909 helped topple Zelaya and install a more cooperative regime. In order to protect its canal monopoly, the United States sent marines into Nicaragua to help the conservatives, who dutifully produced a treaty giving the United States canal rights in Nicaragua. However, the United States then had to keep marines in Nicaragua for most of the next two decades to keep the conservatives in power. When the United States attempted to settle yet another civil war in 1927 by switching sides to the liberals, an anti-intervention resistance movement arose, led by A. C. Sandino. The United States escalated its military presence in Nicaragua and established a National Guard to help fight Sandino, but eventually withdrew in frustration in 1933.

The principal legacy of twenty-four years of U.S. military intervention in Nicaragua was the National Guard, headed by Anastasio Somoza García, who used it to depose the president and rule as a dictator until his assassination in 1956. Control of the National Guard and the government passed to his sons Luis and Anastasio Somoza Debayle, who continued the family dynasty while promoting industrialization and economic growth. Increasing social diversity and political frustration at four decades of dictatorship, combined with

Anastasio Somoza Debayle's heavy-handed repressiveness and corruption, re-sulted in a destabilized country in the early 1970s. The 1972 Managua earth-quake and its aftermath intensified hostility toward the government, which became rapidly more repressive. A growing opposition gradually united and demanded an end to the Somoza dynasty. Most opponents of the regime joined forces with the Marxist-Leninist rebel group the Sandinista National Liberation Front (FSLN) as the National Guard made war on Nicaragua's population in 1978 and 1979. In July 1979 the FSLN-led coalition defeated Somoza's guard after a fight that featured, on the rebel side, widespread participation and support by much of the Nicaraguan populace.

The Sandinistas dominated the coalition government, but permitted more moderate groups to organize and participate in ruling. As Sandinista control over the revolutionary government grew in 1979 and 1980, other political groups began to break with and criticize the FSLN so that elite consensus on the regime broke down. The Sandinistas set out to establish in Nicaragua a unique program for a Marxist-Leninist government; rather than full socialism and a single-party regime as in Cuba, they promoted a mixed economy and "political pluralism."[9] A broad array of programs and services was developed to benefit the poor majority of Nicaraguans. Many of these programs sought public input on policies and required citizen participation in administration, particularly the literacy drive and health and neighborhood security programs. The FSLN also built support for itself by establishing neighborhood, youth, women's, labor, peasant, small farmer, and professional organizations (Walker, 1985). Opposition to Sandinista rule from former allies grew as the FSLN continued to gain political power.

The advent of the Reagan administration led to U.S. efforts to oust the FSLN from power. The United States encouraged former National Guard elements, some Somoza allies, and opposition elements that had broken with the revolu-tionary government to form a political-military counterrevolutionary ("contra") movement. With overt and covert U.S. aid, the contra movement grew to a peak of about 15,000 rebel troops based in Honduras and Costa Rica. Contra forces conducted guerrilla operations in Nicaragua and sabotaged economic and political targets in hopes of fomenting economic chaos and mobilizing an internal resistance to the revolutionary government. The United States also placed a trade embargo on Nicaragua and conducted an energetic campaign designed to isolate Nicaragua from the West, prevent a negotiated settlement of the war, and cut off trade and aid.

The principal effects of these U.S. policies and the development of the armed opposition to the revolution have been several. Nicaragua has turned increasingly to the Soviet bloc for military and economic assistance and has massively built up its armed forces for a counterinsurgency war and a feared U.S. invasion. It has curtailed civil liberties and restricted press and opposition party freedoms, deferred many social programs, and accelerated agrarian reform to build its political base. In 1984 Nicaragua restored most civil liberties and held a national election under rules that the opposition parties had helped draft. Virtually all observers characterized the election as procedurally fair and free.

The United States sought to prevent the consolidation of a new consensus on a regime by successfully pressuring certain groups to refuse to take part, by denouncing the election as a sham, and by continuing its aid to the contra war. The Sandinista regime won a substantial majority of the vote, but U.S. pressure and the regime's own policies have continued to fan opposition to the revolution. With considerable public and opposition input, the new Nicaraguan National Assembly wrote a constitution (accepted in 1987) that embodies extensive civil liberties and democratic procedural norms. Despite this the government of the victorious FSLN candidate Daniel Ortega Saavedra in 1985 and 1986 restored numerous restrictions on civil liberties, closed the principal opposition newspaper, and continued to defend the revolution militarily.

The contra war presently bars Nicaragua from promoting its own, potentially quite distinctive, model of democracy. The Sandinista Revolution's effort to promote a broader, deeper, and wider range of democracy through mass participation in policymaking and implementation has achieved some notable successes, as Jonas points out in her contribution. As is common in revolution, however, popular mobilization and some regime elements have often been intolerant of and intimidated opposition. The 1984 election created opportunities for participation that had not existed for many decades, and the new constitution promised Nicaraguans a continuation of these opportunities. The suspension of civil liberties because of the war, however, called into doubt the permanence of such participatory opportunities and their potential for nurturing commitment to electoral rights and procedures. The war, U.S. efforts to disrupt the election and encourage the FSLN's domestic opponents, and the deep ideological differences between the various contending factions in Nicaragua have so far prevented the emergence of a consensus that would permit us to label the 1984 election as democratizing.

Until peace can be achieved, Nicaragua seems unlikely to move forward toward achieving the potential of its participatory goals or establishing a climate of respect for civil liberties. Slow and painful progress toward settlement of the war and restoration of civil liberties began in late 1987 under the terms of the Central American peace accord, but Nicaragua remained far from an emergent consensus on a new regime. Many observers believed that the Central American accord provided at least a framework under which the government, the contras, the Church, and the domestic opposition parties and groups in Nicaragua could begin to negotiate about their differences. As of early 1988, however, despite having commenced indirect negotiations with the contras, the Nicaraguan government remained adamant that it would not fully restore civil liberties until foreign assistance to the contras had been ended.

Conclusions

Although Central America's five major nations now have civilian governments and constitutions providing for representative government, extensive participatory rights, and civil liberties, one must not conclude that democracy has been enthroned in the region. Defining democracy as citizen participation in rule permits one to conclude, however, that recent elections have brought modest increases in the breadth and range of political participation in several countries. This cursory review and the following chapters, however, raise numerous questions about the procedures of recent Central American elections and of their contributions to democratic political culture and the establishment of stable regimes committed to participatory rules of the game.

As a general proposition, the advancement of democracy in Central America is obviously better served by fairly elected civilian governments than by dictatorial military governments. Nevertheless, progress in the 1980s toward fulfilling the specific requisites of effective and lasting systems of democratic rule in Central America—systems potentially vastly different in structure and style—has been uneven and halting.

The Central American peace accords signed on 7 August 1987 at Esquipulas, Guatemala, required that all the Central American countries negotiate with armed rebels who will accept amnesty and undertake a dialogue with domestic opponents, fully restore civil liberties, and hold democratic elections for a Central American Parliament by mid-1988. The Esquipulas accord thus created both internal and international pressures upon the Central American governments to take steps that could move each nation toward greater democracy. The construction of both peace and more democracy in Central America remained highly complex processes, however, each beset by powerful enemies both within and outside Central America.

Notes

1. Pateman (1970) notes that "classical" democratic theory is a somewhat inaccurate designation because the theorists she includes in the category span three millennia from Aristotle to J. S. Mill. I am using the term classical very loosely here, as did she, for the sake of convenience.

2. This provision notwithstanding, almost all democratic models exclude from participation persons incapacitated by youth, lunacy, or criminality.

3. See also Rosenberg (1985:23–33).

4. I am using this term as Paul Drake and Eduardo Silva do in "Introduction: Elections and Democratization in Latin America, 1980–1985," (1986:2–3) rather than as Petras (1986:1–15) and Rabine (1986:59–64) do. The latter approach suggests that the election of civilian regimes in Latin America can mean nothing more than a more effective mechanism by which an old regime continues to exploit the poor and block popular democracy. I would argue that if such occurred, no true "democratization" as intended here would have taken place.

5. Note that not all democratic theories would weight votes equally. J. S. Mill, for instance, preferred a system of unequal votes based on political knowledge and experience. Pluralist-elitists celebrate elite dominance of most choices because of distrust for the mass public's capabilities. The U.S. Constitution gave electors, not citizens, the right to elect the president; state legislators chose U.S. senators; and the principle of "one-person, one-vote" was violated by giving the votes of senators from small states a weight equal to that of senators from more populous states.

6. See Seligson and Gómez chapter in this volume. Also see Carvahal Herrera (1978) and Booth and Seligson (1984).

7. See also Carvahal Herrera (1978).

8. I participated in an observer mission to Guatemala in April–May of 1987, sponsored by the Washington Office on Latin America and the International Human Rights Law Group, to examine political conditions after the election. The team interviewed dozens of party, human rights, and labor activists, as well as social workers, lawyers, and government officials. See also Booth et al. (1985) and Carliner et al. (1988)

9. Their model has most of the traits of Macpherson's "underdeveloped variant" of democracy: a heavy emphasis on popular participation and distributive justice issues (Macpherson, 1966:23–34).

References

Aristotle. 1962. *Politics (Aristotle's Politics)*. Translated by Richard Robinson. Oxford: Clarendon Press.

Bachrach, Peter. 1966. *The Theory of Democratic Elitism*. Boston: Little, Brown.

Baloyra, Enrique. 1982. *El Salvador in Transition*. Chapel Hill: University of North Carolina Press.

Barber, Benjamin. 1974. *The Death of Communal Liberty*. Princeton: Princeton University Press.

Berelson, Bernard R. 1954. Democratic Practice and Democratic Theory. In *Voting*, edited by Bernard R. Berelson et al. Chicago: University of Chicago Press.

Booth, John A. 1986. Election amid War and Revolution: Toward Evaluating the 1984 Nicaraguan National Elections. In *Elections and Democratization in Latin America, 1980–85*, edited by Paul Drake and Eduardo Silva. La Jolla: Center for Iberian and Latin American Studies, University of California at San Diego.

———. 1988. Costa Rican Democracy. In *Democracy in Developing Countries: Latin America*, edited by Larry Diamond, Juan Linz, and Seymour Martin Lipset. Boulder: Lynne Reinner Publishers.

Booth, John A., and Seligson, Mitchell A. 1984. The Political Culture of Authoritarianism in Mexico: A Reexamination. *Latin American Research Review* 19, no. 1, 106–24.

Booth, John A., et al. 1985. *The 1985 Guatemalan Elections: Will the Military Relinquish Power?* Washington, D.C.: International Human Rights Law Group, Washington Office on Latin America.

Carliner, David, et al. 1988. *Political Transition and the Rule of Law in Guatemala*. Washington, D.C.: International Human Rights Law Group, Washington Office on Central America.

Carvahal Herrera, Mario. 1978. *Actitudes políticas del costarricense*. San José, Costa Rica: Editorial Costa Rica.

Cohen, Carl. 1971. *Democracy*. New York: Free Press.

———. 1982. *Four Systems*. New York: Random House.

Contemporary Marxism. 1986. Vol. 14 (Fall), special issue on Latin America.

Cornelius, Wayne A. 1986. Political Liberalization and the 1985 Elections in Mexico. In *Elections and Democratization in Latin America, 1980–85*, edited by Paul Drake and Eduardo Silva. La Jolla: Center for Iberian and Latin American Studies, University of California at San Diego.

Dahl, Robert A. 1956. *A Preface to Democratic Theory*. Chicago: University of Chicago Press.

———. 1971. *Polyarchy: Participation and Opposition*. New Haven: Yale University Press.

El Día (Mexico). 1987. 1 February.

Diamond, Larry; Linz, Juan; and Lipset, Seymour Martin. 1988. Preface. In *Democracy in Developing Countries: Latin America*, edited by Larry Diamond et al. Boulder: Lynne Reinner Publishers.

Dillon Soares, Glaucio Ary. 1986. Elections and the Redemocratization of Brazil. In *Elections and Democratization in Latin America, 1980–85*, edited by Paul Drake and Eduardo Silva. La Jolla: Center for Iberian and Latin American Studies, University of California at San Diego.

Drake, Paul W., and Silva, Eduardo, eds. 1986. *Elections and Democratization in Latin America, 1980–85*. La Jolla: Center for Iberian and Latin American Studies, University of California at San Diego.

Drake, Paul, and Silva, Eduardo. 1986. Introduction. In *Elections and Democratization in Latin America, 1980–85*, edited by Paul Drake and Eduardo Silva. La Jolla: Center for Iberian and Latin American Studies, University of California at San Diego.

García Laguardia, Jorge Mario. 1986. Prólogo. In Augusto Hernández Becerra et al. *Legislación electoral comparada: Colombia, México, Panamá, Venezuela, y Centroamérica.* San José: Centro de Asesoría y Promoción Electoral—Instituto Interamericano de Derechos Humanos/Instituto de Investigaciones Jurídicas—Universidad Nacional Autónoma de México.

Herman, Edward S., and Brodhead, Frank. 1984. *Demonstration Elections: U.S.-Staged Elections in the Dominican Republic, Vietnam, and El Salvador.* Boston: South End Press.

Jefferson, Thomas. 1935a. Letter to John Taylor (28 May 1816). In *The Jeffersonian Tradition in American Democracy*, edited by Maurice Wiltse. Chapel Hill: University of North Carolina Press.

————. 1935b. Letter to Peter Carr (10 August 1787). In *The Jeffersonian Tradition in American Democracy*, edited by Maurice Wiltse. Chapel Hill: University of North Carolina Press.

Jonas, Susanne. 1986. Introduction. *Contemporary Marxism* 14 (Fall): i–v.

Karl, Terry. 1986. Imposing Consent: Electoralism vs. Democratization in El Salvador. In *Elections and Democratization in Latin America, 1980–85*, edited by Paul Drake and Eduardo Silva. La Jolla: Center for Iberian and Latin American Studies, University of California at San Diego.

Latin American Studies Association (LASA). 1984. *The Electoral Process in Nicaragua: Domestic and International Influences.* Report of the Latin American Studies Association Delegation to Observe the Nicaraguan General Election of 4 November 1984. Austin: Latin American Studies Association.

Lijphart, Arend. 1977. *Democracy in Plural Societies: A Comparative Exploration.* New Haven: Yale University Press.

————. 1984. *Democracies: Patterns of Majoritarianism and Consensus in Twenty-One Countries.* New Haven: Yale University Press.

Macpherson, C. B. 1966. *The Real World of Democracy.* Oxford: Oxford University Press.

————. 1977. *The Life and Times of Liberal Democracy.* Oxford: Oxford University Press.

Madison, James. 1961a. *The Federalist Papers*, No. 10. New York: Mentor.

————. 1961b. *The Federalist Papers*, No. 14. New York: Mentor.

Magleby, David B. 1984. *Direct Legislation: Voting on Ballot Propositions in the United States.* Baltimore: Johns Hopkins University Press.

Malloy, James M., and Seligson, Mitchell A., eds. 1987. *Authoritarians and Democrats: Regime Transition in Latin America.* Pittsburgh: University of Pittsburgh Press.

Mesoamerica. 1987. July.

Miami Herald. 1985. 18 September.

Middlebrook, Kevin J. 1986. Political Liberalization in an Authoritarian Regime: The Case of Mexico. In *Elections and Democratization in Latin America, 1980–85,* edited by Paul Drake and Eduardo Silva. La Jolla: Center for Iberian and Latin American Studies, University of California at San Diego.

Mill, John Stuart. 1958. *Considerations on Representative Government.* Indianapolis: Bobbs Merrill.

Nohlen, Dieter. 1987. *La reforma electoral en América Latina: Seis contribuciones al debate.* San José: Instituto Interamericano de Derechos Humanos—Centro Interamericano de Asesoría y Promoción Electoral.

O'Donnell, Guillermo. 1979. *Modernization and Bureaucratic Authoritarianism.* Berkeley: Institute of International Studies, University of California.

O'Donnell, Guillermo; Schmitter, Philippe; and Whitehead, Laurence, eds. 1986. *Transitions from Authoritarian Rule.* Baltimore: Johns Hopkins University Press.

Pateman, Carole. 1970. *Participation and Democratic Theory.* Cambridge: Cambridge University Press.

Paz, Octavio. 1985. La democracia en América Latina. In Octavio Paz et al. *Frustraciones de un destino: La democracia en América Latina.* San José: Libro Libre.

Peeler, John. 1985. *Latin American Democracies: Colombia, Costa Rica, Venezuela.* Chapel Hill: University of North Carolina Press.

Petras, James. 1986. The Redemocratization Process. *Contemporary Marxism* 14 (Fall).

Przeworski, Adam. 1985. *Capitalism and Social Democracy.* Cambridge: Harvard University Press.

Rabine, Mark. 1986. Guatemala: "Redemocratization" or Civilian Counterinsurgency? *Contemporary Marxism* 14 (Fall): 59–64.

Rosenberg, Mark B. 1985. Democracia en Centroamérica? *Cuadernos de CAPEL,* No. 5. San José: Instituto Interamericano de Derechos Humanos-Centro de Asesoría y Promoción Electoral.

Rousseau, Jean Jacques. 1962. *The Social Contract.* Excerpted in *Communism, Fascism and Democracy,* edited by Carl Cohen. New York: Random House.

Schumpeter, Joseph A. 1943. *Capitalism, Socialism, and Democracy.* London: Allen and Unwin.

U.S. Department of State. 1985. *Guatemala's 1985 Elections: Presidential, Congressional, and Municipal.* Washington (October).

———. 1987. *Democracy in Latin America and the Caribbean: The Promise and the Challenge.* Washington, D.C.: Bureau of Public Affairs (March).

Walker, Thomas W., ed. 1985. *Nicaragua: The First Five Years*. New York: Praeger.

Wiarda, Howard J., ed. 1974. *Politics and Social Change in Latin America: The Distinct Tradition*. Amherst: University of Massachusetts Press.

Yates, Douglas. 1982. *Bureaucratic Democracy*. Cambridge: Harvard University Press.

2 Can Democracy Survive the Democrats?
From Transition to Consolidation in Honduras

Mark B. Rosenberg

Much of the recent research on the return to democracy in Latin America has focused on the transition from authoritarian to democratic governments (Malloy and Seligson, 1987; Baloyra, 1987; Drake and Silva, 1986). Less attention has been given to an equally important process: the *consolidation* of new democracies.

Examining the process of consolidation directs our attention to important questions about the democratic uses and abuses of power. Greater attention to the formal, institutional qualities of political organization will help us to understand how the political process itself works and why (Valenzuela, 1985). The establishment and consolidation of working democratic procedures and institutions is a formidable task, as Booth suggests in his opening analysis. Indeed, the process of democratization only begins when two conditions are met: (1) civilian groups can establish and maintain a working consensus on how their disagreements will be resolved, and (2) they can provide operationally for mechanisms to manage their differences. Ultimately, the content of democracy in the sense of *how* things get done is just as important as the *form* of governance. Being democratic involves adhering to democratic principles, even if they undermine the basis for personal rule.

This chapter focuses on the difficulties of consolidating democracy in Honduras, where orderly governance, whether by civilians or the military, has been rare during the past three decades. Since 1954 the country has had nine heads of state. Only three have left office following elections, and two of these made serious and disruptive efforts to prolong their rule. One of them, a civilian, Roberto Suazo Córdoba, almost succeeded. Suggesting that civilians have been as apt to ignore and mutilate constitutional pretense and democratic aspirations as have military officers, this study focuses on the efforts to consolidate democracy during President Suazo's four-year term (1982–86).

Politics and Political Style in Honduras

The poorest of Central America's five original republics ($720 GDP per capita), Honduras has had little success in establishing and maintaining an enduring democratic order (Morris, 1984). Its difficulties in consolidating democracy can be explained in general terms by examining Honduran political style, which exhibits several important characteristics.[1]

First, Honduran politics are not yet governed by regulations that prevent the arbitrary exercise of power. The formal rules of political life do not effectively govern the conduct of officeholders. Institutionalized public politics have not yet taken precedence over "palace and barracks politics." Noninstitutionalized government is the norm; persons take precedence over rules. The public system of rules is subject to continual abuse, neglect, and whim in accordance with momentary needs. Because no single set of rules is accepted, key authority roles are subject to continual redefinition in accordance with particularistic needs of the moment. The political system in Honduras is thus more akin to a game, where power for power's sake is often the primary objective.

Second, Honduran politics during the last three decades has generally been a personal struggle to control or influence the national government through the search for stable, but often short-lived, political coalitions. Such coalitions are critical. Through networks based on party affiliation, they give organizational coherence to a political aspirant's efforts. And they help to define the aspirant's power relations, both horizontally with other elites (and their respective coalitions) and vertically to the bases of society (Kenworthy, 1970). This effort is characterized by private and tacit agreements, prudential concerns, and personal ties and dependencies rather than public rules and institutions. Politicians emphasize competition and power, not rule making and problem solving. Political leaders spend as much of their time looking backward to protect themselves as looking forward to anticipate programs. Accordingly, political rewards are related to groups jockeying for power, not to their consequences for society.

Third, personal rule in Honduras is a dynamic world of political will and action that is determined by personal authority and power instead of by institutions. It is a system of relations based on shifting coalitions that links rulers and would-be rulers with patrons, associates, clients, supporters, and rivals. The military is a critical actor in coalition formation through both "push" and "pull" factors (Rosenberg and Colburn, 1986). Like other actors in the

Honduran political system, it is subject to factionalism and divisiveness, both of which can be critical impediments to the formation of stable coalitions. Nonetheless, the military plays the key role because power is typically checked by countervailing power, not by institutional rules.

With rare exceptions, the political process in Honduras is almost totally absorbed with issues directly related to the maintenance and use of power. Strategies for development are reduced to minimal efforts at incrementalism. Leadership tends to respond to particularistic interests of the moment; there is no tradition of public interest that can be defined beyond the narrow interests of the personal ruler and his coalition in power.

The necessity of meeting specific client needs, and the intensity of those clients' expectations and demands, militates against general pressure for responsive government. Shortages of human and material resources impose imperatives on public officeholders that work against any notion of the public good. *Chamba*, the provision of employment, becomes a principal modus operandi of government (Contreras, 1970). Indeed, government jobs are viewed as entitlements and rewards for personal loyalty rather than as public trusts and responsibilities. There are few incentives to perform official duties with probity because the personal imperative of meeting clients' needs takes precedence.

In this context the state becomes the object of power not so much because of its ability to promote the image of the larger good but because it is the mechanism through which private need can be addressed. Power is ultimately defined in terms of the ability to turn public authority into private benefit, in both a material and a symbolic sense. The state is an arena in which individuals and factions struggle for power and position; it is not an arena in which groups or parties compete for policies and constitutional norms. In fact, state power in Honduras has historically been the major arena of privilege, far exceeding in importance the economic, social, and religious arenas where elites normally interact.

Political Style and the Consolidation
of Democracy in Honduras

Even though civilian and military governments have alternated in power for the last three decades, Honduras's prevailing political style has been invariable. Both military and civilian groups have had difficulty adapting to democracy. In the setting of authoritarian political arrangements, the military has tended to be more responsive to mass demands than civilian political parties in power following popular elections. Only civilian parties, however, have been able to engender political mobilization and consciousness, though in a highly partisan and divisive fashion (Salomón, 1980). Both groups have had difficulty adapting to democracy. Civilians have shown as much resistance to responsible self-government as has the military. Elections have often been preludes to the reduction of participation. For example, in 1963 the military stopped the October presidential election and established itself in power. Civilian discord following the 1971 presidential elections ushered in yet another military government in late 1972.

The election of Liberal party leader Roberto Suazo Córdoba to the presidency in 1981 brought a new opportunity for civilians to consolidate their political hegemony over the military, which had gradually discredited itself while in power from 1972 to 1981. Elected by a clear and decisive mandate, Suazo promised a "revolution in honesty and work." Yet the 1981 elections merely provided the newly elected leadership with the legal framework and political legitimacy necessary to establish a system of democratic governance; political will would be necessary to implement it.

Although Suazo governed a full four years and completed his constitutionally mandated term in early 1986, he was almost forcibly ejected from office. Few of his political efforts were designed to strengthen, nurture, and expand the country's nascent democratic interests; on the contrary, they were designed to consolidate his style of personal rule. Much of his last year as president witnessed a furious political game of checkmate and intrigue, resulting in his ultimately unsuccessful efforts to stay in power. The cost to the Honduran polity was high. By the time Suazo left office, the Honduran electorate was debilitated and disillusioned with a political process that seemed only to reinforce the worst aspects of Honduran political style.

The actions that Suazo took to undermine democracy during his four-year presidency cannot be understood without considering the added difficulty of governing during a period of intensive U.S. intervention in Honduras. U.S. security managers in Washington and Honduras were prepared to support a transition from authoritarian to democratic rule, but they could not accept wide-ranging pluralism in the country that was the linchpin of U.S. security policies for Central America. The primary objective of U.S. policy was to keep

Honduras a loyal and unquestioning ally, prepared to support the United States in its efforts to overthrow the Sandinistas (Shepherd, 1986). Critical to this policy were agreeable civilian and military elites and an apathetic Honduran polity.

Using and abusing the powers of the presidency, and relying on his own cunning and wit, Suazo ably protected U.S. interests in a neat quid pro quo: Honduran national security policy would be dominated by pro-U.S. concerns; in exchange there would be very little U.S. interference in the country's internal political affairs. Suazo's rule was geared not to playing the political game within consensually derived procedural norms but rather to the maintenance of his own power. Thus, he simultaneously served U.S. and Honduran military objectives, both of which could show little tolerance for a serious political opening in the country. As described below, the Honduran president used a number of instruments to further his political ends. The promise of elections as a vehicle to contribute to enhanced participatory politics was unfulfilled, as we will see below.

Political Intervention in the
Legislative and Judicial Branches

The Honduran constitution of 1982 provides for the legal division and independence of powers. Deputies in the unicameral National Congress are elected every four years on the basis of proportional representation, and Supreme Court justices are elected by the National Congress. In turn, the Court appoints all other judges and court-related officials.

Honduras lacks a strong legislative tradition. While two political parties have tended to dominate the country's political life, clientelism and patronage have effectively limited political initiative and reinforced the tendency to centralization. The National party had been dominant since the 1930s, with the exception of a brief period of Liberal rule in the late 1950s. Since the early 1970s, the military has been the dominant political force, initially in coalition with urban and rural labor, but later in loose alliance with the National party. As a result, there has been little bipartisanship in decision making and public policy initiatives. Some of the most important state policies in recent years have been formulated privately through decrees or presented to the National Congress as a fait accompli. There is little confidence in the value and utility of open debate.

Suazo's Liberal party had a slight majority in the National Congress during his presidency; more important, the president of the Congress, Bu-Girón, was a Suazo loyalist and confidant who really functioned as the president's executive manager of the legislative body. Bu-Girón controlled the congressional agenda; few deputies seemed concerned about this and even fewer understood the implications. The Congress, largely reactive and deliberative, had little initiative in matters of public policy. One of the few activist deputies in Congress, a Christian Democrat, stated in June 1983 that "the Congress legitimizes all that the executive power wants. . . . It is not an independent power" (*Honduras Update*, 1983:5). Indeed, there was little serious debate in the Congress until Bu-Girón, whose presidential aspirations could not be contained, broke from Suazo near the end of the latter's term when it became apparent that Suazo would support another party loyalist for the presidency.

While Bu-Girón's vapid leadership helps to explain much of the Congress's lethargy, other more enduring factors reveal why democratic consolidation has been so difficult in Honduras. There is but a nascent sense of professionalism and corporate identity among legislators. Only a small number of the country's eighty-two deputies have had any prior experience in the legislative process, and the Congress has no staff to conduct research and draw up bills. Though each deputy nominally represents one of the country's eighteen departments, in reality they represent their parties to their departments. They have little incentive to be responsible to their constituencies because their political longevity is settled in the executive committees of the parties. They have virtually no role in helping to build community participatory norms. Indeed, the centralized system of proportional representation guarantees that they be the antithesis of community input and activism.

Democratic consolidation has also been difficult because of the tradition of intraparty competition and conflict (Molina, 1986). Coalition building is an ongoing phenomenon in the Honduran political system. As a result, both the National and Liberal parties tend to be more concerned with the vagaries of internal leadership in the often fractious parties than with the establishment of enduring procedures for governance that enjoy the confidence of contending elites. The tendency toward intraparty factionalism of both an ideological and personalistic nature has been one of the enduring characteristics of political party life in Honduras, especially within the Liberal party. Some of Suazo's most serious political battles arose from challenges by dissident groups within his own party.

Even though Suazo's Liberal party enjoyed a slim majority in the Congress (see table 2.1), the president had difficulty maintaining party cohesion among members of a splinter faction known as the Rodistas (*Tiempo*, 1983). The faction's source of leadership was personalistic rather than ideological. Its leader, Modesto Rodas Baca, son of a former Liberal party caudillo, had an intense personal dislike for Suazo.

In response, Suazo cultivated deputies from the National party as a means to ensure a legislative majority. Throughout his presidency, he was able to blunt the few serious legislative challenges by crafting a cross-party alliance of Liberal loyalists and National opportunists. The latter were attracted by Suazo's willingness to deliver jobs for their followers as well as direct cash payoffs. In one case, Suazo offered a National party deputy an ambassadorship to a European country in exchange for a favorable vote. Like Machiavelli's prince, Suazo was "lavish only with other people's money."

While nominally independent, the Honduran judiciary has always been an important source of presidential control and political pork barrels. Under Suazo, politicization of the nine-person Supreme Court reached new levels: Suazo's hand-picked Supreme Court president used the judiciary to protect Suazo politically and to ensure that Suazo loyalists stayed above the law.

Many of the problems with the judicial branch are structural: deficient legal training for judges and paralegals, poor or nonexistent record keeping, rudimentary investigatory capabilities, low budgets that are inadequate for the judiciary's work load, and virtually no job security (Salas and Cira, 1985). Other problems derive from a lack of respect for the legal system at the country's highest political and judicial levels.

Suazo directly and openly contravened Congress's right to elect Supreme Court judges. When Suazo was unhappy with some judges, he illegally forced them from their seats. When the Court attempted to remove from power a Suazo appointee, the president reacted by imprisoning the congressional nominee named to follow the Suazo loyalist. When opposition political parties or groups challenged the validity of Suazo-supported official "rump leadership factions," the Court inevitably ruled for the government.

It was just such a device that Suazo used to ensure his control of the

Table 2.1. Distribution of Seats in the Honduran National Congress, 1982–1986

Liberal Party	44
National Party	34
Innovation and Unity Party	3
Christian Democratic Party	1

country's election agency, the National Electoral Tribunal (TNE), which was composed of delegates representing each of the four main parties and a representative of the Supreme Court. Suazo was continually able to distort outcomes in his own favor by controlling the votes of the Liberal, National, and Supreme Court representatives. He could thus determine which leadership factions of parties, labor unions, and professional associations would be legally recognized.

Another measure of continuing politicization of the judiciary can be found in Suazo's reluctance to implement a judicial career law promulgated by the military in 1980 (Pérez, 1986). This law, which would engender the formation of a professionalized, career-oriented judiciary, would begin to provide the court system with a regularized process of judicial selection and tenure. Recognizing the political sensitivities involved in judicial politics, however, the law excludes Supreme Court appointments from professional regulation. Yet as a recent survey of Honduran lawyers suggests (see table 2.2), one of the main impediments to judicial independence is perceived to be interference from Supreme Court justices.

Thus two institutions critical to the consolidation of democracy in Honduras—the legislature and the judiciary—contributed little to the political opening inherent in the transition from authoritarian to democratic rule. President Suazo's leadership style reinforced inherent organizational weaknesses by continual interference and politicization from key elites both within and outside the two organizations. While this aggressive behavior can be conducive to forging a programmatic consensus within government, it can also be selfishly oriented to the enhancement of personal rule and the appropriation of public office for private gain. The latter outcome more aptly fits the Suazo legacy.

Table 2.2. Lawyers' Perceptions about Judicial Behavior

Perceived Situation	Percent[a]
Judges have become partisan because of political pressure	13
Judges have become partisan, but only as a secondary consideration	13
Judges have become partisan because of pressure from the Supreme Court, whose justices pressure judges to resolve issues in specific ways	26
There have been cases in which contending parties paid justices or judges to make favorable rulings	23
Specific cases are unknown	25

a. Unfortunately, the total number of lawyers interviewed was not indicated.
Source: CONSUPLANE, "Diagnóstico Administrativo del Poder Judicial de Honduras,"
Tegucigalpa, December 1985, p. 105.

Political Imposition and the Politicization
of the Supreme Electoral Tribunal

Transition to democratic rule in Honduras was marked by elections for a Constitutional Assembly in 1980 and presidential elections in 1981. In contrast to previous elections, both were relatively devoid of the politicization of voter registration lists, ballot-box stuffing, and physical intimidation that has normally characterized Honduran voting. By almost all accounts, the conduct of both elections was fair.

Despite periodic elections in Honduras, there has been little consensus on basic issues associated with the procedural aspects of democracy: the legal recognition of parties and their candidates, the compilation of voter registration lists, and the distribution of voter registration cards. Governed by an administrative board with representatives from each of the four parties and a delegate from the Supreme Court, the National Electoral Tribunal (TNE) was established as an autonomous agency to organize and conduct elections in Honduras. An equally important function of the TNE is the certification of the parties' official leadership cadres, which in Honduras has been a source of considerable attention, given the patronage opportunities and expectations.

From the party leadership comes the all-important *recomendación*, which is necessary if a *chamba* is to be secured.

The TNE also supervises the National Registry of Persons, which has jurisdiction over the creation of a national electoral census, the actual working list which determines a citizen's right to vote. Immediately after the 1981 election, the Registry was charged with developing a new census for the municipal elections of 1983 and then with the preparation of the final voting list for the presidential elections of 1985.

The TNE was a constant source of political conflict throughout Suazo's presidency. Because of his well-developed skills of political manipulation, the TNE became an important instrument for his opportunism and intrigue. While his party ostensibly had but one vote on the five-person panel, Suazo was able to co-opt the National party representative; with his control over the Supreme Court, he could effectively control its delegate to the TNE, giving him the majority necessary to ensure his influence in decision making.

By controlling the TNE, Suazo was able to impose on the National party an unpopular leader whom he maintained until the presidential elections of 1985. The TNE also certified his arbitrary machinations within his own party and the evolution of an unpopular leadership cadre whose primary virtue was its loyalty to the president. Perhaps in alliance with military commander General Gustavo Alvarez, he was also able to legalize the imposition on labor unions of rump leadership factions. The aggrieved parties had little recourse, as an appeal to the Supreme Court would only result in a deaf ear being turned by Suazo's cronies.

Through delays which Suazo engineered, the TNE could not complete its electoral census in time for the planned 1983 municipal elections to be held. Indeed, extreme politicization in the organization almost impeded the completion of the census in time for the 1985 presidential elections.

Political Imposition in Political Organizations

Unlike several Central American countries, Honduras has developed a set of mediating political institutions which have helped to channel and direct conflict and mobilization. Even though Honduras has one of the best-established party systems in Central America, stable civilian governance has been elusive in the post–World War II era. The Liberal and National parties, both dating from the early 1900s, have much in common, including broad, cross-class appeal, as well as a mixture of urban and rural support. They also share a history of factionalism that has lead one analyst to suggest that intraparty competition is greater than interparty competition (Sevilla, 1986).

When Suazo took office in January 1982, he enjoyed immense popularity and legitimacy. By the time he left office in 1986, he was feared and reviled for the damage he had done to the country's political system. He not only promoted internal divisions in his party and the main opposition party but, illustrating his love for power, also intervened in a number of unfriendly labor unions.

The president's leadership had two distinct phases. For the first two years he was eclipsed by the aggressive, hard-line chief of the Honduran armed forces, General Gustavo Alvarez Martínez (Salomón, 1984). Upon the general's ignominious ouster by his own officer corps in March 1984, the outlines of Suazo's political behavior emerged from the long shadows cast by Alvarez.

Neither Suazo nor Alvarez had much respect for the democratic process or its implications for state-society relations. During the first phase, Alvarez purposefully constructed a national security apparatus which was unprecedented by Honduran standards (Americas Watch, 1984). Despite the political opening implicit in the return to democratic rule, the breadth and depth of democracy (to use Booth's terminology) in the country declined. Politically related disappearances and murders, linked directly to Alvarez by a dissident senior military officer, became a new part of the political landscape. Progressive interest groups and associations either went underground or disbanded altogether. A short-lived but serious proto-corporative organization, with General Alvarez as its head, formed to promote "democratic" interests both at home and abroad.

Suazo showed little concern for the political deterioration that characterized the first two years of his rule. Only upon Alvarez's ouster was it clear why: the president himself demonstrated only minimal amounts of the statesmanship necessary to confront the political and economic problems of a country directly involved in the festering Central American conflict. Rather than promote national interests with his electoral mandate, he preferred to diminish and weaken democratic forces and organizations (including his own) for the apparent purpose of promoting his political monopoly.

Suazo's project was power, not democracy. Self-serving efforts to enhance his administrative and political primacy with other branches of his government, as described above, could have been expected, if for no other reason than the patronage imperative. However, the president's cynical and opportunistic efforts with both the military and nongovernment civilian sectors matured and ripened as his experience in office grew. An analysis of the specific features of Suazo's efforts can be instructive about the limits of democratic consolidation.

First, Roberto Suazo Córdoba was a typical, rural-based Liberal party leader who had been trained as a medical doctor. During the 1970s he had emerged as a member of the inner circle of one of the Liberal party's two main factions, the Rodistas, followers of the stubborn Liberal autocrat Modesto Rodas Alvarado, who was an antimilitarist. When the latter died unexpectedly in 1979, Suazo outmaneuvered another Rodas insider, Efraím Bu-Girón, for the party's leadership. The party's other important faction, the social reform Liberal Alliance of the People (ALIPO), had been eclipsed in the early 1970s by the Rodistas, whose coarse appeals were far more appealing to Honduran rural folk than was the ALIPO's urban, professional, reformist orientation.

Despite the growing public mandate for a return to civilian rule, Suazo's first serious efforts to build a solid base of support were with sectors in the military rather than with other civilian groups. This strategy, followed for years by the National party, had been a successful formula for securing political power. Suazo sought out Alvarez, a senior army colonel who enjoyed the confidence of the United States; but Alvarez's most attractive qualification from Suazo's viewpoint was the officer's deep dislike for the National party's likely presidential candidate. When Suazo was elected, the colonel was rewarded with the highly coveted top leadership post in the armed forces and with promotion, over the heads of more senior officers, to the rank of general. Even after Alvarez was thrown into exile, Suazo craftily maintained key senior officers' loyalties by providing financial inducements and other material incentives.

Once in office, President Suazo's governance style was rough, if not crude. His public rhetoric was often tactless, and he frequently derided urban values. He unabashedly made use of his *partida confidencial* (confidential fund), and he publicly admitted financial payoffs made to hold important supporters in place (*La Prensa*, 1985a). He often relied on budget transfers from other agencies, including the National Registry of Persons, to help finance political campaigns (*La Prensa*, 1985b). Suazo also used and withheld the limited foreign exchange from the Central Bank to reward friends and punish enemies (*El Heraldo*, 1985). One summary analysis described Suazo as "having been raised in the most 'rancid' political tradition, where caudillismo, compadrazgo, and bribery were the main elements of action" (*Boletín Informativo Honduras*, 1985:8).

During his four years in office, President Suazo used an array of resources to promote factionalism in the dominant political parties and in labor organizations which were perceived as unfriendly. In his own party, Suazo's unpredictable decision making, often contrary to Liberal customs and rules, resulted in the gradual marginalization of leading Liberal insiders and in the further factionalization of the party. Top Liberals such as José Azcona, Carlos Montoya, and Efraím Bu-Girón all gradually broke from the Suazo coalition as a result of the president's arbitrary and highly centralized conduct of the party and their own unfulfilled political ambitions.

By mid-1985 the party had undergone profound fission: from just two main factions in 1981, the organization had split into five contending factions (see table 2.3). The ALIPO movement split apart when Suazo engineered official recognition for the moderate wing by the Liberal party's central committee. Not wanting to risk political oblivion by separating themselves totally from the Liberal banner, the Reina brothers then formed their own political movement within the party. The José Azcona movement was the logical result of his marginalization from the party hierarchy in 1983; Efraím Bu-Girón's faction emerged from Bu's disgust at Suazo's ceaseless machinations and, worse, the likelihood that Suazo would not reward Bu-Girón's loyalty with nomination to the presidency. The noteworthy feature of this factionalization is that it developed in response to the presidential ambitions of party leaders rather than over substantive issues of party platform, ideology, domestic politics, or foreign policy.

Long the country's dominant political organization, the National party was thrown into profound disarray as a result of the voters' stampede to support the Liberal party in the 1981 presidential elections. The crisis of the National party was perhaps deserved. Its dominant force since the early 1960s was an aging lawyer, whom one observer known for his mild hyperbole labeled as "the most corrupt person in the universe."[2] While this aging autocrat was able to hold on to power in the party for a short period after the November polling, it was clear that new leadership would have to emerge if the National party was to be a viable opposition force.

But such opposition was not immediately forthcoming. In mid-1983 an obscure National party deputy seized the party's leadership and was given official recognition by the National Electoral Tribunal (TNE) as the party's

Table 2.3. Political Factions in the Liberal Party, 1981 and 1985

Faction	Leadership	Dominant Interests
November 1981		
Rodista	Roberto Suazo Córdoba	Rural, traditional
	Efraím Bu-Girón	
	José Azcona	
	Carlos Montoya	
	Carlos Flores Facusse	
ALIPO	Carlos Roberto Reina	Urban, professional,
	Jorge Bueso	developmentalists
	Jaime Rosenthal	
	Jorge Arturo Reina	
September 1985		
Rodista (in power)	Roberto Suazo Córdoba	Rural, traditional
	Oscar Mejía Arellano	
	Carlos Flores Facusse	
Rodista Dissidents	José Azcona	Urban, traditional
	Carlos Montoya	
	Modesto Rodas Baca	
Movement of Bu-Girón	Efraím Bu-Girón	Rural, traditional
ALIPO	Jorge Bueso Arias	Urban, professional,
	Jaime Rosenthal	moderates
M-LIDER	Carlos Roberto Reina	Urban, professional,
	Jorge Arturo Reina	reformers

leader. Because he was often sympathetic to Liberal party causes in the Congress and because he had little serious backing in the National party's leadership hierarchy, there was a general feeling that the main source of the deputy's support came directly from Suazo. Recognition by the TNE, controlled by Suazo, confirmed for many this suspicion, especially because it fit a familiar pattern of imposing rump leadership on organizations which could present opposition to the president of the country.

Democrat versus Democrat: Continuismo

Continuismo has a long and respected tradition in Honduras. Once in office, few Honduran presidents, whether civilian or military, have wanted to leave the perquisites, status, and power of the presidency when their mandated terms ended. When President Ramón Villeda Morales was removed from office by the military in 1963, his followers later criticized him for not "fighting" to stay in power (Contreras, 1970:17). Throughout his presidency, Suazo had been laying the basis for his continuation in power. His most important ally, the United States, was dependent on his good will to sustain logistical support for the contras. The military had retreated from the high political profile it had had under Alvarez and, like many civilian institutions, was highly factionalized around issues relating to its role with the United States, support for the contras, relations with El Salvador, and corruption. Suazo himself was quietly working with several senior-level officers who commanded troops to ensure the military's loyalty.

Most important, President Suazo had gradually created a situation in which government and nongovernment institutions were incapable of promoting and maintaining a working consensus about how disagreements should be resolved and what mechanisms would be used to manage conflict. Both the National Congress and the judiciary, as well as the election agency, were effectively serving very narrow interests rather than broad community interests. Political parties (and oppositionist labor unions), rarely paragons of a programmatic consensus, were penetrated and further divided as a result of Suazo's efforts. As the final constitutionally mandated year of Suazo's presidency approached, democratic institutions in the country were in far worse shape than before the election of 1981.

The political struggle during the last year of Suazo's presidency was more akin to the furious efforts in some countries to oust a recalcitrant dictator than to a peaceful transition from one civilian to another. President Suazo's machinations and the counterefforts on the part of elements in his own party, leaders from opposition parties and labor unions, the private sector and the military, as well as the United States, left the Honduran electorate debilitated and disillusioned with the politics of the country's democracy.

Critical to Suazo's continuation in office was the generation of a crisis over the issue of the forthcoming elections. By insisting on selecting his own successor in the Liberal party, Suazo had gradually alienated many of his key coalition partners, including Efraím Bu-Girón, who was his logical successor in the Rodista faction (*Boletín Informativo Honduras*, 1985). Suazo's handpicked successor in the National party was legally certified by the Supreme Court, thereby blocking the emergence of a more popular candidate in that party. Frustrated and finally understanding that he would not be Suazo's successor, Bu-Girón moved in early 1985 to promote an electoral reform which insisted on primary elections in all parties as a means to designate presidential candidates. He also engineered a constitutionally correct procedure by naming a new Supreme Court. Suazo vetoed the new electoral law and jailed the new Supreme Court chief justice.

The ensuing political crisis drew the military even more directly into the political arena. In the process the military's chief officer, General Walter López Reyes, emerged as a critical power broker and interlocutor between Suazo and a coalition of political forces led by organized labor and the private sector (members of which were quietly working in close collaboration with the military). The military was under pressure: many important leaders wanted Suazo ousted from power to ensure elections and an orderly transition of power. In essence they supported the notion of breaking the constitutional order to preserve it.

When a compromise was finally arranged, a modified electoral procedure was agreed upon which resulted in a campaign with multiple candidates from the dominant parties (Delgado, 1986:50). The elections would serve at once as a primary and final election. The party with the highest total number of votes would win the presidential election, even if the leading vote getter from this party had fewer votes than a rival candidate from the other dominant party. While it has often been the norm in Central America that the candidate with the highest number of votes is not the candidate who takes office, seldom have civilians openly agreed on this possibility in anticipation of the event (Solórzano, 1983:46). Disgust with Suazo was the key element in forging this consensus.

Thus the Honduran citizenry was confronted in the November 1985 elections with a dizzying array of nine candidates, four from Suazo's fractious Liberal party, three from the leading opposition National party, and individual candidates from the Christian Democratic and Innovation and Unity parties. Suazo's imposed candidate was so unpopular that above his name on the official ballot was a picture of the old Liberal party caudillo Modesto Rodas, who had been dead for six years. When the votes were counted, the National party's charismatic Rafael Leonardo Callejas had outpolled all other candidates. But the total number of votes cast for the Liberal party was greater than those for the National (see table 2.4), and an old Suazo crony-turned-antagonist, José Azcona Hoyo, was declared president by the TNE.

Callejas could have challenged the results of the election by asking the Supreme Court to review the compromise agreement that determined the winning formula, particularly given the difference in votes between him and Azcona. However, the National party understood that a challenge to the elections could allow Suazo to postpone his departure from office. When Azcona approached Callejas with the possibility of a "pact of national unity," allowing for a kind of co-government, the Nationals opted for the certainty of that arrangement. Azcona was inaugurated in late January 1986. Shortly thereafter, General Walter López Reyes, the military commander who had in essence stood against Suazo by negotiating the compromise election agreement, was ousted by the military, as his predecessor, Gustavo Alvarez, had been. Suazo-watchers, now firmly dazzled by the Liberal party leader's political acumen, aptly concluded that the former president had achieved his final revenge for not being able to continue in office.

Can Democracy Survive the Democrats?

Even though civilians were given a firm electoral mandate to govern Honduras in 1982, this study shows that they were unable to consolidate their political control because of the personal rulership style of Suazo, with the resultant civilian mismanagement and abuse.

A perceptive book written by Carlos A. Contreras addresses one of the central dilemmas of political life in Honduras: "power for power, cost what it does, has been the reason for the existence of the two traditional parties in Honduras" (Contreras, 1970:17). In many newly emerging or reemerging democracies, there is a vast gulf between a general commitment to democratic norms and an adherence to those same norms. Rules and statutes are as easily abused and neglected under democratic governments as they are under authoritarian ones.

The very fragility of the political environment in new democracies promotes

Table 2.4. Voting Results from the 1985 Presidential Elections in Honduras

Party/Faction	Candidate	Votes Cast
Liberal Party		786,594
Liberal Azconista Movement	José Azcona	424,358
Liberal Rodista Movement	O. Mejía Arellano*	250,519
Liberal Rodista Movement	E. Bu-Girón	62,230
Lib. Dem. Rev. Movement	C. Roberto Reina	43,373
(for the party itself)		4,114
National Party		701,406
MONARCA	R. L. Callejas	656,882
Unity and Change	J. P. Urrutia*	20,121
Movement	F. Lardizábal G.	22,163
(for the party itself)		2,240
Christian Democratic Party	H. Corrales P.	30,173
Innovation and Unity Party	E. Aguilar P.	23,705
Null Votes		27,733
Blank Votes		28,230
TOTAL VOTES		1,597,481

*Imposed by Suazo
Source: Foreign Broadcast Information Service, 26 December 1985.

personal rule and the continual search for powerful coalitions. If democracies are to be responsive to their citizens, these coalitions should progressively become inclusionary—gradually incorporating new groups as consensus over common concerns grows—while at the same time providing institutions to manage their inevitable differences. In Honduras, President Suazo's ruling coalition gradually diminished in size; institutions that could have mediated broader conflicts within the society became personal instruments for Suazo's own power needs.

Notes

1. For this section, I have drawn on the concepts developed by Jackson and Rosberg (1982).

2. This source asked that the remark not be directly attributed to him. The comment was made in June 1986 in Tegucigalpa.

References

Americas Watch. 1984. *Honduras on the Brink*. New York: Americas Watch.

Baloyra, Enrique, ed. 1987. *Comparing New Democracies*. Boulder: Westview Press.

Boletín Informativo Honduras. 1985. June.

Contreras, Carlos. 1970. *Entre el marasmo: Análisis de la crisis del Partido Liberal de Honduras, 1933–1970*. Tegucigalpa: n.p.

Delgado, Aníbal. 1986. *Honduras: Elecciones 85 (más allá de la fiesta cívica)*. Tegucigalpa: Editorial Guaymuras.

Drake, Paul W., and Silva, Eduardo, eds. 1986. *Elections and Democratization in Latin America, 1980–85*. San Diego: Center for Iberian and Latin American Studies.

FBIS (Foreign Broadcast Information Service). 1985. 20 May.

El Heraldo. 1985. 13 April.

Honduras Update. 1983. No. 10 (June).

Jackson, Robert H., and Rosberg, Carl G. 1982. *Personal Rule in Black Africa*. Berkeley: University of California Press.

Kenworthy, Eldon. 1970. Coalitions in the Political Development of Latin America. In *The Study of Coalition Behavior*, edited by Sven Groennings. New York: Holt, Rinehart and Winston.

La Prensa. 1985a. 2 July.

La Prensa. 1985b. 25 October.

Malloy, James M., and Seligson, Mitchell A., eds. 1987. *Authoritarians and Democrats: Regime Transition in Latin America*. Pittsburgh: University of Pittsburgh Press.

Molina, Guillermo. 1986. The Politics of Democracy in Honduras. In *Honduras Confronts Its Future: Contending Perspectives on Critical Issues*, edited by Mark B. Rosenberg and Philip L. Shepherd. Boulder: Lynne Rienner Publishers.

Morris, James. 1984. *Honduras: Caudillo Politics and Military Rulers*. Boulder: Westview Press.

Peeler, John. 1985. *Latin American Democracies: Colombia, Costa Rica and Venezuela*. Chapel Hill: University of North Carolina Press.

Pérez, Guillermo. 1986. Enhancing the Instruments for Human Rights Protection in Honduras. In *Honduras Confronts Its Future: Contending Perspectives on Critical Issues*, edited by Mark B. Rosenberg and Philip L. Shepherd. Boulder: Lynne Rienner Publishers.

Rosenberg, Mark B., and Colburn, Forrest D. 1986. Ruling from the Barracks: Honduras' Military. Miami: Florida International University.

Salas, Luis, and Cira, Carl. 1985. The Central American and Spanish Caribbean System of Justice: A New Focus for U.S. Development Assistance. Miami: Florida International University, Latin American and Caribbean Center.

Salomón, Leticia. 1980. Honduras: de los militares en la política a la política entre los militares. Unpublished ms., Tegucigalpa.

———. 1984. La doctrina de la seguridad nacional en Honduras: Análisis de la caída del General Gustavo Alvarez Martínez. *Boletín Informativo Honduras* no. 11 (May).

Sevilla, Edgardo. 1986. The Limits of Democracy in Honduras. In *Honduras Confronts Its Future: Contending Perspectives on Critical Issues*, edited by Mark B. Rosenberg and Philip L. Shepherd. Boulder: Lynne Rienner Publishers.

Shepherd, Philip L. 1986. Honduras. In *Confronting Revolution: Security through Diplomacy in Central America*, edited by Morris J. Blachman, William LeoGrande, and Kenneth Sharpe. New York: Pantheon Books.

Solórzano, Mario. 1983. Centroamérica: democracias de fachada. *Polémica* no. 12 (November–December).

Tiempo. 1983. 1 October.

Valenzuela, Arturo. 1985. Political Science and the Study of Latin America. Paper presented at the 12th International Congress of the Latin American Studies Association, 18–20 April 1985, Albuquerque, New Mexico.

3 El Salvador
Recent Elections in Historical Perspective

José Z. García

This chapter explores the evolution and political significance of elections in El Salvador's mercurial political system from 1948 to 1988.[1] The coup against General Romero in 1979 constitutes a major break point in the analysis because, as subsequent events have revealed, it ended a political regime created after 1948 and began the efforts by many centrist groups to create a new regime while fighting a civil war. The elections of 1982, 1984, 1985, and 1988, when viewed in historical context, should be seen as elements of a successful strategy against guerrilla insurgents devised by an alliance between the armed forces of El Salvador, the Christian Democrats, and the U.S. government.

This strategy consisted of efforts to employ military force against the guerrillas effectively enough to avoid defeat, to buy time to initiate policy reforms designed to co-opt sectors thought to be vulnerable to guerrilla appeals, and to create a more viable political system that could institutionalize democratic legitimacy through electoral and governmental reform. The strategy appears by and large to have succeeded. Elections should thus be seen as a necessary but not sufficient ingredient in preventing what one might call the "Sandinization" of Salvadoran politics, a minimum goal consciously shared by the three forces —U.S. government, Christian Democratic party, Salvadoran armed forces— that formed the alliance.

The Historical Context:
Elections from 1948 to 1979

The 1948 Osorio Revolution

The first relatively free election in Salvadoran history occurred in 1930. Several candidates contested the presidential election, policy differences between candidates were clear, and the votes were counted honestly

(Anderson, 1971:chaps. 3–4; Guidos Véjar, 1980). The winner was a wealthy, quixotic civilian, Manuel Araujo, who organized a populist government designed to accommodate the demands of a small but vocal middle class chafing under the jackboot of an arrogant and armed coffee-growing elite which preached an extremely narrow version of laissez faire doctrine. This experiment with both procedural democracy and reformist policy ended in disaster in late 1931 and early 1932. A serious financial crisis (caused principally by the global economic troubles of that epoch) sapped government revenues, leading to a political crisis that resulted in Araujo's overthrow by General Maximiliano Martínez in December 1931. A Marxist rebellion against Martínez headed by Farabundo Martí failed a few weeks later when the armed forces discovered the plot, arrested the leaders, and assassinated thousands of suspected participants after localized violence, presumably organized by Martí's followers, broke out in the western portion of the country, which had a heavily indigenous population (Anderson, 1971:chaps. 5–10; Gómez, 1972; Guidos Véjar, 1980).

In retrospect it is easy to see that the middle classes in those days were too small and too dependent upon coffee revenues to have had much chance of reformist success under the best of conditions. Under the circumstances of the Great Depression this first experiment with the pluralist and procedural imperatives of democracy was bound to fail. The legacy of the effort, however, was to have a profound impact on the course of Salvadoran history. From that moment on the coffee barons viewed free elections as a concession they had once "allowed" (in truth they did not take Araujo's preelectoral promises of reform seriously) in a moment of generosity but which had led to two great affronts to their power. The first was a reformist assault on their absolute control over government policy making, and the second—this point is less historically sound—an armed revolutionary assault on their property. For the middle classes, too, the legacy of this electoral episode was lasting—they began to equate free elections with pluralist reform. In short, free elections in El Salvador became the central issue of political conflict for at least the next half-century. Members of the armed forces were not immune to the impact of these tensions. Military officers were formally in charge of the government for the next fifty years.

An extraordinary growth in the cotton industry of El Salvador between 1930 and 1960 greatly enlarged the size of the middle classes (Browning, 1971). Unlike coffee, which is extremely labor intensive, the successful cultivation of cotton in El Salvador required extensive capital-intensive investments and forward and backward linkage networks such as textiles, imports of agricultural implements and chemicals for insecticides and fertilizers, credit-granting institutions, crop-dusting, and so on. All of these activities stemming from the growth of the cotton industry caused a significant expansion of the middle classes. And as these grew, they once again began to articulate the need for enlargement of the scope, range, and magnitude of government in order to address a set of demands commonly associated with the middle classes: educational investment, transportation and communication improvements, legislation governing labor-management relations, modern banking practices, and so on (White, 1973). These changes were resisted by the coffee barons, who backed General Martínez as president from the time he took power in 1932 until he was ousted in 1944.

General Martínez used his power in 1939 to amend the constitution to allow himself to be "elected" (the Martínez machine brooked no opposition) to another term of office. In 1944, Martínez tried to use his clout once again to amend the constitution for the same purpose. This time, however, a small group of dissident coffee growers joined a large group of cotton entrepreneurs and junior military officers in a full-scale civil-military revolt against Martínez and his clique of aging officers and coffee barons. The rallying call was "free elections," a password for middle-class reform.

The revolt failed. The senior military leaders of the coup attempt proved incompetent. Several officers were executed, several civilians were condemned in absentia, and order was restored (García, 1983; Parkman, 1988). General Martínez resigned after some confusion, but power over the government was secured by senior officers who represented a continuation of Martínez's rule.

A second effort by sectors of the middle class to seize power by force succeeded in 1948. Again backed by middle-class civilian interests, junior officers overthrew and purged the aging army leadership clique. They placed at the head of the government an astute lieutenant colonel, Oscar Osorio, whose foreign experience had included assignments in Mexico City, Washington, and fascist Italy. Osorio forged a coalition between the armed forces and the new middle class that would last until the early 1970s. A third middle-class effort to seize power by force would not take place until 1980.

Osorio's genius lay in his ability to institutionalize military rule by precariously balancing middle-class interests with agrarian property interests (Castro Morán, 1983; López Vallecillos, 1979). This was accomplished by greatly enlarging the scope, range, and magnitude of government through modern tax policies; government revenues were increased by taxing new sources of wealth. A military-controlled political party, elected periodically, provided a formidable base of legitimacy for both the government and the regime that backed it. Taxing new wealth was a relatively easy matter during the 1950s when commodity prices rose to unprecedented levels and during the 1960s when the growth of the Central American Common Market greatly stimulated industrial growth in El Salvador. It would become more difficult when commodity prices fell and the Common Market failed during the 1970s.

The New System

The rules of the game of politics in El Salvador as established in 1948 and operative until 1979 included the following: (1) an officialist party representing Osorio's power base among civilians was formed to compete in periodic elections. This was headed during the first presidential term following a constitutional convention by Osorio himself, and members of the armed forces were to be allowed to compete for later presidential candidacies within the party. The officialist party was first called the Revolutionary Party of Democratic Unification (Partido Revolucionario de Unificación Democrática—PRUD) and was later renamed the National Conciliation party (Partido de Conciliación Nacional—PCN); (2) other political parties were to be allowed to compete for legislative and presidential positions and to debate the relative merits of the expansion or contraction of the government sector; (3) there was to be no reelection of the president, thus assuring some political opportunity for unincorporated sectors of the polity. "Out-groups" would have some incentive to remain loyal and to jockey for position in future administrations because the no-reelection provision would assure periodic circulation of top power holders.

In other words, Osorio created a new political machine. It was more inclusive and had more support mechanisms and democratic trappings than the previous machine organized by General Martínez. Its policies were dramatically successful in expanding the role of government (the national bureaucracy more than doubled from 1948 to 1958, while salary expenditures tripled) through increases in the tax burden imposed on coffee growers. Public works, education, and social programs flourished.

Structurally the Osorio system represented a shift away from a narrow alliance between the armed forces and coffee growers in which officers represented the interests of a single agrarian elite, toward one in which officers mediated between the demands of two agrarian elites and the middle classes (López Vallecillos, 1979; White, 1973). Domestically it was quite successful in eliciting support. Internationally the Osorio system was viewed as a successful effort by the armed forces to modernize an agrarian society. It is said that President Kennedy saw El Salvador's regime as a model and remarked that he would like to see the armed forces play a similar role in other areas of the less developed world.

This was the political regime that collapsed in 1979 when rifts developed within the coalition of forces that had sustained it since 1948. These rifts were marked by a concatenation of events in which (a) a violent conservative reaction occurred when commodity prices leveled out; (b) it subsequently became evident that the armed forces—still formal mediators between the component parts of the regime—had abandoned their own evenhanded rules of the game in favor of the rich; and (c) a guerrilla revolutionary movement became viable with the increasing support of the laboring classes. Ultimately, procedural violations in several fraudulent or exclusionary elections destroyed the middle-class base of support for the regime when it became clear that major policy disputes could no longer be resolved or compromised through electoral means. The rule of force prevailed.

Elections and the Collapse of the Osorio System

Although the system enjoyed support, especially in the early years, problems of legitimacy began to plague the government as early as 1960. The most nagging problems centered around the question of elections. Osorio made clear when he left office that the president would make the final decision over his own replacement. In 1956 he made a fateful decision to replace himself with a fellow military officer. He apparently believed that he could control his successor, Colonel José María Lemus. Osorio was also probably pressured by fellow officers and perhaps members of the agrarian elite (fearful for their perquisites) to protect the system of patronage and other benefits for officers.[2]

Osorio's choice of Lemus had major implications. If officialist candidates would in the future be military officers selected by the president, then as long as the regime remained popular enough (or devious enough) to be the probable winner, civilians would court the upper ranks of the officer corps. The armed forces would inevitably be politicized and factionalized by various and sometimes contradictory civilian interests. Indeed, such factionalism did plague virtually every government until the regime's collapse in 1979. Internally, the officer corps became seriously divided over succession issues. Externally, it became increasingly clear that military leaders were much more accessible to the rich than to others. Middle-class civilians who had backed presidential losers and were bereft of governmental access soon resented the unfairness of the system. During moments of economic stagnation or decline, when government revenues could not support as many public employees and programs as during moments of prosperity, the size of the "out" groups grew large indeed.

In 1960 a military coup backed by left-of-center middle-class groups overthrew Lemus, but this was followed a few weeks later by a successful conservative countercoup headed by Colonel Julio Rivera. In dispute in both coups were procedural and policy issues revolving around the presidential selection system. After some confusion a compromise was struck whereby Rivera would remain at the head of the government to supervise elections for a constitutional convention, after which political parties would be allowed to compete in presidential and then legislative elections.

Constitutional provisions stipulated a winner-take-all rather than proportional representation electoral system. The officialist party was well organized. It won a plurality of the votes in each district, resulting in a constitutional convention in which all members belonged to the officialist party. Rivera thus controlled the convention; he decided to offer himself to the public as a presidential candidate. A young Christian Democrat, José Napoleón Duarte, and other potential presidential aspirants decided not to dignify this electoral process by participating, and Rivera found himself the only candidate on the ballot. University students jestingly "nominated" a donkey, reasoning publicly that only a donkey would be fool enough to run in such elections (Webre, 1979).

Rivera's military faction represented a continuation of the Osorio system, but under the circumstances Rivera was forced to promise significant reforms. Rivera recognized the damage done to the legitimacy of the political system in his bid to become president and tried to remedy it through electoral reforms that guaranteed political opposition through proportional representation in subsequent legislative elections. To emphasize his sincerity he changed the name of the officialist party to the Party of National Conciliation (PCN).

Moreover, he tried to mollify the middle classes through substantive policies: he doubled the size of the government bureaucracy by the end of his administration,[3] and took other measures to accommodate the middle class. But the system whereby military officers became officialist candidates remained intact, and many officers and civilians felt betrayed by Rivera as his and subsequent governments drifted steadily toward greater accommodation with the rich.

In the 1972 presidential election the military declared PCN candidate General Armando Molina the victor, even though centrist Christian Democrat candidate Duarte had clearly won. Duarte was sent into exile, but the Osorio system lost all vestiges of procedural legitimacy. The only potential source of support for the regime among democratic sectors lay in the substantive policy changes the government might make. Recognizing this, Molina, president from 1972 to 1977, tried to mollify middle-sector interests by announcing plans for a comprehensive agrarian reform. By this time the extreme right had consolidated its position, however. Sectors of the armed forces allied with the coffee-growing elite threatened a coup, and Molina was forced to abandon his program in 1976 in order to save his presidency.

Guerrilla groups, active in El Salvador since 1970, began to expand their activities, especially against the rich. Sectors of the Church began openly to defy the government, speaking out against abuses and in some cases openly organizing agrarian labor unions. When the right responded with a wave of repression, including widespread death squad activity against clergy and labor organizers, the international community began publicly to condemn the government. All of these tensions were exacerbated when General Humberto Romero, head of the dreaded ORDEN (Nationalist Democratic Organization—Organización Democrática Nacionalista) paramilitary squads, became president in 1977 in elections that had become meaningless except as symbols of a total lack of governmental legitimacy. On 15 October 1979 moderate factions in the armed forces overthrew Romero.

Elections after 1979

The Dilemma Facing the Armed Forces

The fall of Romero in fact represented the collapse of the entire Osorio system. The officialist party and large sectors within the armed forces—the two key mediating institutions of the post-1948 political system—were tainted by several fraudulent elections. The net result was that the extreme right wing could monopolize power in blatant contradiction of the fundamental power-sharing premises of the Osorio system. Virtually no group in Salvadoran society seriously believed the presence of active Marxist guerrillas justified this ham-fisted violation. On the contrary, many were beginning to feel that systematic violations by the government justified a Marxist revolt.

As death squads acting with the complicity of government and military officials used the label "subversive" to justify the elimination of thousands of previously legitimate political actors—teachers, labor union leaders, progressive priests, and middle-sector politicians—they were also in fact assuring the destruction of the regime. In neighboring Nicaragua in 1978 and 1979 a network of international support had made possible a multiclass overthrow of Somoza. As human rights violations made the Salvadoran regime an international pariah, portions of the middle classes began to join with the guerrillas.

As they had done under less dangerous circumstances in 1948, younger officers in the armed forces again sought to accommodate the interests of the middle classes within a centrist government by overthrowing Romero and instituting certain reforms. The Junta established after the 15 October coup incorporated prominent opposition leaders in the government. By the end of 1979, however, some in the opposition decided they could not trust the armed forces to constitute a new regime. The middle classes split: some, led by the Christian Democratic party, hoped to reconstitute democratic reformism in alliance with a reformist military, while others hoped to destroy the armed forces altogether. A small party headed by Guillermo Ungo, sections of the Christian Democratic party, and much of the labor movement broke with the government. These defectors established the Revolutionary Democratic Front (Frente Democrático Revolucionario—FDR), which allied itself with the guerrilla coalition the Farabundo Martí Liberation Front (Farabundo Martí para la Liberación Nacional—FMLN).

Thus began the Salvadoran civil war. Just months after the defeat of Somoza in neighboring Nicaragua, the Carter administration was denying any military aid to the government of El Salvador, Church members were attacking the government for complicity in gross human rights abuse, and international ostracism was growing. Many observers believed the guerrillas would win the civil war.

Constructing a Counterinsurgency Strategy

The armed forces, still formally in charge of the new government, were left with two potential but incompatible allies: the extreme political right wing, whose behavior over the years (with the help of large sectors of the armed forces) had destroyed the Osorio regime, and the Christian Democratic party (PDC). The latter had been rejected by the armed forces from 1962 to 1972 as a legitimate player in the regime, but most of the party members appeared still willing to bargain. Alliance with both groups at once would have been impossible. Alliance with the right wing would have implied continuation of state-sponsored terrorism and invited rejection by the United States and most of the international community. Without foreign assistance the armed forces of El Salvador might lose to the FMLN guerrillas, who could count on considerable levels of international support. On the other hand, alliance with the Christian Democrats would imply acceptance of substantive and procedural reform, but it also would secure the backing of the U.S. government. The armed forces opted for reform.

The fateful decision taken in early 1980 to constitute a new, centrist, more legitimate government involved a strategy consisting of the following elements: (1) the creation of an alliance between the Christian Democratic party, the armed forces, and the United States to create an emergency government capable of short-term survival against an increasingly serious guerrilla threat; (2) the adoption of policies designed to reduce the power of the extreme right, quickly legitimize the government with the middle sectors through substantive policy reforms, defeat the guerrillas in combat, and maintain the government's long-run legitimacy through free elections; and (3) the restitution of significant amounts of U.S. assistance devoted both to political and military objectives.

The first actions of this coalition involved substantive policy reform. In March 1980 the government decreed a comprehensive agrarian reform program that would confiscate lands in excess of five hundred hectares held in large estates; army troops were sent into affected estates. That same month the government nationalized the banking sector, allowing the state to control foreign exchange transactions and lending policies. Government monopoly of export sales was also decreed, enabling the government to tax exports effectively for the first time in history. All of these measures were tangible, not just symbolic, efforts by the new government to secure some autonomy for itself over the extreme right wing oligarchy and to serve notice that a centrist government had taken control. Elections were promised for the future, but only after reforms had taken hold. If reform and elections should succeed, the reasoning went, defeat of the guerrillas would follow. Meanwhile, military assistance from the United States, it was hoped, would prevent a short-term victory by the guerrillas.

Elections within the Counterinsurgency Strategy

Elections thus represented only one of several measures taken to legitimize the government, but they were essential. However, the fraudulent elections of the past had become symbolic but vital weapons favoring the opposition. In 1950 the relatively free formal election of Osorio as president had come to symbolize accommodation with the middle class. In 1979 the fact of fraudulent elections had signalled the failure of that very effort at accommodation. Only through free elections could substantive policy reforms, the tripartite alliance structure, and aggressive military actions against the guerrillas be validated.

Free elections had serious military implications as well. It was unlikely that the alliance structure between the armed forces, the PDC, and the United States could remain intact without massive military assistance from the United States. This level of assistance, however, was unlikely to be granted by a post–Vietnam era U.S. Congress until free elections in El Salvador were a fact. Elections thus had, in a purely military sense, a direct impact on the ability of the coalition of forces backing the new government to survive.

A number of unproven assumptions formed the underpinning of this heavy, one might even say excessive, reliance on elections to perform critical tasks in the drive to avoid defeat by the guerrillas. First, it was assumed that free elections, under the intense scrutiny of highly skeptical international news media representatives, could be held in the middle of a civil war. Second, it was assumed that the electorate in El Salvador would respond to elections in numbers large enough to make credible the effort to reconstruct a democratically legitimate government. Third, it was assumed that elections would result in a generous dispersal of military and economic assistance by the U.S. Congress. And fourth, it was assumed that elections would result in the coming to power of a popular, centrist government that could survive long enough to build a lasting support base that would permit future governments to consolidate the program of middle-class reform. That is, elections would curtail the extreme right while helping secure aid to defeat the guerrillas. It now appears that the strategists were correct about their first three assumptions, but only partially correct about the last.

The 1982 Elections

On 28 March 1982 a national election was held for a constituent assembly. In an effort to encourage a high turnout no voter registration system was used. All voters with identification were allowed to vote. Six political parties contested the election. Voters were asked to cast a ballot for the candidates of a single party. Parties would be allocated seats in the assembly in proportion to their national vote. All but the Christian Democratic party represented the right or center-right of the political spectrum. Out of 1.36 million votes counted, the Christian Democratic party received 40 percent, followed by ultra-right ARENA with 29 percent, and the PCN with 19 percent (see table 3.1).

The middle-class democratic groups who had begun the civil war when they defected to the guerrillas had formed the Revolutionary Democratic Front (Frente Democrático Revolucionario—FDR) and identified themselves roughly as social democrats in a European sense. This group encountered strong cross-pressures because of the elections. As a democratic organization, the FDR could hardly denounce elections, but to endorse this electoral effort would be to betray their FMLN allies. In the end many FDR members simply ignored the elections as much as possible, asserted their disbelief that they could be successful, and, somewhat awkwardly, sometimes argued that their own lack of participation should be seen as proof that the process was not legitimate.[4] In truth, participation in the elections in 1982 or 1984 would have been impossible for the FDR. To the FMLN guerrillas this would have been a clear betrayal. To the right, FDR participation would have appeared to legitimate treason. To the public it would have seemed cynical opportunism. To members of the FDR it would have been downright dangerous.

FMLN guerrilla commanders, who never professed a belief in democratic elections, were nevertheless hamstrung by their democratic allies. If they attacked the voters with military force, they might succeed in disrupting the electoral process and demonstrating strength, but only at great political cost at home and abroad. El Salvador was, after all, one of the major news stories of the day. Elections in El Salvador would certainly receive major coverage in

Table 3.1. 1982 Election Results

Party	Percent Valid Votes	Valid Votes	Valid Seats
PDC	543,150	40	24
ARENA	395,086	29	19
PCN	258,305	19	14
AD	100,372	8	2
PPS	39,363	3	1
POP	12,453	1	0

Note: Turnout was 80 percent (estimate): 1,551,687 persons voted; 1,362,339 votes were considered valid; 8 percent were invalid; 3 percent were blank.
Source: *Estudios Centroamericanos* (April 1982, p. 324).

Europe and the Western Hemisphere, where political culture imbues elections with almost sacred symbolism. News of disruptions might well lead to repudiation of antidemocratic tactics and a consequent reduction in funds available from democratic sources to pursue the war. Worse, they might lead to increases in military aid to the Salvadoran armed forces.

In the end the guerrillas compromised. Radio Venceremos, the guerrilla radio for the militant ERP, broadcast threats against the security of citizens who wanted to vote, but guerrilla activity before, during, and after the elections seemed restrained. Attacks did take place on election day in various places, including an early morning series of attacks in San Salvador, but 90 percent of the polling places were open to voters. In the Department of Usulután the military commander did not take prescribed preventive measures to protect voters from guerrilla sabotage. Guerrillas prevented people from voting in most of the province. Despite these incidents it seems clear the guerrillas could have engaged in far more disruptive tactics.

The 1982 election was reasonably free. Parties willing to participate were free to organize and field candidates. There were no organized impediments to free speech. The media was free to comment, support, and withhold support. Intermediary groups such as unions and business associations, which are quite well developed in El Salvador, were active in the campaign both as supporters of various parties and as pressure groups. Although death squads were still assassinating suspected guerrilla sympathizers, they did not intimidate campaign workers or candidates. In interviews with Christian Democratic party organizers the author was told that in isolated instances in 1982 National Guardsmen intimidated their candidates enough to influence the results in an occasional ballot box but that the overall results were not significantly affected. One Christian Democratic candidate, now a legislator from Sonsonate, told the author there were areas in his district (in the coffee-growing region, one of the most reactionary areas in the country) in which he was afraid to campaign. Nevertheless, he was able to win and was reelected in 1985. Such practices were even more isolated in the 1984 and 1985 elections. If the elections cannot be said to have taken place in an atmosphere entirely free of coercion and fear, this could only be expected in a country fighting a civil war.

Moreover, the very climate of war in many ways served the interests of those trying to bolster the government through elections. After the elections voters were reminded not only by the national news media but especially by reports from abroad that 80 percent of the potential voters had participated in the elections, a fact that, by itself, became a political weapon against the guerrillas. The results were said by U.S. and Salvadoran government officials—joined by a large and sympathetic press corps—to prove guerrilla threats did not work; they were said to prove the electorate was brave; they were said to prove that the brave electorate was large. The very act of voting at such a scale was said to represent a collective democratic event of major proportions, the first in many decades, a national celebration of democratic aspirations in action. Every citizen who voted could look back on the experience, through the eyes of the news media, and indulge in a moment of self-congratulation for this ordinary act made brave in the context of civil war.

In this sense the election of 1982 created a kind of patriotism through participation where none had existed before; the event became a national unifying experience, like an earthquake or military victory—at least for those who participated in it. In short, the 1982 elections helped define political reality in El Salvador in ways that very much helped legitimize the government at the expense of the guerrillas.[5] Certainly Washington was pleased with the elections. The day after the event the *New York Times* described U.S. embassy officials as "euphoric" over the turnout.

One of the assumptions in the strategy outlined above was that free elections would result in a centrist government. As it turned out, however, the only centrist party, the PDC, was outnumbered by the extreme right in the constituent assembly, which was charged with legislative powers as well as with writing a new constitution. Indeed, ultra-right retired Major Roberto D'Aubuisson, accused by many of active complicity in death squad activity, was elected president of the constituent assembly in a compromise in which Alvaro Magaña, a centrist, would be elected interim president of El Salvador until 1984. In effect, then, the radical right wing had been legitimized in power through elections, a somewhat embarrassing and unexpected outcome. With human rights abuses still high and the military situation still precarious, many skeptics felt the substantive reforms such as agrarian reform initiated by the preelection junta would be reversed, weakening the legitimacy of the government among members of the middle class.

There was reason for concern. Shortly after the elections, for example, the right tried to suspend implementation of the Decree 207 program, which allowed land tillers to purchase land they were renting, a policy move felt to be important as a means of securing peasant support. The measure failed only with indirect pressure from the United States and some members of the high command of the armed forces. Rightist landowners began expelling Decree 207 peasant beneficiaries at gunpoint. The right wing, which commanded several key ministries in the government, began a full-scale offensive to prevent the reforms the Christian Democratic party felt necessary to consolidate a moderate government.

The right, however, was in a precarious position. In 1982 the guerrilla war was going badly for the government. Only an increase in U.S. military support was likely to result in a government victory. But the Congress of the United States was highly skeptical of the Reagan administration's strategy in El Salvador and was unlikely to increase military assistance to levels sufficient to destroy the guerrillas without tangible evidence that human rights improvements and centrist reforms were firmly under way. Should the guerrillas win, the right understood that it would be destroyed. Only a certain amount of cooperation with the centrist designs of the tripartite alliance would prevent this from happening. Predictably, the right responded to this challenge by ceding only what it thought to be the minimum price for its own survival.

If elections had created a legitimate government, they had not created a viable regime, since no system yet existed whereby major policy disputes—

especially between centrist and rightist interests—could be worked out within a framework of basic cooperation. The right refused to cooperate with centrist policy designs, and the centrists, believing reform to be the only long-term solution to the civil war, believed the right to be as much an enemy as the guerrillas. As long as this lack of cooperative effort persisted, the guerrillas would have a chance to win, at least in the long run. For this reason efforts were made following the elections to forge some sort of consociational pact that would produce at least some measure of coherence in government policy.

On 3 August 1982, under pressure from several quarters, representatives of four political parties—the PDC, ARENA, PCN, and the Popular Salvadoran party (Partido Popular Salvadoreño, or PPS)—met in the small town of Apaneca to seek an agreement on fundamental policy matters involving democratization, human rights, economic recovery, social and economic reforms, pacification, and international support (Campos, 1982:865–79; Baloyra, 1984). Although a "Pact of Apaneca" was adopted, the right wing, in control of the assembly, maintained its offensive designed to prevent the passage of any of the substantive measures the Christian Democratic party felt were necessary to legitimize the government with the popular classes. In fact, by late 1983 the stalemate was underscored by a new wave of violence, directed against labor leaders, clergy, and intellectuals, just before a constituent assembly discussion of agrarian reform. Murders by death squads shot up to 116 in August (tripling the usual monthly totals for that time), and in the assembly conservatives threatened to vote against a measure to incorporate an agrarian reform plank into the new constitution. The extreme right simply did not adhere to the spirit of the Apaneca pact.

On the military front, guerrillas began a strong offensive in which they recaptured effective control over about one-third of the country. U.S. congressional leaders of both parties and high-level Reagan administration officials demanded an immediate effort on the part of the armed forces to curb death squad activity. Vice-President George Bush was sent to San Salvador essentially to make a deal with the armed forces: in return for specific measures to be taken against right-wing human rights abuse, the Reagan administration offered substantial increases in military assistance to the Salvadoran armed forces—enough to reduce the guerrilla insurgency to manageable proportions. The armed forces accepted. Death squad murders declined to 25 in December 1983, and 22 in January, 58 in February, 46 in March, 34 in April, 14 in May, and 11 in June 1984.

Moreover, early in 1984 the Reagan administration signalled strongly that it was concerned about the future electoral power of the right wing. Presidential candidate Roberto D'Aubuisson was refused a visa to the United States, a strong public signal of disapproval. The *New York Times* reported that the Central Intelligence Agency had spent $1.4 million to assist the electoral fortunes of the PCN and PDC in the upcoming presidential election. Other signals from Washington strongly indicated that an election victory for D'Aubuisson would jeopardize U.S. assistance (García, 1985). It is within this context that the 1984 presidential elections were held.

One might well inquire about the source of the electoral strength of the extreme right. While some have simply asserted that this strength must somehow be related to an underlying unfairness in the electoral process, there is good reason to believe that it is real. As indicated above, the Osorio machine was well organized. Patronage was extended not only to the upper classes in the way of favorable legislation but also to the middle and lower classes in the form of jobs. While the economic difficulties of the government during the 1970s meant that the machine could not keep up with the huge surge in the urban population—and this helped cause the downfall of the regime—it did not mean that the machine ceased to function effectively altogether. In many small communities throughout the country government jobs were extremely important sources of loyalty to the regime. Some of this loyalty to the machine has persisted in rural areas.

After 1979 the right wing inherited the remnants, some quite strong, of the officialist machine. Moreover, the guerrillas in the countryside were often seen as intruders against fairly well established order: skirmishes between the armed forces and guerrillas near villages disrupted daily life.[6] The penalties for collaboration in conflictive areas not secured by the guerrillas did not need documentation. Many of El Salvador's peasants, often highly conservative, hoped that the guerrilla conflict might end with a reestablishment of the old, familiar order. D'Aubuisson's campaign speeches also emphasized—sometimes chillingly, to outside observers—that if he were president the guerrilla war would come to a rapid end and life would continue as before. For all of these reasons D'Aubuisson's greatest electoral support came from conflictive rural areas where the PDC was not firmly established and where the old machine had functioned efficiently. This can be seen in table 3.3, where the runoff vote between Duarte and D'Aubuisson is compared. D'Aubuisson received a majority of votes in ten of the fourteen departments. The most conflictive departments in the civil war were Morazán, San Miguel, Chalatenango, Cuscatlán, Usulután, and San Vicente. D'Aubuisson carried each of these.

The 1984 Elections

Presidential elections were held on 25 March 1984, and although eight candidates entered the race, it was clear that only three had the organizational capacity to make a strong bid: Christian Democratic candidate José Napoleón Duarte, ARENA candidate Roberto D'Aubuisson, and PCN candidate Francisco ("Chachi") José Guerrero. This time a complex registration procedure was devised with the assistance of U.S. technicians, who spent $3.4 million in setting up an electoral system. Voters were assigned to specific polling places, and their names were checked against a national registry. Those whose names did not appear could not vote.

The system led to some confusion. Some voters ended up waiting in long lines at the wrong table. In some places voting began late because ballot boxes arrived late or not at all. Some names that were to be checked against a computer list appeared twice. Eventually the Electoral Commission decided voters would be allowed to vote at any polling place. Guerrilla efforts to disrupt the elections also contributed to confusion: they set up road blocks and sometimes confiscated national identity cards. In other cases voting boxes and ballots were destroyed. Voting did not take place at all in forty small towns controlled by the guerrillas. Nevertheless, these anomalies apparently were viewed by the vast majority as technical deficiencies which did not rob the event of its overall validity (see tables 3.2 and 3.3 for results).[7]

Since no candidate received 50 percent of the total vote, constitutional provisions led to a runoff election, held a few weeks later, between the top two vote-getters. Duarte received 54 percent of the total vote of 1,404,366; D'Aubuisson received 46 percent. While this election added depth to the legitimacy of the government—an elected constituent assembly was now supplemented by an elected president—it did not resolve the legislative dispute between the right wing and the center. Elections for a new legislative assembly would not take place until 1985.

The 1985 Elections

On 31 March 1985 national, legislative, and municipal elections were held in El Salvador to contest all sixty seats in the legislature and

Table 3.2. March 1984 Presidential Elections Results, First Round

Party	Votes	Percent Valid Votes
PDC	549,727	43.4
ARENA	376,917	29.8
PCN	244,556	19.3
AD	43,929	3.5
others	51,147	4.0

Note: Turnout was 75 percent: 1,419,493 persons voted; 1,266,276 votes were considered valid; 11 percent were considered invalid; 7.4 percent were spoiled; 2.9 percent were blank.
Source: *Estudios Centroamericanos* (April–May 1984, p. 366).

Table 3.3. Geographic Breakdown of 1984 Runoff Election

Department	Votes for D'Aubuisson	Votes for Duarte
San Salvador	156,460	278,786
Santa Ana	66,663	87,015
San Miguel	42,611	41,786
La Libertad	71,279	82,756
Usulután	42,147	34,842
Sonsonate	57,019	61,597
La Unión	28,236	26,087
La Paz	39,269	35,093
Chalatenango	20,019	18,183
Cuscatlán	32,580	15,913
Ahuachapán	39,051	32,264
Morazán	15,988	13,044
San Vicente	19,428	15,317
Cabañas	20,991	9,942

Source: *Estudios Centroamericanos* (April–May 1984, p. 366).

262 municipal mayorships. Again guerrilla efforts to disrupt the elections were unsuccessful, at least partly because of the effectiveness of the armed forces in guaranteeing security. Voter turnout, however, was lower, at 59 percent (see table 3.4 for results). The Salvadoran government invited representatives from fifty-one countries to observe the elections. The U.S. government sent an official delegation, as it had in 1982 and 1984, composed of congressmen and prominent private citizens and allocated around $4.5 million to support the costs of preparing for and administering the elections. While eight parties had competed in the 1984 elections, nine parties competed in 1985. No significant anomalies were reported.

Unexpectedly, Duarte's Christian Democratic party increased its representation in the legislature from twenty-four to an absolute majority of thirty-three of sixty seats. It also won control of about 200 of 262 municipal governments. With this victory a centrist government had at last been elected.

The 1988 Elections

By the time of the 1988 elections the successes and failures of the strategy outlined above were much clearer than they had been even a year or two earlier. If the armed forces had not defeated the guerrillas militarily, the guerrilla army no longer represented a major threat to the government. Few people still believed that the guerrillas would win the civil war. Equally important, although the guerrillas began the civil war with a moral edge (it was after all government and military fraud and abuse that precipitated the rebellion in the first place), by 1988 they had lost it, as they too took to killing innocent civilians, damaged hundreds of millions of dollars of national economic assets, and made every effort to sabotage sincere efforts at reform.

These changes had a profound effect on the act of voting and the context in which those votes were cast, for voters and observers alike. Casting a vote when one believes the to-be-elected government may—or should—fall to an insurrection if things go wrong is quite different—and will be so interpreted by observers—from casting a vote assuming the elected government will survive until the next one. Decision making for a voter under the former conditions is likely to revolve around a constellation of issues bearing on the survival of the government. The act of voting itself will inevitably be seen as a powerful political statement: of faith that the act of voting is meaningful; of hope the

Table 3.4. 1985 Legislative Election Results

Party	Number of Votes	Percentage of Votes	Number of Seats
PDC	505,338	52.3	33
ARENA	286,665	29.7	13
PCN	80,730	8.4	12
AD	35,565	3.7	1
PPS	16,344	1.7	—
PAISA	36,101	3.7	1
MERECEN	689	.1	—
POP	836	.1	—
PAR	2,963	.3	—

Source: *Estudios Centroamericanos* (April 1985, p. 221).

next government will survive; of judgment the political system of which elections are a part *deserves* to survive; and somehow of the belief that the act of voting will *help* the government survive. All of these imply that the elections are largely a test of loyalty. And viewed as an act of loyalty under conditions of armed threat, the voters' choices of candidates will be seen as a judgment on which leaders can best help ensure regime survival.

Once survival seems assured and loyalty to the regime is taken for granted, these dimensions of the act of voting recede into the background. Voting becomes more banal as an act as it takes on less dramatic meanings. It reflects judgments about a vast range of many kinds of past performances and articulated policy alternatives, and it is more likely to reflect a narrower, more immediate, and perhaps more identifiably selfish view of the voters' self-interest. In short, voting becomes far more complicated to interpret, both for the voter and the observing audience. Ultimately the only way a voter or analyst can interpret the meaning of a single act of voting or the results of an election is by its overall context.

In 1988 the context did not help the Christian Democratic party. Rumors of widespread corruption in highly placed government circles abounded. Military commanders complained that their national plan—funded largely by the U.S.

government—for restoring government services to areas in conflict as a means of winning over local populations was ineffective because of government inefficiency, corruption, or lack of will. In the agrarian sector the government for the first time in memory had been forced to import basic food staples. Inflation was high, over 30 percent. Unemployment was also high. Wage rates for workers had fallen in real terms by 50 percent since the beginning of the war. While some of the economic problems of the government could be attributed to guerrilla sabotage—guerrillas during the first seven years of the war destroyed about $2 billion in crops, electrical facilities, equipment, and so forth, about the same as the total amount of U.S. assistance during the same time period—by 1988 there was a strong feeling among voters that the government could be doing much better. The major beneficiary of these feelings was the right-wing ARENA party, whose leaders blamed the nation's problems on the reformist policies of the government.

Guerrilla action was stronger in 1988 than in previous electoral years. They announced early they would not tolerate voting in populations over which they exerted control. They seized and burned voting cards in several villages. They took credit for blowing up a delivery truck and an office owned by two leading members of the Christian Democratic party. In one village under their frequent control they publicly executed two civilians after finding out they had applied for and received voter registration cards. The cards were left in the victims' mouths after the executions to make certain the point was not lost on witnesses. Guerrillas also timed their second 1988 transportation stoppage to coincide with the elections. In an announced rehearsal of the stoppage in February guerrillas machine-gunned civilian buses and bombed three gasoline stations to prove they could enforce a ban. On the night before the elections guerrillas set off six bombs in San Salvador, enforced the traffic ban wherever they could, attacked outlying villages, and blew up electric lines cutting energy to an estimated 80 percent of the country. When voter turnout was lower than in 1985, guerrillas claimed this proved the government was losing legitimacy.

The outcome of the elections was not completely unexpected. Corruption scandals almost certainly affected the outcome of the mayoral election in San Salvador, an office held by a Christian Democrat since 1964. The Christian Democratic candidate, the president's son Alejandro Duarte, lost to the ARENA candidate after a campaign in which he was accused of trying to use his influence to protect a close friend implicated in large-scale government corruption. All in all, ARENA won around 200 of the 262 municipal races, a reversal of the proportions of three years earlier. In the legislature the Christian Democratic party won only 29 of 60 seats, losing their absolute majority and returning power to ARENA.

Evaluating the Elections

Using the criteria developed by Booth in chapter 1, what can be concluded about the meaning of the electoral episodes since 1982 in El Salvador? Did the elections consolidate a stable regime that can last through at least several democratic elections?

First, as indicated above, the conduct of the elections was fair and the environment was as free as could be expected during civil war. Given the symbolic importance of elections in El Salvador's history and worldwide attention, intense scrutiny of the electoral episodes was to be expected. Any indication of governmental insincerity or fraud would have been counterproductive under the circumstances. The relative freedom of the electoral episodes in the context of guerrilla war very much helped legitimize the current government of El Salvador. At home, most Salvadoran citizens consider the president and the legislative and municipal representatives to be legitimately elected, if not always wise, leaders. Abroad, support for the regime has increased in the form of assistance from Europe and the United States. Countries that ostracized the early postcoup Junta, such as Mexico, have acknowledged the legitimacy of the government. Few people seriously associate the current government with the old regime.

Second, the regime has evolved in positive directions that have helped strengthen it. The strongest and certainly the most ironic indicator of strengthened legitimacy is the relative calm with which observers accepted the verdict of voters who handed the ruling Christian Democratic party a stunning defeat in the 1988 legislative and municipal elections—in favor of the right-wing ARENA party. One of the assumptions underlying the U.S.-backed strategy for victory was that if given a choice voters would support a centrist, reformist program that would address some of the major problems which led to the civil war: the concentration of land, the monopoly of power of the right, fraudulent elections, and the like. Only the Christian Democratic party in 1982 was willing to address these issues in an electoral context, and for the next few years ARENA party activists tried everything possible to thwart the reformist program many observers thought imperative in the battle for hearts and minds. For this reason many began to equate the success of the regime with policy control by the Christian Democratic party. Many U.S. congressmen would have found it difficult to vote for a continuation of aid to El Salvador had the ARENA party decisively won the 1985 legislative elections. By 1988 this was no longer the case, to the dismay of the guerrillas.

Documents captured from guerrillas in 1988 indicated they thought an ARENA victory would undermine the case for U.S. assistance in Congress and create policy disarray during the crucial months prior to the 1989 Salvadoran presidential elections. Whether guerrillas helped "campaign" for ARENA (in their own peculiar ways) during the 1988 elections is not known, but that their writings suggest they believe the outcomes of elections have strategic implications is an astonishing tacit acknowledgment that they have come to accept many of the postulates of the original centrist strategy employed against them. A victory by the right, however, was unlikely to affect the regime's ultimate continuation because of changes within the right and the left of the political spectrum which have strengthened the regime.

In 1985 the party system was greatly flawed. While the centrist Christian Democratic party was formally in power, neither the democratic right nor the democratic left would cooperate with it in creating a viable regime. The right-wing parties (principally ARENA) had spent three years trying to thwart all vestiges of centrist reform, using legal and extralegal means to do so. Sometimes death squads would intervene; sometimes obstructionist parliamentary tactics would prevail; sometimes expensive propaganda was employed to lash out against reform. The right wing seemed to cooperate with the government only to the extent its members felt was essential to maintain U.S. economic and military assistance to prevent a victory by the guerrillas.

The democratic left had joined the guerrillas in early 1980 and steadfastly refused to break their alliance with the FMLN. By refusing to participate in elections the democratic left robbed the regime of legitimacy. The Duarte government, then, was sandwiched between a right wing that often equated the reformist policies of the Duarte government with the potential program of the guerrillas and the democratic left, which equated the policies of the Duarte government with those of the right-wing governments of the past. Had this situation remained in 1988, the guerrillas would have been justified in believing an electoral victory by the ARENA party would point out the essential failure of the centrist strategy. Fortunately for the regime two things within the party system had changed by 1988.

First, the right wing began to change. Hoping to broaden their electoral appeal, ARENA leaders purged the most reactionary—and certainly the most notorious—of their members. Roberto D'Aubuisson was replaced as the effective head of the party by a more moderate conservative, Alfredo Cristiani. Cristiani made an effort to convince his constituents that they had to accept the newly evolving rules of the game, in which they could succeed only by winning a mass following and criticizing government action by argument rather than violence. To a large extent he was successful in this effort. The party began to argue that the problems facing the country had less to do with guerrilla insurgency than with inept distributional policies designed during the early 1980s when it was thought a guerrilla victory was imminent. They argued that the collectivist assumptions of the agrarian reform program caused agricultural production to fall, since peasants lost motivation when they didn't own their identifiable parcel of land. Further, state monopoly of the sale of coffee and mismanagement of the crop by government technicians, they argued, should be stopped. Planters should be paid market prices and laws covering investment and export incentives should be revised. In short the party's overall viewpoint sounded remarkably like "privatization" arguments among U.S. conservatives during the same period, hardly an extremist program. ARENA party leaders began to criticize government policies in less strident, less ideological, and far more policy-specific ways. Party leaders also began to lobby for understanding among respected conservative groups in the United States, and with some success. The *Wall Street Journal*, for example, began to comment favorably about ARENA criticisms of government policy. In short, the right wing improved its image at home and abroad.

Second, the democratic left began to make efforts to accommodate to electoral politics. Beginning in 1986 and 1987 FDR leaders began to return to El Salvador to explore electoral possibilities, a tacit acknowledgment that they felt the regime would outlast the guerrilla rebellion. This change in posture required great skill and delicacy. They were allies of and fundraisers for the guerrillas—who, as mentioned above, do not profess any commitment to electoral politics under capitalist conditions. A return of the democratic left to electoral politics would represent a betrayal of the guerrillas, whose weapons had kept their hopes alive—and put constant pressure on the government to reform itself—for more than five years.

More concretely, the absence of the democratic left among their allies would deny the guerrillas the aura of democratic moderation, making it more difficult to maintain sympathy for their cause at home and abroad. At the same time it would be a major step toward fully legitimizing the government, making it that much more likely that the regime would succeed. As the democratic left began to return to El Salvador to explore electoral possibilities, then, it was another sign that the overall counterinsurgency strategy had worked.

As it turned out, the democratic left did not participate in the 1988 elections, but in late July 1988, after a top-level strategy meeting in Managua, FMLN leader Joaquin Villalobos declared the guerrillas would not oppose the participation of the democratic left in the 1989 presidential elections. Guerrillas would continue the guerrilla war, but would also negotiate with the government through the Esquipulas Accords. With the democratic left about to defect to the electoral process, this declaration in effect constituted the first announcement of a phased withdrawal by the guerrillas from the war.

Breadth, Depth, and Range of Democratic Participation

There appears, then, to be a strong trend toward an expansion of the breadth, depth, and range of political participation. If the democratic left does indeed participate in the 1989 elections, the political space within the regime will have been inflated significantly. The views of labor union members will be represented far more fully than before, as will those of agrarian workers, students, government workers, and others who identify with the views of the democratic left. An increase in participation by these sectors in the elections is to be expected, particularly if the guerrillas do not discourage voting. Increases in the number of voters during the next few elections should thus be seen as evidence that the breadth of participation is increasing. That labor and other sectors will be more fully represented is an indicator that the range of participation is increasing. And increases in the kinds of issues and proposals for alternative solutions to problems that surfaced during the 1988 elections should be even more evident during the 1989 elections; this should increase the depth of participation by a significant degree.

The Armed Forces and Political Culture Favoring Democracy

The most important difference between the regime structure under the Osorio system and the current one lies in the role of the armed forces. Under the old system military officers served as candidates for the presidency while an officialist civilian party sought support for the government through control of patronage. Under the current system there appears to be at least a tacit understanding that military officers will not run for president. Nor is there an officialist party: patronage is controlled in direct proportion to the ability of a party to receive votes. This civilianization of the party system has major implications.

Procedurally, it democratizes the system: in removing the armed forces from direct participation in partisan affairs all political parties are placed on the same competitive level. This has imbued the new system with a legitimacy the old system sorely lacked. Partisan factionalism within the armed forces has been reduced drastically, and civilian political actors no longer have the same need to calculate the potential consequences of momentary intrigues within the armed forces. While these measures do not by any means guarantee good or democratic government, they certainly eliminate a problem that plagued the prior regime. The system is now more normal, in democratic terms, with the army officially nonpartisan.

Substantively, the withdrawal of the armed forces from partisan politics has meant that the extreme right has had to learn to appeal to a broader public. Although the financing and skills rightist parties enjoy in this endeavor still outweigh those of centrist parties, for the first time in their history they are finding that they must speak seriously to the electorate and to political elites representing different interests. This new set of constraints could well contribute to the development of an elite political culture more amenable to dialogue.

How sincere is this new military nonpartisanship? Historically, the armed forces have had a strong tendency gradually to gravitate to the side of the agrarian elite. Is this tendency likely to reappear? If not, will traditional military interventionism reappear in some other guise? These questions are exceedingly difficult to answer, in part because of the significant structural changes that have taken place within the armed forces during the civil war and in part because it is too early to evaluate the lasting impact of changes in the overall power structure of the country. In the short term, however, there are some hopeful signs.

First, the painful lessons of history appear to weigh heavily on the minds of the senior officer corps. Those now in command of troops were junior officers during the bleak days of the 1970s. As long as the current regime can continue to expand its civilian base of support, it seems unlikely that officers will risk a repetition of the disastrous course of events that threatened their very survival only a decade ago.

More important than the lessons of history in forging a new mentality is the effect of armed combat upon the officer corps. Military sociologists (Janowitz, 1960; Huntington, 1957; Coates and Pellegrin, 1965) underscore the importance of combat in producing new ideologies within the armed forces. At the time of this writing the armed forces of El Salvador have spent nearly a decade learning, with some success, how to operate as a counterinsurgency unit. While it is easy to dismiss this success as "U.S.-imposed," it should be remembered that training and weapons alone do not defeat guerrillas: it also takes willpower. In 1981 the Salvadoran armed forces were woefully unprepared for guerrilla war. Today they are among the best counterinsurgents in the world.

It is still unclear what effect success in warfare will have on the political behavior of the Salvadoran armed forces. To what extent has combat changed their views about the peasants they were forced to shoot or the coffee growers they used to protect? To what extent were they influenced by the political alliances they were forced to make outside the institution in order to survive? While the evidence is sketchy, the author has interviewed dozens of officers and many have repeated a similar theme: "I did not risk my life and those of my men to defeat an enemy only to turn power back to a coffee-growing oligarchy that fled to Miami with their millions and their families when the first shots were being fired."

But if they did not fight for this, for what did they fight? I believe that the institution has not formulated a clear answer to this question beyond the visceral one of survival. A period of profound introspection is likely to ensue before a clear political identity emerges. And in a deeper sense the political future of the armed forces in El Salvador may depend more upon civilian groups in the new regime than it does upon an institutional identity. Students of military politics point out that the level of political involvement of the armed forces is inversely proportional to the strength of civilian political institutions.[8]

Conclusion

Underlying the strategy devised in 1980 for the survival of the government of El Salvador was the notion that military force could be applied both to stop a revolutionary challenge and to buy time for democratic roots to take hold through electoral processes. Critics argued that it was too late for military force to prevent revolutionary change or that military force *should* not prevent a revolution, or that the effort through elections to nurture democracy was bound to fail for lack of sincerity, flawed domestic policies, or inept intervention by the U.S. government. After more than nine years it is clear that military force—funded by the U.S. government—prevented the violent overthrow of the regime by Marxist-Leninist guerrilla insurgents. It is equally clear that at least some democratic roots are beginning to take hold, as evidenced by the successful completion of several rounds of national elections which selected the first civilian governors in over half a century, major improvements in government respect for human rights, the tentative emergence of a competitive party system, and strong evidence from survey research that the vast majority of Salvadorans applaud the democratic character of the regime, if not the performance of the government itself.

These successes notwithstanding, Salvadoran democracy still has a number of serious problems. First, even though at the time of writing it appears certain the presidential elections of 1989 will include the participation of members of the democratic left (thus making the electoral system inclusive of most sectors of the population), it is not at all certain the various actors will act with a minimum of cooperation in the joint ventures of rebuilding the nation's economic infrastructure, restoring faith in the regime, and improving governmental performance in such basic functions as taxation and law enforcement. During the first years of the regime even purported allies within it had serious difficulties getting along. Sometimes the armed forces cooperated with the government only to the extent necessary to fight the guerrilla war; sometimes the Christian Democratic government did not cooperate sufficiently with the armed forces in counterinsurgency. Often the right wing cooperated with the government only as a means of preventing a cutoff of U.S. assistance.

Now the democratic left has joined the electoral fray. To make Salvadoran democracy "take," some sort of consociational pact among most members is needed whereby all actors agree on a minimum program of action for the future, possibly including some sort of alternative power-sharing agreement such as emerged in Colombia in 1957. Perhaps such a pact might emerge formally or informally as the guerrillas conclude their insurrection.

Second, a consociational pact is unlikely to emerge until all actors understand they cannot reach an artificial modus vivendi supported indefinitely by the outside world. One of the most striking phenomena of the Salvadoran conflict has been the internationalization of the local power struggle. Virtually every institution in El Salvador—the armies of both sides, the parties, labor unions, the Church, the business community—has received significant amounts of international support. The left in El Salvador has pointed to the role of the United States in propping up the government. The right counters that the FDR, the guerrillas, the progressive Church, and other elements that comprise the left have received vital international support.

Thus, foreign assistance has been granted for humanitarian, geopolitical, economic, and political reasons. The full effect of this aid has not yet been seriously studied, but it seems certain to have had unintended results, including the extension of war long after the logic of local interests dictated a cessation of hostilities.[9] One possible eventual outcome of this lengthening of the war might well be an upsurge of a unifying but virulent nationalism, a rejection of certain forms of international pressure. On the other hand, it is also possible that structures of international support might become so entrenched that national solutions to national problems would become impossible. Since the U.S. government was one of the major pillars of support for the centrist strategy for many years—but cannot continue so forever—it seems likely that creative disengagement will remain a major challenge to U.S. policymakers and Salvadorans during the immediate post-Reagan administration. Major problems in this regard might lead to serious structural problems in the consolidation of a viable regime.

Moreover, international scrutiny of the Salvadoran process has been intense, from the news media, the Church, human rights groups, and the international community at large. Without this scrutiny events—including electoral episodes or human rights abuse—would almost certainly have taken a different turn. It would therefore be absurd to evaluate the entire process solely as a function of the interaction of Salvadoran actors. In a real sense, in the future Salvadoran affairs will continue to depend to some degree upon international actors. This places a certain responsibility upon the shoulders of all international actors because increased international encouragement of a centrist, democratic regime might well be decisive in determining whether it succeeds or fails. If the centrist regime fails, some responsibility for that failure will lie with international actors.

Elections in El Salvador have accomplished what they were intended to accomplish. They helped legitimize a regime enough to enable it to withstand a guerrilla challenge. By themselves elections cannot be expected to accomplish much more. As in all democratic societies elections are a necessary but not sufficient condition for success. Future problems in Salvadoran democracy are to be expected. After all, if in the United States our civil war produced the eloquence of Abraham Lincoln, the aftermath was not pretty, as evidenced by the negative connotations Southerners still attach to the term "Reconstruction." If in El Salvador the civil war produced the eloquence of Archbishop Oscar Romero, the aftermath is likely to be problematic as well.

This chapter should therefore be seen as a rejection of the views of Herman and Brodhead, who argued some time ago that elections in El Salvador fall into the category of "demonstration" elections, more for external consumption than for genuine democratic purposes. Although the elections were indeed important to the U.S. government as symbols for external consumption, they appear also to have had a profound influence in helping to alter some fundamentally undemocratic and unrepresentational Salvadoran realities. That this was possible during the intense fighting of a civil war and under conditions in which the elections themselves were held up to widespread ridicule is a testimony to the strength of democratic ideals among millions of Salvadoran citizens.

Notes

1. The author thanks the Wes and Nadine Handy Fund at New Mexico State University for support during 1987 for research on this topic. The author also thanks the NMSU Arts and Sciences Research Council, the NMSU–University of New Mexico Latin American Consortium, and the Mellon Foundation for support during the past few years on his ongoing research on El Salvador.

2. Interviews of the author with Colonel (retired) Mariano Castro Moran and Colonel (retired) Alberto Funes, San Salvador, July 1984.

3. The growth of the government bureaucracy is recorded for the 1948–78 period in López Vallecillos (1979:562).

4. *Estudios Centroamericanos* (*ECA*), a superb social science journal published by the Jesuit-run Universidad Centroamericana Simeon Cañas in San Salvador, whose editorial stance can best be described as often in accord with the views of leading FDR members, did not write an article analyzing the results of the 1982 elections. In January 1982,

Prof. Segundo Montes wrote an article about the forthcoming elections in which he argued that even free elections would not change the fundamental reality of national life (see p. 65); in April the journal editorial section refused to concede that "national elections" had taken place, expressed serious doubt that the relatively large turnout figures were correct, but nevertheless conceded a certain degree of legitimacy had been gained by the government (see *ECA* 1982:233–58). The same edition published the official election results without further comment. The May–June edition contained an article alleging that turnout figures may have been inflated. The allegations received considerable attention in the international news media, were denied vigorously by Salvadoran electoral officials, and were not pursued or repeated after that. The journal devoted considerable space to analyzing election results for the 1984 and 1985 elections, a tacit acknowledgment of their legitimizing success.

5. See for example the editorial in *America* (1982:271), *New Republic* (1982), Hoge (1982), *Christian Science Monitor* (1982). For a detailed account of U.S. media coverage of the elections see *Time* (1982).

6. In May 1980 the author interviewed peasants who had been attacked by guerrillas in San Jose de Cancasque, Chalatenango, El Salvador. The peasants in that village had a long history of participation with the officialist party. From these interviews the general pattern of support for the officialist party described in this paragraph became evident.

7. CIDAI (1984:218) makes this point in an article describing the technical efforts to avoid fraud in the elections.

8. See, for example, Janowitz (1964).

9. Terry Karl ("Exporting Democracy: The Unanticipated Effects of U.S. Electoral Policy in El Salvador," in *Crisis in Central America: Regional Dynamics and U.S. Policy in the 1980s*, edited by Nora Hamilton et al. [Boulder: Westview Press, 1987]) asserts that U.S. assistance prolonged the civil war, presumably because the guerrillas would have defeated the armed forces quickly or else caused the government to negotiate with them. It is of course equally true that without foreign assistance for the guerrillas or the human rights restraints imposed upon the armed forces by the U.S. government the Salvadoran army might have defeated the guerrillas even more quickly; these external factors also "caused" the war to be prolonged. In an earlier work (García, 1985) I argued that U.S. policymakers may have deliberately prolonged the war by extending the military just enough assistance to avoid defeat by the guerrillas but not enough to win, on the grounds that a quick defeat of the guerrillas might encourage the right and the armed forces to resume their antidemocratic and violent ways. In truth the civil war lasted a long time for highly complex reasons and all sides—the Salvadoran military; the U.S. president and Congress; the guerrilla armies, sympathizers, funders, and suppliers, including the Nicaraguan government; and the extreme right wing—can be said to bear some responsibility.

References

America. 1982. 10 April.

Anderson, Thomas. 1971. *Matanza.* Lincoln: University of Nebraska Press.

Baloyra, Enrique. 1982. *El Salvador in Transition.* Chapel Hill: University of North Carolina Press.

————. 1984. Political Change in El Salvador? *Current History*, February.

Browning, David. 1971. *El Salvador, Land and Society.* Oxford: Oxford University Press.

Campos, Tomás R. 1982. El Pacto de Apaneca. *Estudios Centroamericanos* 37, no. 407–8 (Sept.–Oct.): 865–79.

Castro Morán, Mariano. 1983. *Función política del ejército Salvadoreño en el presente siglo.* San Salvador: UCA Editores.

Christian Science Monitor. 1982. 1 April.

CIDAI. 1984. Destapando la "Caja Negra": condicionamientos técnicos del proceso electoral 1984. *Estudios Centroamericanos* 39, no. 426–27 (April–May): 187–218.

Coates, Charles H., and Pellegrin, Roland. 1965. *Military Sociology.* University Park, Md.: Social Science Press.

CUDI. 1982. Las elecciones de 1982: realidades detrás de las aparencias. *Estudios Centroamericanos* 37, no. 403–4 (May–June): 573–96.

Estudios Centroamericanos. 1982. Editorial: Las elecciones y la unidad nacional, diez tesis críticas. Vol. 37, no. 402: 233–58.

García, José Z. 1983. Political Conflict within the Salvadoran Armed Forces: Origins and Consequences. Unpublished paper delivered at the Inter-University Consortium on the Study of the Armed Forces, Annual Convention, Chicago, Ill., October.

————. 1985. El Salvador: Legitimizing the Government. *Current History*, March, pp. 101–36.

Gómez, Arias. 1972. *Farabundo Martí.* San José: EDUCA.

Guidos Véjar, Rafael. 1980. *El Ascenso del Militarismo en El Salvador.* San Salvador: UCA Editores.

Herman, Edward, and Brodhead, Frank. 1984. *Demonstration Elections: U.S.-Staged Elections in the Dominican Republic, Vietnam, and El Salvador.* Boston: South End Press.

Hoge, Warren. 1982. Salvadorans Jam Polling Stations; Rebels Close Some. *New York Times*, 29 March.

Huntington, Samuel P. 1957. *The Soldier and the State.* Cambridge: Harvard University Press.

Janowitz, Morris. 1960. *The Professional Soldier.* New York: Free Press.

————. 1964. *The Military in the Development of New Nations.* Chicago: University of Chicago Press.

López Vallecillos, Italo. 1979. Fuerzas Sociales y Cambio Social en El Salvador. *Estudios Centroamericanos* 34, no. 369–70 (July–August): 557–90.

Montes, Segundo. 1982. *Estudios Centroamericanos*, January.

New Republic. 1982. 12 July.

Parkman, Patricia. 1988. *Nonviolent Insurrection in El Salvador*. Tucson: University of Arizona Press.

Schlesinger, Jorge. 1946. *Revolución comunista*. Guatemala City: Editorial Castañeda, Avila, y Cia.

Time. 1982. 12 April.

Webre, Stephen. 1979. *José Napoleon Duarte and the Christian Democratic Party in Salvadoran Politics, 1960–1972*. Baton Rouge: Louisiana State University Press.

White, Alastair. 1973. *El Salvador*. New York: Praeger.

4 The Guatemalan Election of 1985
Prospects for Democracy

Robert H. Trudeau

If democracy is defined strictly in terms of elections resulting in a civilian president, there is now democracy in Guatemala. But in spite of official optimism in both Guatemala and the United States, there are troubling and persistent reports that the civilian government may have much less power than other institutions in the country and that human rights violations continue to be a salient feature of daily political life. In other words, the degree and nature of democracy is being questioned. More important, future prospects for Guatemalan democracy are uncertain; we need to ask if recent elections are helping to increase (or, in an apparent paradox, decrease) the level of democracy there.

Guatemala's recent elections were not held in a vacuum; the historical, economic, and political context must be part of any comprehensive analysis. This chapter undertakes to sort through a wealth of contextual, and often contradictory, information on Guatemala's military forces and their central role in the political process, with the hope of clarifying the relationships between recent elections and future prospects for democracy in Guatemala.

Guatemala's recent history includes several examples of elections and of vigorous party activity. Some of these elections were fraudulent, for example, the imposition of General Laugerud in 1974 and the attempted imposition of General Guevara in 1982. Other elections were honest, including the 1945 election of Juan José Arévalo, the 1966 election of Julio Méndez Montenegro, and the 1985 election of Vinicio Cerezo, all of which are discussed in this chapter. Yet through it all, even during the reformist civilian administration of Méndez Montenegro, the underlying thread has been the growth of the political and economic power of the military officer corps relative to other organized sectors of society. Understanding Guatemala's 1985 elections, therefore, requires an examination of the development of the Guatemalan military's role in the political economy.

History and Context of Guatemalan Elections

The Election of 1966

The roots for understanding today's Guatemala are many and complex, and have been treated in depth elsewhere.[1] One very important element of the history of electoral politics, however, is the election of 1966.

That election, in which Julio César Méndez Montenegro came to power, is considered the first honest election in Guatemala after the 1954 coup that terminated the reformist politics of the 1944–54 period. A reformist civilian, Méndez was the candidate of the Revolutionary party (Partido Revolucionario—PR), a party that sought to identify itself with the governments of the 1944–54 period by characterizing itself as the "third government" of the 1944 revolution.

Although the fact of a civilian reformer taking office as a result of relatively fair ballot counting seemed a positive step after protracted military rule, the conditions of the election reflected the real limits of civilian power in relation to the strength of the military. In the 1966 campaign the only other parties allowed to participate were the National Liberation Movement (Movimiento de Liberación Nacional—MLN), an oligarchic party that emerged after the 1954 coup, and the Democratic Institutional party (Partido Institucional Democrático—PID), the party of the armed forces. Other political parties were excluded by a law promulgated during military rule that restricted parties with "exotic ideologies," such as social democracy and Christian democracy, and outlawed opposition further to the left (Black, 1984:21). Moreover, the PR itself had shifted to the right in the late 1950s when its leader, Mario Méndez Montenegro, "purged the entire left wing of the party" (Jonas, 1974a:196). Julio César Méndez Montenegro became a presidential candidate only after his brother Mario had been assassinated. From the beginning, then, the electorate's choices were narrowly constrained and the "reformist" credentials of the PR, open to question.

Once elected, the Méndez government was severely constrained by the military and the oligarchy. First, Méndez was not allowed to take office until he agreed to guarantee the military "a free hand in counterinsurgency, autonomy in such matters as selection of the defense minister, chief of staff, budgets, etc." Méndez also had to promise "to exclude 'radicals' from the government, but not to retire too many generals" (Jonas, 1974a:195). Second, threats from the oligarchy prevented Méndez from carrying out even relatively mild, U.S.-supported tax reforms, let alone taking the initiative on more serious land reforms (Jonas, 1974b:104–8).

Perhaps most seriously, Méndez was powerless to stop a new wave of repression unleashed by an anxious military and paramilitary death squads controlled by the oligarchy. A wave of official terror swept eastern Guatemala during the Méndez administration. The repression, directed by Colonel Carlos Arana, was presented to the outside world as a counterinsurgency campaign. The army's campaign crushed several hundred guerrillas, but also killed between three thousand and ten thousand civilians (Sharckman, 1974:196).

U.S. support for Guatemala's economy during this period resulted in improved macroeconomic performance. The decade of the 1960s was a period of economic growth. Real gross national product grew at about twice the rate of the population until the late 1970s (WOLA, 1983:2; World Bank, 1978:27). New export commodities flourished, and economic integration via the Central American Common Market stimulated economic prosperity for Guatemala's business sector.

But growth without reform produced growth with misery for large sectors of the Guatemalan population, with almost no "trickle-down effect."[2] The renewed stress on agricultural exports resulted in increased concentration of land; land distribution, already one of the most inequitable in Latin America, actually worsened between 1964 and 1979 (Amigo, 1978:125–27; Mendizábal et al., 1979).

The social consequences in rural areas of this pattern of development were severe: a growing landless population confronted declining access to food and reduced purchasing power from wage and migrant labor.[3] With the assistance of the Alliance for Progress a largely self-sufficient rural peasantry had been converted into a rural proletariat, subject to the vagaries of world demand for Guatemala's export commodities and to the vagaries of local elites controlling the plantations. The deteriorating situation generated by this "growth without reform" fostered popular pressures for change. Opponents of social change, supported by the military, responded with increasing violence to crush reformers, whom they usually branded as "communists."

In spite of the existence of elections and parties during this period, political power remained in the hands of the military and economic power remained in the hands of the military and the oligarchy. From the perspective of the deprived sectors of society, the socioeconomic picture worsened, for the export-oriented agribusiness economic growth spurred by U.S. aid and private investment had primarily enriched the military and oligarchy while decreasing the food supply. Using terror as a weapon, the oligarchy and the military stifled discontent, and as a result the political system became more closed during the "reformist-centrist" period of Méndez Montenegro and remained closed during the "authoritarian" administration of Colonel Arana Osorio which followed.

The Military in Office, 1970–1981

The military awarded Colonel Arana the presidency in 1970 largely because of his successful tenure as director of the counterinsurgency program during the Méndez government. Between the 1963 coup of Colonel Peralta Azurdia and the 1970 election, the military had been transformed into a formidable political and economic actor. Reformist civilian parties and popular organizations were repressed. Stability, or at least the appearance of stability, had been achieved, with economic growth. During the Arana presidency, the military consolidated its position politically and economically.

Arana began by declaring a state of siege during his inauguration address and followed this by unleashing a wave of terror in urban Guatemala. The targets were, for the most part, the very people who represented the possibility for nonviolent reform of the political and social system—leaders of the Christian Democratic and Social Democratic parties, major trade unions, and peasant organizations. During the Méndez regime, some of the "reformers" had taken office but not power; under Arana many of the reformers were eliminated.

In 1974 General Kjell Laugerud García was imposed as president in a fraudulent election generally thought to have been won by the Christian Democratic candidate, former army chief of staff General Efraín Ríos Montt. Within a decade, the army had institutionalized its direct control over the political system by rigging elections and controlling appointments in the public bureaucracy. After the election of 1974 one Christian Democratic party leader, Daniel Barillas, admitted that "in Guatemala, it is useless to think of governing, except as the result of a political decision by the Army" (Black, 1984:31).

The military establishment continued to solidify its economic position as well. Corruption has always been rife in the Guatemalan army, but in the early 1970s military officers started becoming entrepreneurs as well. For more than a decade military policy has melded the state's interests with the economic interests of individual military officers, using the threat (and application) of force to acquire wealth. As the Guatemalan military was taking advantage of U.S. military assistance to become a formidable internal security force, it was also using its political control of the government (and of U.S. economic assistance) to become an economic elite.

By the early 1980s the army controlled forty-six "semiautonomous state institutions," including its own investment and pension fund and a "private" bank, called, appropriately enough, the Bank of the Army (Banco del Ejército) (Black, 1984:52). Government appropriations capitalized the bank, and its funds assisted entrepreneurial officers as they invested in such businesses as hotels, housing projects, the cement industry, and especially real estate. Officers have been particularly prominent in acquiring land for livestock, agriculture, and forestry in the development area known as the Northern Transversal Strip. One former president, General Romeo Lucas, is reported to own over 100,000 acres in what has come to be known as the "zone of the generals." Corrupt military leaders had acquired millions of dollars through weapons trading (Black, 1984:52–55).

Firmly in control both economically and politically, the military relaxed its grip on society. The period from 1974 to the late 1970s showed a marked increase in popular organizing and in the level of open activity by reformist political parties, labor unions, peasant groups, and student groups. In the urban areas a new generation of political leaders had matured by the mid-1970s, and the political process began to show signs of increasing tension as urban middle-class reformers confronted upper sectors who felt threatened by reform. Although electoral fraud continued, moderately reformist political parties began to organize. From 1976 to 1980 there was marked growth in several political movements.

The responses of the army and major sectors of the oligarchy to this new surge of popular organizing and reformist pressure was repression. In the rural areas the army and landowners reacted violently to reform efforts.[4]

In urban areas violence against political party and labor union leaders increased dramatically after the fraudulent election of General Romeo Lucas García in 1978.[5] Guatemala's two centrist-reformist political parties, the Social Democrats (Partido Socialista Democrático—PSD) and the United Front of the Revolution (Frente Unido de la Revolución—FUR), were crushed following the 1979 assassinations of their leaders, former foreign minister Alberto Fuentes

Mohr and former Guatemala City mayor Manuel Colom Argüeta, respectively. The grass-roots leadership of the centrist Christian Democrats was decimated, and the murders of 150 party organizers in 1980–81 silenced all but a handful of party activists.

The Military in Power, 1982–1986

The military's economic power has sometimes created serious conflicts with civilian economic elites who see their interests challenged by a government whose corruption now favors military officers and bureaucrats. The National Liberation Movement (MLN), for example, has increasingly challenged the military and its political candidates; indeed, conflict among elite factions is behind many of the daily political events in Guatemala.

The military therefore finds itself in competition not only with the bulk of the population that is living in economic and social misery but also with sectors of the economic elite. This competition has become especially contentious since the late 1970s, owing to the combination of a prolonged economic crisis and the drying up of foreign sources of capital, which is at least partly due to the terrible human rights record and pariah status of the Guatemalan state.

In this situation the military's goals are essentially to retain, and if possible expand, its economic position in society and to prevent threats to this position from any social sector. Preventing threats from competing sectors has meant not only fraudulent elections but massive repression at times, in addition to military coups. Since the late 1970s the strategy has included a vicious counterinsurgency campaign, especially in indigenous areas. As these stratagems have become more intense, they have often provoked factionalism within the military itself. One good example is the fraudulent election of 1982. Violence had struck the political parties of the moderate center as well as those of the "Left" in the period leading up to the 1982 election. As a result the campaign was distinctly conservative and antireform, in spite of the fact that all the candidates save one were civilians. That one, however, was General Aníbal Guevara, the candidate of the dominant faction of the army. Guevara was declared the winner, and Guatemala witnessed the unusual spectacle of a protest march led jointly by members of such disparate political parties as the extreme right-wing National Liberation Movement and the Christian Democrats.

These events and others helped bring about the military coup of 23 March 1982, which installed the messianic General Efraín Ríos Montt in power at the head of a three-person junta.[6] The Ríos Montt coup signified a shift in the military's strategy. The economic assistance needed to maintain the military's wealth could be obtained if lip service, at least, could be paid to international pressures on protecting human rights, ending corruption in government, and fashioning a transition to democracy by holding elections. Lucas García had been intransigent in the face of such pressures; Ríos Montt pledged to guarantee all three.

By August 1983, Ríos Montt's legitimacy as a guarantor of foreign economic assistance had been jeopardized by his eccentricities. He was ousted in a military coup led by General Oscar Mejía Víctores. Mejía continued to apply the same brutal counterinsurgency techniques as his predecessor—burning of crops, civilian massacres in villages suspected of guerrilla sympathies, forced resettlement into camps, and forced service in paramilitary civil patrols.

The counterinsurgency campaign was largely successful in at least temporarily stemming the growth of popular armed insurgency. But publicity about the continuing brutality impeded the renewal of international assistance. To overcome this impediment, the military undertook to legitimate its counterinsurgency activities by in effect legalizing the de facto counterinsurgency structures and behavior of the army. Three institutional mechanisms merit scrutiny, for they reduce the need for obvious repression while seeking to ensure reduced levels of popular participation and democracy.

The first of these is the Civilian Self-Defense Patrols (Patrullas de Auto-Defensa Civil—PAC). In most rural areas, membership and rotating duty in the PACs is in effect mandatory for all males. The civil patrols, whose membership was estimated at between 750,000 and 850,000 by 1984, ostensibly serve the purpose of protecting local villages from guerrilla attacks.[7] The real purpose of these ill-equipped patrols, however, is social control: they are a means to account for and regulate the whereabouts of villagers.[8]

One underreported aspect of the civil patrols is that they form a labor pool for forced labor projects, usually building roads and other infrastructure projects that make land more valuable for, among other things, export agriculture; transforming agricultural land for export production is part of the coordinated development plan for these regions. This process of creating new wealth in previously isolated areas, which is of course totally under military control, is frequently ignored by observers concentrating on the counterinsurgency aspects of these activities. Some members of Guatemala's civilian elite have objected to this "unfair" competition (*Ceri-Gua*, 7–13 January 1985, pp. 5–6).

The second institutional mechanism, which complements the first, is the creation of model villages as part of the "poles of development" program. This plan is described as one of coordinated development aimed at bringing social progress and basic quality-of-life improvements to highland areas previously marked by isolation and extreme poverty.[9] In fact, in addition to offering military officers control over adjacent agricultural lands and individuals desperate for work, the model village program appears very similar to the "strategic hamlets" developed by the United States in Vietnam. The development possibilities blend nicely with the military officers' quests for wealth, but the basic intent is one of counterinsurgency—of population control.

A third mechanism for maintaining a degree of permanent military control over rural Guatemala was a structure to regulate political affairs, the "National Interinstitutional Coordinator" (Coordinadora Inter-institucional Nacional—CIN), established in each department and presided over by military zone commanders. Because it coordinated and regulated all normal civil governmental functions under direct military supervision (to "reduce corruption" and "increase efficiency"), the CIN was in essence a parallel government that allowed the military to continue to rule the nation even though Guatemala was to return to "civilian rule" (Krueger and Enge, 1985:53–59; *Ceri-Gua*, 7–13 January 1985, p. 6; and Counterinsurgency . . . , 1985:5, 8).

Like active repression, the CIN was designed to inhibit independent community organization and control over local political affairs, to counter the threat the military sees in the creation of self-help organizations, and to ensure that the "democratic opening" of 1985 and the civilian government inaugurated in 1986 would not threaten military dominance.

Elections and Civilian Government, 1984–1986

By 1984 the military's three mechanisms for social control had led to an environment in which fear, terror, and totalitarian control replaced murder as the primary mechanism for social domination. In 1985 these mechanisms were integrated into the new constitution by military decree, which in effect legitimized the repression. The strategy of attending to Guatemala's tarnished international image was completed by scheduling national elections in 1985, which culminated in the inauguration of Vinicio Cerezo in January 1986.

During his tenure as chief of state, Ríos Montt had begun the process of preparing Guatemala for elections. Under the guise of purging the system of corrupt and undemocratic elements, he took several steps that effectively reduced the formal level of democratic participation in the Guatemalan system. He established secret summary military trials before the Tribunals of Special Jurisdiction, and executions of suspected "enemies" continued. He announced that no civilians would be allowed to hold executive government positions. He removed from office all elected mayors, most of whom had been elected in the relatively honest municipal elections of 1980, and replaced them with military appointees. Another decree permitted the president to act as the legislative as well as the executive power.

Using a campaign to end corruption as the rationale, Ríos eliminated the major political parties from meaningful political participation. He decreed a new election and political party law which allowed for the registration of new political parties with far fewer signatures than formerly had been required, resulting in a proliferation of new political parties, much to the dismay of the established ones. He announced that all citizens would have to reregister as voters and that the army would be in charge of this census. The 1983 coup that installed General Mejía led to no major changes in the implementation of the electoral strategy, just as it made few in the counterinsurgency campaigns (Inforpress, 1984:21–43; Rosada Granados, 1985:13–24).

In July 1984 voters went to the polls to elect eighty-eight members of a constituent assembly. The bulk of these, sixty-five, were elected by districts corresponding to Guatemala's twenty-three departments; the remaining twenty-three were elected on an at-large basis from national lists. The new assembly's task was to write a constitution in preparation for the national and municipal elections on 3 November 1985. The campaign for this preliminary election was vociferous, but none of the major parties seemed willing to take positions on concrete issues (Rosada Granados, 1985:24).

In the new assembly twenty seats were held by the Christian Democrats, compared to twenty-one for the newly organized "centrist" party, the National Union of the Center (Unión del Centro Nacional—UCN), and twenty-three for an alliance of the MLN and its fellow party of the right, the Authentic National-ist Center (Central Auténtica Nacionalista—CAN). The remaining seats were distributed among seven other parties.[10]

The 3 November presidential election was contested by eight candidates. In addition to the presidential election, organized on a plurality and runoff basis, a new congress of one hundred members was elected (seventy-five of these by electoral districts corresponding to Guatemala's twenty-three departments and twenty-five elected at large on a national basis). At the local level, 328 munici-palities held elections for mayors and municipal councils. A total of fourteen political parties participated in the elections (Embassy of Guatemala, 1985:1; Stix et al., 1985).

Vinicio Cerezo of the Christian Democrats outdistanced Jorge Carpio Ni-colle of the UCN, obtaining almost 39 percent of the vote to Carpio's 20 percent. The Christian Democrats won a slim majority of seats in the new National Congress (Christian Democrats . . . , 1985:1–2). There being no ma-jority in the presidential vote, a runoff was held on 8 December. Cerezo won handily, and he was inaugurated in January 1986.

Although flawed by earlier and continuing human rights violations, unequal press coverage, and intimidation of voters from various sources, the election campaign, balloting, and vote counting appeared to have been conducted in accordance with Guatemalan electoral law. The election was "procedurally correct" (Booth et al., 1985:vii–xvi).

Conceptualizing Democracy

Whatever its particular institutions, any democracy must be based on the idea of widespread distribution of decision-making power in the society. There must be a balance of power between rulers and ruled. There must be clear evidence that democratic procedures allow the general populace to have a visible, tangible impact on policy, producing outcomes that favor the general populace.

This initial formulation stresses both procedures and outcomes of the politi-cal process. Liberal democratic models, however, usually stress procedures, assuming, perhaps unconsciously, that the presence of properly democratic procedures is adequate evidence for the existence of democracy, or at least for the beginning of a transition to democracy.

Although this is problematic in the case of Guatemala, where there are obvious examples of poverty, inequality, and the ruthless use of power by dominant sectors of society, I will review Guatemalan democracy from within the liberal conceptualization, looking at two types of structures and procedures commonly associated with liberal democracy: the representational model and the pluralist model. The most conventional way to measure democracy is through the occurrence of regular elections and the existence of opposition parties—the principal features of the "liberal-representative" or "republican" conceptualization of democracy (Dahl, 1966:xviii; Carr et al., 1971:151). But this model centers on elections themselves as the key structure (Kirkpatrick, 1982:2–3).

Nonetheless, attention is also paid to the quality of other types of linkages between the masses and the rulers in a society. The principal historical fear of representational democrats (or "republicans") is that, once elected, rulers will have no restraints on their behavior, there being no structure to hold them in check between elections, and that such a group might become a class unto itself. Consequently, emphasis is placed on limits such as civil liberties and other protections from arbitrary governmental action, including governmental activities that might have a direct impact on the future participation of citizens seen as opponents of a ruling group (Greenberg, 1983:34).

The second type of democratic structural arrangement is the pluralist model, which posits that the influence of citizens affects governmental policy between periods of electoral activity through the medium of access to policymakers. For most pluralists, the relevant vehicle is groups, especially organized interest groups or institutional groups with activities directed at policymakers. Generally, the Guatemalan constitution defines "politics" in terms of electoral and party behavior. This means that seeking access to policymakers is a "nonpolitical" activity. To pluralists these attempts to exert influence are part of the procedural complexity of politics, and such arrangements tell us something about the level of democracy in a polity.

A superficial analysis of the 1984–86 period in Guatemala, especially one that focuses only on the conduct of the elections, narrowly defined, and on the presence and activity of the several political parties, including even a Democratic Socialist party (the PSD) would conclude that the situation is democratic, especially in comparison with earlier and recent Guatemalan electoral episodes. This analysis would be more or less consistent with the position of the U.S. government—that the 1985 election, if not the "final step" in establishing democracy in Guatemala, is certainly a major and important step in that direction. The elections would then be described as "democratizing" events, as the term is used in the introduction to this volume. A more careful analysis of Guatemalan events, however, raises questions about whether the criteria for either representational or pluralist democracy have been met. A more sophisticated analysis of the electoral events requires answers to some hard questions and an extended time frame, questions such as those posed by John Booth in chapter 1 of this volume.

Herman and Brodhead suggest six "core requirements" that must be met if an election is to be considered "real." These criteria include (1) freedom of speech, including the opportunity to openly criticize governmental and other leaders; (2) freedom of the media, including the absence of censorship and intimidation; (3) freedom to organize interest groups that serve as a medium for allowing "organized pressure on the state" and also serve to "restrain state power"; (4) "absence of highly developed and pervasive instruments of state-sponsored terror"; (5) freedom to organize political parties and to field candidates; and (6) absence of coercion and fear on the part of the general population (Herman and Brodhead, 1984:11–14).

None of these criteria was met in Guatemala in the period leading up to the election of 1985. Two, however, *seem* to have been met, the third and the fifth, that is, the criteria of political parties and "intermediate" interest groups. The Guatemalan political system gives the appearance of competition because of the constant press coverage accorded to a variety of political parties and interest groups. On the question of political parties, the historical context, which becomes relevant if the time span of the analysis is expanded, shows that several major political parties have had their leadership groups decimated since the late 1970s, and only a very tame "opposition" participated in the 1985 election. The existence of a multiparty system during recent election campaigns, therefore, provides a superficial resemblance to a "democratic" society marked by openness. There is the suggestion that a multiplicity of issues is being represented.

The vocal participation of many interest groups also supports the image of an open system in Guatemala. But how is influence via group pressure distributed? What are some of the outcomes? In Guatemala the efficacy of these group activities varies with class. As societies become more complex, governments often turn to private organizations for assistance in governing, and Guatemala is no exception. Many governmental functions, such as business regulation, for example, are carried out by organized interest groups through a variety of legal mechanisms, ranging from ad hoc arrangements to permanent congressional commissions. Groups representing the economic elite are much more success-ful in this process than those representing the working class (Maldonado, 1980). As evidence, one need but mention the successful blocking of any but the most superficial agrarian reform policies, the successful avoidance of pro-gressive tax reform, at least until 1987, and the overall absence of social legislation protecting the working class.

Because working-class groups have been unsuccessful in having their needs and demands met via electoral participation, "popular" groups have used a variety of means to gain access to policymakers. But without the direct access that comes with the privatization of governmental functions, popular groups must use rallies, marches, personal visits to policymakers, appeals through the press, and so on.

The public articulation of interests by working-class groups, however, has lead to reactions far out of proportion to their scanty effects on policy deci-sions. The Guatemalan elite has consistently responded to attempts by work-ing-class groups to affect the policy process by seeking to eliminate partici-pants. The repression that Amnesty International has referred to as a "gov-ernment program of political murder" is not a situation in which a group of psychologically aberrant individuals have run amok but a systematized attempt to reduce political democracy by eliminating participants from certain interest groups and by sowing terror in the process.

In short, participation by the poor in Guatemala has not been efficacious, and observers can "see" successful evidence of pluralistic democracy only if they limit their scope to elite groups and groups organized to support elite programs. Such a conclusion does not, of course, mean that there is no competition within the elite. It does mean that the majority of the populace is not represented in the process and that by this standard Guatemala cannot be considered democratic.

If the Herman and Brodhead indicators allow us to incorporate a variety of criteria regarding the context in which an election takes place, Greenberg's four criteria allow us to speculate about the quality of an election in terms of its impact on public policy. The representational approach to democracy suggests that elections matter in terms of policy, and Greenberg's criteria posit that an election can be considered "democratic" if, at a minimum, "(1) candidates and parties . . . present clear policy choices . . . [on] . . . important issues. Elections

... should be *competitive* and *nontrivial*; (2) once elected, officials should try to carry out what they promised during their campaign; (3) once elected, officials should be capable of transforming campaign promises into binding public policy; (4) elections should generally influence the behavior of those elites who are responsible for making public policy" (Greenberg, 1986:169).

Very little evidence exists to suggest that these criteria have been met in the recent Guatemalan elections. During the presidential campaign, no candidate touched on such issues as corruption within the military or its human rights violations; none suggested that such violators be punished for past crimes or proposed dialogue with the insurgents. All contenders pledged not to pursue major socioeconomic reforms, and all acknowledged the special status of the military. Although there were differences of style and rhetoric, there were few major programmatic differences on nontrivial issues. The campaign resembled a "beauty contest" (Gleijeses, 1985:22–23).

Having promised little of substance during the campaign, the administration of President Cerezo has done little since its inauguration in January 1986. This is not to deny the Christian Democratic desire to implement some reforms. But the major stumbling block is Greenberg's third criterion. From the evidence presented earlier, it is clear that no elected civilian government has the power seriously to affect the institutional, economic, and political influence of the military and of some sectors of the civilian elite.

Although various elites can be seen to be accommodating each other's presence in the political system in recent elections, this does not necessarily mean that democracy is on the increase. Given the historical and social contexts, and the power of the military and some interest groups, the burden of proof for the existence of democracy has to rest on those who would assert that democracy exists because an election took place. No such proof exists. Indeed, few positive signs of any evidence of "democracy" exist.

In sum, a more intensive probing of the data on Guatemalan elections, even within the limited scope of conventionally accepted models of liberal democracy, reveals a shaky foundation. Recent elections—even with multiparty participation and nonfraudulent vote tallies—provide weak evidence of democracy. One delegation of electoral observers noted both that the 1985 election was "procedurally correct" and that the "prospects for civilians gaining true control of the armed forces remain extremely questionable given the historic, tragic, and violent role the military has long played in Guatemala" (Booth et al.,

1985:vii, xviii). Another source was more straightforward: "Whoever is elected in Guatemala, the army wins" (Goepfert, 1985:36).

Prospects for Democracy

Democracy and Transition in Guatemala

In October 1986, Carl Gershman, president of the National Endowment for Democracy, stated that Guatemala had arrived at the "post-transitional stage" of its democratic development (Gershman, 1986). A contrasting view sees elections "as an integral part of the counterinsurgency plan" (Rabine, 1986:61), meaning that the current civilian government, regardless of the party or ideological affiliation, is a part of a counterinsurgency strategy and hence cannot move toward real democracy (Contrainsurgencia . . . , 1985:26).

As is often the case in complex matters, these opposing positions are plausible on the face, but they mask important details or are too extreme to be accurate. The recent electoral events in Guatemala have in fact created some political space; types of activity are taking place that were not visible a few years ago. The question posed in this volume is whether such events lead to an improvement in the democratic climate, whether "openings" are evidence of democracy or merely masks for newly consolidated elite power.

The concept of "transition to democracy" in the recent work of O'Donnell and Schmitter (1986:48–56) seems useful in studying the current situation. Briefly, their argument is as follows. The transition begins when, for some reason, elite groups become dissatisfied with the functioning of authoritarian regimes. Elite groups, perhaps feeling relatively well protected by their status and their previous support for authoritarian rulers, begin to express demands for change, either in specific policies affecting their interests or in procedures, which means they call for an "opening" of the system.

Once the process of transition has begun, "a generalized mobilization is likely to occur, which we choose to describe as the 'resurrection of civil society'" (O'Donnell and Schmitter, 1986:48). When it becomes apparent that there is indeed an opening in the political process, middle-class and professional groups often emerge with demands that tend to quickly go beyond the strict limits of their particular interests. Lawyers' guilds, for example, may call for broad institutional reform—a demand that is not limited to the narrow interests of attorneys.

The restructuring of public space starts within the elite and then spreads to broader segments of the society, especially to urban middle-class professional groups and to those (such as groups involved in human rights activities) with some international prestige. Only then does the opening extend to the working classes and popular sectors. As O'Donnell and Schmitter (1986:59) point out, "not surprisingly, this is the area to which liberalization is extended most hesitantly and least irreversibly."

Once the popular sector is mobilized, there is likely to be an "explosion" of demands because of earlier repression or corporatist control (or both), earlier economic policies favoring business, or austerity measures aimed at the working classes. Although some of these demands are of the bread-and-butter type, others have much broader implications, such as demands for the restructuring of major societal and political institutions (O'Donnell and Schmitter, 1986:53–55).

An interesting conclusion is intuitively obvious. Once this process is underway, the stakes in the game are raised in two paradoxical ways: first, ever-spreading mobilization is a threat to the interests of the elites, but the more it spreads, the higher the costs of interrupting the process by, say, a coup d'état. Or, as the need (from the perspective of elites and other early opposition groups) to interrupt the transition grows, so does the cost of doing so. These vectors lead to a third paradox: the same moderate leadership groups that have come to power because they are acceptable to, or representative of, the early leaders of the movement against the previous authoritarian regime have an ever harder time staying in office, while at the same time the society's need to keep them in power, because they are moderate, also increases (O'Donnell and Schmitter, 1986:53).

The success of a "transition to democracy" is often expressed as increased opportunities for political participation by groups previously prevented from engaging in such activity by authoritarian regimes. Finally, in yet another paradox, middle-class sectors that come to hold office in transition stages find themselves assailed by both the elite that put them in place and the "popular surge" of the mobilizing masses. Moderate leaders are beset precisely because they symbolize the opening of closed systems, because they hold office, if not power.

It is clear that the current situation in Guatemala is neither equivalent to the brutal dictatorships that preceded it nor to the realization of genuine democracy. Rather, it is potentially a transitional stage, about which some observers are quite optimistic. Their arguments merit attention.

Incrementalism

Incremental arguments present a generally positive evaluation of Guatemala's recent electoral events. In this view, which is consistent with the position of the Guatemalan Christian Democrats, these elections are but a first step in the difficult process of creating a democracy (a "liberal" democracy, that is). The current weakness of the civilian government is acknowledged, but the future is viewed with cautious optimism, because democratic *procedures* have been strengthened. These strengthened institutions will, it is hoped, lead to real civilian power.

In his study of electoral structures and popular consent, Benjamin Ginsberg (1982:21–24) provides some support for this thesis. The use of democratic procedures, he asserts, can often lead to the demand for their continued use. Further, these procedures may become accepted by contending elites who have been kept from power by authoritarian groups. The longer such procedures are in place and found to be useful, the stronger they become and the more difficult it is to remove them from the procedural arena. Authoritarian rulers who have permitted elections or staged them to legitimize their hold over societal power may "discover that they could not restrain the forces they unleashed." In Ginsberg's view, procedures will change the norms adopted by elites, and this will in turn reinforce the existence of the procedures. If this occurs, and if the procedures reflect real democracy, then this process of cultural change would be relevant to the sixth question Booth asks of elections in chapter 1. My view on this, as I shall explain more clearly below, is that new procedures, such as elections, must stand the test of delivering policy changes for the majority before the majority will alter its cultural traditions.

Terry Karl uses an approach more clearly based on changes in the power configuration in a polity, helping us measure the usefulness of incremental arguments on the standard of outcomes. She suggests several ways in which an election *might* incrementally affect an authoritarian regime, thereby increasing the likelihood of a transition to democracy. These dimensions center on concepts such as the following: elections and campaigns can introduce new issues otherwise proscribed by authoritarian rulers; elections can lead to a focus on procedural rules of the game rather than on policy, promoting some unity among differing contenders who at least have in common their opposition to authoritarian rule; the existence of election procedures can limit the options of extremists, who must either compromise if they participate or choose not to participate and risk losing support; elections can, because of the aforementioned, affect (at least temporarily) the political constellation of power, the *coyuntura* of the political system (Karl, 1986:11–13).

The contextual information presented earlier and the apparent power of the military in Guatemala make it relatively simple to refute those who proclaim that democracy exists in Guatemala on the basis of the presence of elections. But these incrementalist arguments are more intriguing, for the notion that we should wait and see is compelling.

To deal with this notion in the present situation, we need to see whether deeper forces in Guatemalan society may act to inhibit democracy, even under the current, improved set of circumstances. According to the incrementalists, the first step has been taken: election procedures are in place. What other dimensions may be changed to enhance the level of democracy? What are the prospects for additional positive change? Several theoretical perspectives have been proposed; these are summarized below.

Developmental Perspectives

The developmentalist explanation argues that the economic correlates of political democracy simply do not exist in Guatemala. Moreover, given the economic crisis that has beset Guatemala for the past eight years and shows no sign of abating, the prospects for economic progress are slim (IADB, 1986:279). A pessimistic (or realistic) response is that the periphery nations are not going to achieve the economic preconditions for democracy through normal developmental processes (Hirschman, 1986:41). A more optimistic view argues that economic progress is possible if adequate infusions of new capital can be obtained, if infrastructure can be developed, and so on (Chilcote and Edelstein, 1974:3–26).

Cultural Theories

Cultural explanations for poor democratic performance are well known to scholars of Latin American politics. One of the prominent theories, the authoritarian culture–corporatist view, often concludes with the idea that Latin America is simply not likely to become democratic, nor do its elites want it to be. Some observers then conclude that corporatist and even "right-wing authoritarian" governments are all—or the best—we can hope for (Wiarda, 1986:142–43).

Other observers remain optimistic, if cautious, about the prospects for some kinds of democracy. Glen Dealy, for example, suggests that part of the analytic problem lies in the concept of democracy employed (Dealy, 1984–85:108–27). In this formulation, to envision democracy in Latin America in pluralistic terms is a mistake. Dealy's persuasive argument is that Latin democracy is much more likely to appear as mass movements oriented toward national unity.

Yet a third type of cultural approach might be called the "attitudinal prerequisites" approach to democratization. Certain attitudes—at both individual and societal levels—must exist, indeed predominate, if a society is to develop democratic structures (Hirschman, 1986:41–42; Dahl, 1956:132–33; Karl, 1986:2; Peeler, 1985:137–40).

Integrated Perspectives

Integrated analyses, those that look to economic preconditions for underlying attitudinal and cultural concepts necessary to a transition, such as consensus and compromise, provide a bridge to a more structural approach. Rosenberg, for example, points to the solution of economic problems, among others, as the sine qua non upon which a social consensus must be based if there is to be any real prospect for democratization (Rosenberg, 1985:27–28).

Lawrence Littwin (1974:8–11), whose work is not explicitly about democratic procedures, asserts that the roots of Latin culture lie in the Thomistic Catholic tradition, which, among other things, stresses the need for a fairly rigid political hierarchy. Assessing the possibilities for social change in Latin America, Littwin hypothesizes that an authoritarian (and therefore culturally acceptable) leader might use his power to ameliorate the adverse socioeconomic conditions afflicting Latin American masses and simultaneously undo the Thomistic Catholic cultural traditions that lead Latin masses to depend on powerful, authoritarian leaders. Cultural norms would be used to produce economic change that would transform those norms.

As applied in the Guatemalan context, both developmentalist explanations and those based on cultural attitudes are wanting. They fail to adequately account for the country's historical experience, and they oversimplify the impact of the power distribution in Guatemalan society at the present time.

For example, there may well be evidence of authoritarian political attitudes throughout Guatemalan society, but the lack of groups willing to compromise as part of their political strategy is not necessarily a result of cultural factors. The absence of such groups may well be the intended result of decades of violent repression by elites unwilling and in some ways unable to share power. Guatemala's experience in repression has operated at several levels: the assassination of opposition elites, the selective murder of members of activist organizations such as labor unions, and the almost indiscriminate massacres in rural Guatemala since Panzós in 1978.[11]

In Guatemala terror has been the predominant style of governance for centuries. Given the climate of state terrorism, it is in some ways irrational for citizens to appear publicly as reformist candidates or supporters of reform programs. It seems more reasonable to suggest, not that attitudes be changed to enhance the prospects for democracy, but that the murderers be removed from the scene. At the very least we need to see why such a style of governance is, tragically, "reasonable" under the circumstances.[12]

A Structural Theory

A structural explanation for the absence of democracy focuses on the relative balance of power between rulers and ruled in Guatemalan society and on the social structures that affect the balance. The measurement of such a balance of power centers on policy outputs of government or on measurable progress of socioeconomic indicators related to the quality of life and to basic human needs—or both. Although procedures are important, outcomes are more so.

This conceptualization is generally consistent with most liberal, representational formulations of democracy, except for the explicit attention given to outcomes. There is no assumption that elections and political parties guarantee an appropriate balance of power. These structures may or may not produce such an outcome; that is precisely what must be investigated. Hence elections can be understood only within a broader context that includes the nature of a society's economic structures and their impact on tendencies towards democratization.

Pre-Hispanic cultures in Guatemala are not normally thought of as democratic, inasmuch as they were based on theocratic, military rule with none of the structures that we normally consider part of democracy. I have come upon no evidence that the Maya societies, for example, allowed the general citizenry to participate in decisions about tribute (taxation), military service, and the like.

Yet the power of the rulers depended to a major extent on the productivity of their citizens. If the people did not produce an adequate surplus or did not pay tribute, the ruling groups had no recourse to external sources. Political decisions perforce were domestic, not international, issues. Decisions had to maintain, if not enhance, the productivity of the citizenry lest the elite lack resources for future rule. Although there was a clear and relatively unbridgeable gap between elites and masses, there was also, in some sense, a balance of power: "democracy" in substance, although certainly without the forms we know today (Gamer, 1982:18–27).

Since the Spanish Conquest, Guatemalan economic elites (which today include the military officer corps) have emphasized exports, particularly agricultural exports. They have thus routinely understood that the ultimate sources of their wealth and power lie outside national borders, in the international markets. To compete successfully it has been necessary to reduce the costs of production, especially labor costs. A direct result of these economic decisions is that the mass of Guatemalan people became, and remain, generally irrelevant to the economy as consumers of the goods produced. Since 1954 no Guatemalan regime has successfully adopted any scheme of income redistribution to turn Guatemalan workers into consumers.

Yet for the poor there were means of survival, the basis of which was the subsistence economy centered in rural areas, helped by opportunities for seasonal migrant labor. In indigenous areas, cultural values assisted in preserving community life. But even these dimensions are changing. Traditional exports, including tourism, have declined as sources of wealth since the late 1970s. At the same time that opportunities for seasonal labor seem to have peaked, if not declined, development plans calling for increases in nontraditional exports have led to new pressures for access to land in rural areas previously devoted to subsistence crops. Indigenous communities have in many cases resisted these trends. The military's role in resecuring these areas was described earlier.

Because workers cannot buy what they produce and because, moreover, there is a surplus of labor due to economic downturns, the Guatemalan economic elite does not depend on its own people as it did in centuries past. As a result, the ruling groups in Guatemala are much more closely allied to international sources of wealth and power and quite alienated from the needs of the Guatemalan populace at large.

Transition . . . to Democracy?

A transition process involves changes in the political structures of a society, including new ways of structuring participation. In other words, transition reflects a new dynamic of power. Evidence of change, however, does not automatically mean movement toward democracy. Moreover, new modes of political activity may not be associated with real shifts in power. We must take care before claiming that new types of activities indicate the development of democracy, of a wider distribution of political power. The transition process should not be merely a change in form; it should also involve new modes of participation, that is, new ways of exercising power, for the majority.

To study the transition process in Guatemala requires a careful examination of the political context in which it is occurring. One critical characteristic is the presence of a military institution that is basically undiminished in its power and presence in Guatemalan society. There is evidence that at least since 1982, counterinsurgency planning in Guatemala has included elections as part of its strategy, suggesting that something other than democracy was the main objective in spite of assertions that the military strategy during the period was "geared to devising a viable framework for the introduction of democratic institutions" (Fauriol and Loser, 1985:6, cited in Rabine, 1986:63).

It is interesting to note in passing that the military, or at least a dominant faction therein, obviously supports the existence of elections and civilian government, even as it is quite likely that the army does not favor genuine democracy. From a strictly political perspective, a cursory look at the situation in Guatemala suggests even less of an opening than that tentatively described by O'Donnell and Schmitter, given the military presence and the continued use of repression to reduce participation by reformers.

Besides the political context a second dimension that merits further study is Guatemala's political culture. As noted earlier, the "cultural impediments" to democracy are consequences, not causes, of policy and opportunity. In spite of acrimonious politics, many political leaders in Guatemala are now focusing on the need for dialogue among parties, a process recently institutionalized in the Instancia Política, formed by representatives of all the political parties in Congress except the National Liberation Movement, which refused to participate (*Boletín*, 1987:4). What may be lacking is a social and economic reality that makes democratic behavior a realistic option. In other words, democratic political culture may follow appropriate performance by the political and economic structures of society. Theorists who predict that cultural change must antedate structural change have the causal arrow reversed.

The third dimension of the study of the potential, and the limits, of the transition process in Guatemala is the political economy, by which I mean the structural nature of the economy and the relationship between a society's economic structures and its political structures.

Observers who focus on the political forms of transition optimistically view the transition as the initial necessary stage in an incremental approach toward creating stronger democracies and more social justice. In this incrementalist perspective, elections are but a first step, and the future is viewed with cautious optimism because democratic *procedures* have been strengthened. These strengthened institutions will eventually lead to real civilian power, and at that time reform programs will be implemented. In their recent work on democratization in Latin America, Drake and Silva advance similar possibilities: "The dictator's dilemma of staging and manipulating a credible election bedevils most authoritarian regimes. Elections concocted for legitimation may unintentionally become instruments for expanding liberalization—and eventually initiating democratization. . . . They provide a powerful (if minimal) vehicle for the government's adversaries to voice demands" (Drake and Silva, 1986:3, 5).

Economic considerations may limit these developments and temper this optimism. Especially in periods of economic crisis, the relationships between the state and sectors that control the productive resources of a nation may well produce a transitional process away from authoritarian rule, but they may also inhibit the democratic potential of that transition. Because of the overall nature of the international economic arrangements within which a nation finds itself operating, the limits on democratic development may not be susceptible to major change, although there will always be some room to maneuver. Guatemala's current situation, in which the nation's economy is beset by international market pressures as well as the pressure of regional U.S. policy concerns, illustrates this perspective very well.

Periods of economic decline generate more demands for reform, and the pressures for change can be substantial. Members of the elite perhaps rightly perceive that change and reform will seriously affect the life-style of the wealthy. Hence, resistance to the pressures for change can be strong. The very economic arrangements that are the source of the elite's wealth produce conditions that imply reform, if not revolution. An elite that fears the power of its own people is not likely to create serious democratic openings, even if there are strong international pressures to do so. On the contrary, it is much more reasonable for such an elite to engage in the sorts of *de*participatory behavior generally conceptualized under the rubric of human rights violations.

In such circumstances, classical liberalism has always seen the role of the state in terms of the protection of property (Green, 1981:52). The state needs to legalize coercion and to falsify the real limits on freedom, in order to guarantee the continuing domination of society by a propertied class using the ideology of liberal democracy (Jalée, 1977:90–99). Finally, there are basic contradictions between the existence of democracy in capitalist, liberal societies, with the state taking an ever more desperate and contradictory role in seeking to preserve the liberal rights of property against the pressures of democracy, and the conclusion that ruling classes in struggling capitalist economies will favor authoritarian politics over democracy (Wolfe, 1977:9–11). Historically, repression has been used in Guatemala with dismaying frequency.

Beyond political repression, a second strategy is the creation of a transition process with democratic forms but without substantive shifts in power. For example, we can imagine elections in which only "safe" candidates are allowed to participate—"demonstration elections" aimed at convincing the population that the new structures do indeed distribute power. Just as one of the United States' most celebrated founding fathers, James Madison, sought a mechanical solution to the inevitable and pernicious (to him) problem of the human tendency to form factions and to seek to control society, leaders in transitional societies might seek to organize political activity so as to preserve "open" systems. Such systems are not likely to respond successfully to demands of the newly participating popular sectors, but instead are designed to *moderate* the influence of the popular sectors.

O'Donnell and Schmitter note this possibility. "In the process of structuring the options of the transitions and taming the popular sector, one event plays a more important and immediate role than all others: the convocation of elections" (1986:56). A recent study has documented a clear plan in Guatemala to create a constitutional state that legitimizes the counterinsurgency activities of the military while simultaneously holding elections (Schirmer, forthcoming).[13] And a good deal of recent evidence suggests that the strategy has been successful. Notes an analyst of the insurgency, "It was easier to fight against a military government elected through fraud than a civilian President who was freely elected" (Norton, 1987:6).

Conclusion

To resolve the tension between democratic pressures for reform and the desire to maintain their economic structures and political influence, dominant elites in Guatemala traditionally have opted to resist reform and seek to reduce the political participation and efficacy of reformers and their followers. It is perfectly logical that such political steps be taken, given the international structures affecting economies and the domestic political position of the ruling class. This strategy, obviously inimical to the creation of any democracy, is likely to continue. The existence of elections does not mean that the desire for privilege or gross inequality will disappear.

Given the economic situation in Guatemala and the government's nonstructural policy responses to demands for land distribution, it may be a mistake to assume that the transition process will continue to expand the distribution of political power even though it may continue to expand the opportunities for electoral participation. Cautious optimism based on incremental approaches to the creation of democracy may be illusory.

Recent history, international pressures, and economic crisis have combined to obviate the continued reliance on traditionally repressive methods of power hoarding. Some Guatemalan elite actors, who perhaps have a broader perspective than others, may understand that oppressive economic conditions coupled with brute authoritarianism create the potential for chronic social instability, in itself an obstacle to economic growth and a threat to elite dominance in the long run. These actors and their international allies seek a political arrangement more consistent with long-range economic growth, one that will provide some economic reform and a good measure of social stability. The transition process we observe in Guatemala is the result of these desires.

The transition from authoritarian regimes is welcome for many reasons. It offers an opportunity for the development of democracy because a transition can lead to opportunities for authentic participation. Intransigent elites, of course, oppose this type of development. But even the enlightened elites and their international allies may not intend that the transition process produce genuine democracy, for the reforms that will be demanded and implemented in a genuine democracy are threats to their privileged position in society.

In chapter 1, Booth asks us to consider the extent to which elections "help consolidate a stable regime under democratic rules." Interestingly enough (from a semantic point of view), the transition process away from authoritarian rule in Guatemala has not produced a less authoritarian situation, although it has helped consolidate a stable regime. In fact, in the new constitution the power of the military has been increased, not reduced, over the situation created by the military in the constitution of 1965. In effect, "exceptional" states of siege and emergency have become normal, and institutionalized, and national security, not democracy or human rights, is the key concept (Schirmer, forthcoming). The result is an authoritarian system that is harder for casual observers to identify—and easier for North American political leaders to "use"—since it can be called democratic.

The continuing policy morass in Guatemala has resulted in few substantive changes in either real political participation or real policy improvements. With the exception of a new tax reform law in 1987, which may mean simply that the military is seeking to weaken the intransigent civilian elites, there has been no substantive change, except that an illegal and pariah regime has been "consolidated" and legitimized internationally. Taken out of context, the new electoral procedures appear democratic, but the social and political reality is certainly not democratic, not simply because it is impossible to undo the human rights violations of the past, but because current human rights violations continue unprosecuted, meaningful land reform remains an illusion, and there has been no reduction in the political or economic power of the armed minority that has governed for decades, the military.

Consequently, the prospects for democracy are quite limited. What we would normally call democratic forms are not necessarily signs of shifts in power, in spite of temporary increases in the levels of political tolerance. New forms of political activity do not necessarily mean a transition toward democratic politics. These new forms may be part of a strategy designed, in fact, to resist shifts in power.

To observe and measure democracy means constantly to be conscious of the question of political power in new forms of political participation. Since democracy is essentially a process by which power is exercised by the society at large, the organization of that power is a key ingredient. Organization is precisely what authoritarian regimes seek to prevent; and when organization begins to take place, it is precisely what authoritarian actors seek to discourage, often using repressive and antidemocratic violence, red-baiting and other delegitimizing techniques, and weak civilian governments as scapegoats. Constitutions and elections can be tools in this antidemocratic adventure.

Since the early 1950s, Guatemala has been a test case in the struggle between democracy and oppressive political and economic structures. "Project Success," the U.S.-led invasion in 1954, successfully stopped an earlier transition to democracy, but events since then have tempered the sweetness of that "success." From it the Cubans learned to dismantle the military after a revolutionary victory, and the United States learned to create stronger militaries with the Alliance for Progress. The Chileans learned that democratic procedures were adequate only until the economic elites (and the middle classes) were seriously threatened, and the United States learned that a Pinochet can be an international liability.

In the 1980s, Guatemala has been the success story in a region fraught with policy failures. Here is the best example so far of how to structure a consolidated regime that institutionalizes authoritarian practices while appropriating for itself the ideology of democracy by creating "demonstration" democratic procedures, and which institutionalizes economic and social oppression using the rhetoric of "development" while creating "model villages" and forced civilian military patrols. The juxtaposition of these dimensions is a masterpiece of political architecture, defusing opponents both in the United States and in Guatemala.

The question that needs to be addressed, then, is not whether Guatemala has become a new democracy since electoral processes have been institutionalized but rather whether these new processes will produce any appreciable movement toward genuine democracy, reflected in significant and prompt socioeconomic reforms of the kinds now being demanded by Guatemala's citizens. Will there be structural changes that can help eliminate the inequalities that make repressive government necessary for the elites?

Honest elections with relatively free participation by reformist parties can be a welcome development in Guatemalan politics if they create openings in which groups can move to make new demands on the government and to organize for future demands. But Guatemala is at a critical stage of its political evolution. The beginning of this transition to democracy is also creating resistance to changes in society, in spite of the efforts of reformist elements in the elite (including the military).

In the past, elite resistance to change has led to repression. The basic structures that are the power source of the repressor are still intact. We must be apprehensive about the future of democratic development in Guatemala. In Guatemala, given its tragic history and its socioeconomic context, it may take more than elections and reformist parties to achieve genuine democracy.

Notes

1. For a thorough historical treatment, see Handy (1984). To focus on the effects of the coffee boom in the nineteenth century, see Cambranes (1985). For detailed treatments of the 1954 CIA-led overthrow of the Arbenz regime in Guatemala, see Schlesinger and Kinzer (1981). For a capsule summary of early Guatemalan history with more detail on political events of the 1980s, see Trudeau and Schoultz (1986).

2. While acknowledging macroeconomic growth, one source says, "[This growth] has not resulted in any substantive increase in the internal market or in the economy's capacity to absorb available labor" (CSUCS, 1978:121).

3. In 1980 AID identified the "very low wage rates paid by commercial agriculture and an extremely low minimum wage established by the government" as the principal causes of Guatemalan poverty (USAID, 1980:6). A 1978 study reported that the per capita income of some 70 percent of the total population of Guatemala was inadequate for the purchase of a minimum diet (Amigo, 1978:124). By the late 1970s, over 80 percent of Guatemala's children were suffering from measurable malnutrition, and approximately 6 percent were *severely* malnourished—about twice the proportion for El Salvador (IADB, 1979:19).

4. For a detailed summary and analysis of this violent reaction by the government and the elite sectors that were affected, see Davis and Hodson (1982); for details from the perspective of the indigenous communities themselves, see Rarihokwats (1982). For a systematic analysis of political violence, especially in rural Guatemala, see Aguilera Peralta et al. (1981).

5. Data in this and other paragraphs describing political violence since about 1978 were obtained from a variety of published sources, including the daily press in Guate-

mala and newsletters and bulletins of various academic, educational, and political organizations.

6. An active member of the evangelical sect Iglesia del Verbo (Church of the Word), Ríos Montt identified himself as a "born-again" Christian and frequently referred to his seizure of power as the will of God. During his administration Ríos delivered weekly televised addresses in the style of homilies invoking divine assistance for his efforts to govern.

7. A good account of the civil patrols is found in Americas Watch (1983) and in Krueger and Enge (1985:23–26). For a good example of how this stated purpose of the patrols can be accepted as real, even in the "responsible" media, see Wright (1983).

8. For an especially poignant description of how civil patrols are a mechanism of social regulation, see Paul and Demarest (forthcoming).

9. For a thorough analysis and description of this program, its model villages, and its implications for Guatemalans, see IGE (1984 and 1986) and Krueger and Enge (1985:17–52). For evidence of U.S. fiscal and ideological support for the program, see NISGUA (1984–85:7) and AID Funds . . . (1984:4). For documentation of the opposition of the Guatemalan Catholic Church hierarchy to this development-counterinsurgency scheme, see *Ceri-Gua*, no. 60, 18–24 March 1985, p. 3.

10. For detailed analyses of voter turnout and results by party and districts, see Rosada Granados (1985:25–34 and 37–46).

11. Panzós, a municipality in eastern Guatemala, saw significant disruption in land tenure in the period after 1976, when economically powerful individuals sought to gain control over lands with mineral and agricultural potential. After a series of protests over these trends, dispossessed individuals, mostly indigenous, were invited to the town square to discuss their grievances. After the crowd had assembled, the square was surrounded by armed groups, allegedly the army, and gunfire broke out. Some one hundred people were killed.

12. For an in-depth analysis of Guatemalan political developments reflecting this point of view, see Torres-Rivas (1981).

13. I wish to acknowledge Professor Schirmer's kindness in letting me preview her manuscript while it is still in preparation.

References

Aguilera Peralta, Gabriel, et al. 1981. *Dialéctica del terror en Guatemala*. San José: Editorial Universitaria Centroamericana.

AID Funds for the Strategic Hamlets. 1984. *Enfoprensa: Information on Guatemala*, 7 December.

Americas Watch. 1983. *Guatemala: A Nation of Prisoners*. New York: Americas Watch Committee.

Amigo, Hugo. 1978. Características de la alimentación y nutrición del guatemalteco. *Alero* third series, no. 29 (March–April): 117–35.

Black, George, with Jamail, Milton, and Stoltz Chinchilla, Norma. 1984. *Garrison Guatemala.* New York: Monthly Review Press.

Boletín ACEN-SIAG. 1987. Mexico City: Agencia Centroamericana de Noticias ACEN-SIAG, 10 April.

Booth, John A. 1980. A Guatemalan Nightmare: Levels of Political Violence, 1966–1972. *Journal of Interamerican Studies and World Affairs* 22 (May): 195–225.

Booth, John A., et al. 1985. *The 1985 Guatemalan Elections: Will the Military Relinquish Power?* Washington, D.C.: International Human Rights Law Group, Washington Office on Latin America, December.

Cambranes, Julio C. 1985. *Coffee and Peasants in Guatemala: The Origins of the Modern Plantation Economy in Guatemala, 1853–1897.* English edition. South Woodstock, Ver.: CIRMA/Plumsock Mesoamerican Studies.

Carr, Robert K., et al. 1971. *Essentials of American Democracy.* 6th ed. New York: Holt, Rinehart and Winston.

Ceri-Gua: Panorama Informativo and *Vistazo Mensual.* Mexico City: Centro exterior de reportes informativos sobre Guatemala.

Chilcote, Ronald H., and Edelstein, Joel. 1974. Introduction: Alternative Perspectives on Development and Underdevelopment in Latin America. In *Latin America: The Struggle with Dependency and Beyond,* edited by Chilcote and Edelstein. Cambridge, Mass.: Schenkman.

Christian Democrats Shellac the Competition. 1985. *Central American Report,* 8 November.

Contrainsurgencia y régimen constitucional. 1985. *Temas de la Realidad Guatemalteca* 1 (October–November). Mexico City: Centro de Estudios de la Realidad Guatemalteca.

Counterinsurgency, Politics, and Instability. 1985. *Central America Bulletin,* April. Reprinted in *Guatemala Network News* 3 (April–May): 5–8.

CSUCS (Programa Centroamericana de Ciencias Sociales). 1978. *Estructura agraria, dinámica de población y desarrollo capitalista en Centroamérica.* San José: Editorial Universitaria Centroamericana.

Dahl, Robert A. 1956. *A Preface to Democratic Theory.* Chicago: University of Chicago Press.

———. 1966. *Political Opposition in Western Democracies.* New Haven: Yale University Press.

Davis, Shelton H., and Hodson, Julie. 1982. *Witnesses to Political Violence in Guatemala: The Suppression of a Rural Development Movement.* Boston: OXFAM-America.

Dealy, Glen C. 1984–85. (Pipe Dreams:) The Pluralistic Latins. *Foreign Policy,* no. 57 (Winter): 108–27.

Drake, Paul W., and Silva, Eduardo, eds. 1986. *Elections and Democratization in Latin America, 1980–85.* San Diego: University of California, Center for Iberian and Latin American Studies.

Embassy of Guatemala. 1985. *General Elections in Guatemala*. Washington, D.C.: Embassy of Guatemala.

Fauriol, Georges, and Loser, Eva. 1985. *Guatemalan Election Study Reports*. No. 1. Washington: Georgetown University Center for Strategic and International Studies.

Gamer, Robert E. 1982. *The Developing Nations: A Comparative Perspective*. 2nd ed. Boston: Allyn and Bacon.

Gershman, Carl. 1986. Address delivered at the Thirteenth International Congress of the Latin American Studies Association, Boston, 23–25 October.

Ginsberg, Benjamin. 1982. *The Consequences of Consent: Elections, Citizen Control and Popular Acquiescence*. Reading, Mass.: Addison-Wesley.

Gleijeses, Piero. 1985. The Guatemalan Silence. *New Republic* 10 (June): 20–23.

Goepfert, Paul L. 1985. Democratic Opening. *Progressive* 49 (November).

Green, Philip. 1981. In Defense of the State (II). *Democracy* 1 (July): 52–59.

Greenberg, Edward S. 1983. *The American Political System: A Radical Approach*. 3rd ed. Boston: Little, Brown.

———. 1986. *The American Political System: A Radical Approach*. 4th ed. Boston: Little, Brown.

Guatemala: News in Brief. 1986. New York: Americas Watch Committee.

Handy, Jim. 1984. *Gift of the Devil: A History of Guatemala*. Boston: South End Press.

Herman, Edward S., and Brodhead, Frank. 1984. *Demonstration Elections: U.S.-Staged Elections in the Dominican Republic, Vietnam, and El Salvador*. Boston: South End Press.

Hirschman, Albert O. 1986. On Democracy in Latin America. *New York Review of Books*, 10 April.

IADB (Inter-American Development Bank). 1979. *Nutrition and Socio-Economic Development of Latin America*. Proceedings of a symposium held in Washington, D.C., 28 June 1978. Washington, D.C.: IADB.

———. 1986. *Economic and Social Progress in Latin America: 1986 Report*. Washington, D.C.: IADB.

IGE (Iglesia Guatemalteca en el Exilio). 1984. Guatemala, "A New Way of Life": The Development Poles. *Guatemalan Church in Exile* (special edition) 4 (September–October).

———. 1986. Development: The New Face of War. *Guatemalan Church in Exile* (special edition) 6 (April).

Immerman, Richard H. 1982. *The CIA in Guatemala: The Foreign Policy of Intervention*. Austin: University of Texas Press.

Inforpress. 1984. *Centro América 1983: Guatemala*. Guatemala: Inforpress Centroamericana.

Jalee, Pierre. 1977. *How Capitalism Works*. New York: Monthly Review Press.

Jonas, Susanne. 1974a. Guatemala: Land of Eternal Struggle. In *Latin America: The Struggle with Dependency and Beyond*, edited by Ronald H. Chilcote and Joel C. Edelstein. Cambridge, Mass.: Schenkman.

———. 1974b. The New Hard Line: U.S. Strategy for the 1970s. In *Guatemala*, edited by Susanne Jonas and David Tobis. New York: NACLA.

Karl, Terry. 1986. Imposing Consent? Electoralism vs. Democratization in El Salvador. In *Elections and Democratization in Latin America, 1980–85*, edited by Paul W. Drake and Eduardo Silva. San Diego: University of California, Center for Iberian and Latin American Studies.

Kinzer, Stephen. 1985a. Guatemala Rivals Look to Transition. *New York Times*, 21 April.

————. 1985b. Guatemalan Rulers Renew Vow on Today's Voting. *New York Times*, 3 November.

Kirkpatrick, Jeane J. 1982. Statement before the Conference on Free Elections, November 4, 1982. In *Promoting Free Elections*. Washington, D.C.: U.S. Department of State, Bureau of Public Affairs, Current Policy, no. 433.

Krueger, Chris, and Enge, Kjell. 1985. *Security and Development Conditions in the Guatemalan Highlands*. Washington, D.C.: Washington Office on Latin America.

Littwin, Lawrence. 1974. *Latin America: Catholicism and Class Conflict*. Encino, Calif.: Dickenson Publishing.

Maldonado, José Rodolfo. 1980. Poder Político en Guatemala de algunos grupos sociales organizados en asociaciones no-políticas. Thesis, Universidad Rafael Landívar, Instituto de Estudios Políticos y Sociales, Guatemala.

Mendizábal, Ana Beatriz; Zepeda, Raúl; and Cardona, Rokael. 1979. *Empleo rural, estado, y políticas públicas en Guatemala: 1960–1979*. Guatemala City: Universidad de San Carlos, Instituto de Investigaciones Políticas y Sociales.

Natchez, Peter B. 1985. *Images of Voting, Visions of Democracy*. New York: Basic Book.

NISGUA. 1984–85. Model Villages and the Development Centers. *Guatemala Network News* 3 (December–January): 5–7, 12.

Norton, Chris. 1987. Guatemala's Insurgency Will Be Tough Test for Region's Peace Plan. *Christian Science Monitor*, 23 September. Cited in *Guatemala: News In Brief*, no. 18, 1 September–14 October.

O'Donnell, Guillermo; Schmitter, Philippe C.; and Whitehead, Laurence, eds. 1986. *Transitions from Authoritarian Rule: Tentative Conclusions*. Baltimore: Johns Hopkins University Press.

Paul, Benjamin D., and Demarest, William J. Forthcoming. The Operation of a Death Squad in a Lake Atitlán Community. In *Harvest of Violence: Guatemala's Indians in the Counter-Insurgency War*, edited by Robert M. Carmack. Norman: University of Oklahoma Press.

Peeler, John A. 1985. *Latin American Democracies: Colombia, Costa Rica, Venezuela*. Chapel Hill: University of North Carolina Press.

Rabine, Mark. 1986. Guatemala: "Redemocratization" or Civilian Counter-insurgency? *Contemporary Marxism*, no. 14, 59–64.

Rarihokwats, ed. 1982. *Guatemala: The Horror and the Hope*. York, Pa.: Four Arrows.

Rosada Granados, Héctor. 1985. *Guatemala 1984: Elecciones para Asamblea Nacional Constituyente*. San José: Centro de Asesoría y Promoción Electoral (CAPEL), Cuadernos de CAPEL, no. 2.

Rosenberg, Mark B. 1985. *Democracy in Central America?* Occasional Papers Series: Dialogues, no. 44. Miami: Florida International University, Latin American and Caribbean Center.

Schirmer, Jennifer. Forthcoming. *Rule of Law or Law of Rule?: Law, Human Rights, and National Security in Guatemala and Chile.* Manuscript in preparation.

Schlesinger, Stephen, and Kinzer, Stephen. 1981. *Bitter Fruit: The Untold Story of the American Coup in Guatemala.* Garden City, N.Y.: Doubleday.

Sharckman, Howard. 1974. The Vietnamization of Guatemala: U.S. Counterinsurgency Programs. In *Guatemala*, edited by Susanne Jonas and David Tobis. New York: NACLA.

Stix, Bob, et al. 1985. *Democracy or Deception?: The Guatemalan Elections, 1985.* Washington, D.C.: NISGUA.

Torres Rivas, Edelberto. 1981. Prólogo: La contrarrevolución y el terror. In *Dialéctica del terror en Guatemala*, edited by Gabriel Aguilera Peralta et al. San José: Editorial Universitaria Centroamericana.

Trudeau, Robert, and Schoultz, Lars. 1986. Guatemala. In *Confronting Revolution: Security through Diplomacy in Central America*, edited by Morris J. Blachman, William M. LeoGrande, and Kenneth E. Sharpe. New York: Pantheon.

USAID. 1980. *Report of the AID Field Mission in Guatemala.* Guatemala City: USAID. Cited in WOLA, *Guatemala: The Roots of Revolution.* 1983.

Wiarda, Howard J. 1986. Political Development in Central America: Options and Possibilities. *AEI Foreign Policy and Defense Review* 5, no. 1 (1984): 6–12. Reprinted as "Democratization in Central America: Possibilities for Democracy," in *Global Studies: Latin America*, 2nd ed., edited by Paul B. Goodwin. Guilford, Conn.: Dushkin.

WOLA. 1983. *Guatemala: The Roots of Revolution.* Washington, D.C.: Washington Office on Latin America.

Wolfe, Alan. 1977. *The Limits of Legitimacy: Political Contradictions of Contemporary Capitalism.* New York: Free Press.

World Bank. 1978. *Guatemala: Economic and Social Position and Prospects.* Washington, D.C.: World Bank.

Wright, Barbara. 1983. Guatemala's Civilian Patrols Help Quash Leftist Rebels in North. *Christian Science Monitor*, 13 December.

5 Elections and Transitions
The Guatemalan and Nicaraguan Cases

Susanne Jonas

"Elections . . . are the central institution of democracy. . . . Democratic elections guarantee that laws will not be made simply in the name of a community but with the consent of the community. No substitutes are acceptable. . . . "—Jeane Kirkpatrick

This essay attempts to assess the significance of recent elections in Guatemala (1985) and Nicaragua (1984) and to interpret them in light of larger questions regarding democracy. In so doing, I hope to develop a cogent alternative to the model explicit and implicit in the Kirkpatrick–Reagan administration view—a model which is widely held even among critics of Reagan policy in Central America. My purpose here is not to present an empirical study of those elections but to use them to examine four broad arguments.

1. *Framework*. The theoretical framework for interpreting democracy and elections should be broadened. If we are to address seriously the significance of elections, our starting point should not be (as in Kirkpatrick's view) their simple occurrence. Rather, elections should be interpreted and evaluated in relation to the broader question of what constitutes a genuine "transition to democracy" at the level of the state and civil society. Moreover, I share John Booth's view that the concepts commonly accepted in U.S. social science (which tend to overstress institutional, representational democracy) should be augmented by concepts of substantive, participatory democracy from other political traditions. Finally, I argue for a structural approach to political development.

2. *Guatemala*. Reagan administration officials and supporters maintain that, having held nonfraudulent elections that returned the country to civilian rule in 1985, Guatemala under the presidency of Christian Democrat Vinicio Ce-

rezo is now "posttransitional" and in the phase of "democratic consolidation"—the implication being that the election itself represented the passage to democracy. In contrast, this chapter argues that ever since the 1954 U.S. intervention which ended the Revolution of 1944–54—Guatemala's uncompleted bourgeois-democratic revolution—the context for politics has been the counterrevolutionary state. Since the 1960s this has taken the specific form of what we shall call the "counterinsurgency state." Because it is designed for control, the counterinsurgency state is incompatible with true pluralism, although it has proven more flexible (and more contradictory) than previously thought.

The 1985 Guatemalan election, far from being a rupture with the past, can best be understood within that framework. It was not openly fraudulent, but was severely restricted and nonrepresentational of large sectors of the population. That election, therefore, opened up a period, not of democratization, but of liberalization—at best a real opening, at worst not much of an opening, but in no sense a fundamental change in the nature or class basis of state power. More than anything else, it should be viewed as a necessary adjustment for dealing with Guatemala's economic and political crises.

3. *Nicaragua.* This chapter analyzes the 1984 elections both from the perspective of pluralism and representational democracy and from the perspective of participatory or popular revolutionary democracy. While paying attention to the effects of the U.S.-inflicted war and "rollback" policy, it also examines the construction of democracy as an internal process of the Nicaraguan Revolution. I agree with the vast majority of international observers that the 1984 election conformed very closely to Western standards of fairness and pluralism—more so than most other elections in recent Central American history. Furthermore, when viewed from a broader perspective (participatory democracy, socioeconomic justice, and so forth), the election was a genuine advance, part of a larger process subsequently expressed in other political experiences, such as the writing and ratification of the 1987 constitution.

I shall argue that, far from being the totalitarian or Stalinist state Reagan would have it, revolutionary Nicaragua has embarked upon a transition process which has the potential for constructing a democratic state. There are significant issues of how to interpret this experience, but those correspond to the problems and contradictions of the transition process. The process is restricted, above all, by the exigencies of war and external aggression, and the legacies of underdevelopment and of the pre-1979 counterinsurgency state cannot be overlooked. Even within the limits imposed by total mobilization for war, however, the Nicaraguan attempt to integrate pluralistic with popular, participatory democracy contributes a new experience to the evolution of Third World revolutions.

4. *U.S. Policy.* It is impossible to understand the experience of either Guatemala or Nicaragua outside the context of U.S. actions and policies. One pillar of U.S. policy in Central America is the Reagan Doctrine, which is designed to "roll back" (overthrow) governments deemed "Communist." In Nicaragua this policy is reflected in the administration's promotion of counterrevolutionary insurgency against the Nicaraguan government. Far from promoting democracy, this policy represents the greatest threat to the development of democratic processes in Central America and is in many respects incompatible with it. (The U.S. attempt to disrupt the Nicaraguan election is only the clearest example.)

The other pillar of U.S. policy (for example, in Guatemala) is to establish "counterinsurgency democracies"—anti-Communist governments, military or civilian, authoritarian or liberal, which can serve as bulwarks against nationalist or socialist revolutionary movements. Far from promoting or consolidating democracy in Central America, as it claims, the United States is responsible for strengthening the antidemocratic elements in the security forces and inculcating an anti-Communist ideology which defines "the people" as "the enemy." An examination of U.S. policy suggests that there are in reality three conceptions of democracy: apart from representative and participatory, there is a counterinsurgent conception of democracy, which is presented as representative democracy (hence, Kirkpatrick's emphasis on elections), but which in reality means smashing Communism by any means necessary, no matter how undemocratic.

Conceptual and Methodological Issues

Democratization is very much the object of attention in academic as well as political circles concerned with Central America; however, the discussion is often limited, conceptually and ideologically, to paradigms of representational democracy that make elections the central (or only) criterion. To broaden the range of discussion on the question of democracy, I shall introduce some countervailing perspectives that are frequently excluded from discussion in the United States, but that are, in many respects, both methodologically and substantively more appropriate.[1]

The following are some methodological premises:

1. The analysis here is structural in that it examines political issues in relation to socioeconomic factors, for example, underdevelopment, economic crisis, class, and class conflict. More particularly, my starting point is the proposition that representative or political democracy should be analyzed in relation to issues of socioeconomic equality—a prime consideration in a region like Central America, where such gross inequalities of distribution prevail. (See note 1 above.)

2. In addition to "regimes," we are concerned with the nature of the state. The state is not an isolated political creation, independent of class or other social forces; it can only be fully understood in relation to its social base and its articulation with civil society. The significance of any given shift—for example, from a military to a civilian regime—depends primarily on whether or not there is a change in the class basis of state power. Only a major and lasting change at this level, I shall argue, makes possible a significant "transition."

3. I shall examine both internal factors (for example, social structure, underdevelopment, nature of the state) and external factors (for example, U.S. policy, world capitalist accumulation and crisis) affecting the current political evolution of Central America. While not primary or determinative, external factors have had a singular importance in setting the context for politics in the region. Perhaps that is obvious, but it bears emphasizing today, since we are dealing with a fundamental challenge to U.S. power from Central American popular and revolutionary movements and the U.S. military response (counterinsurgency wars, and now the war against Nicaragua).

4. The focus is regional in scope, recognizing that in some respects Central America is a structural unity, with dynamics that differ from those of the Southern Cone. Developments in individual countries are affected by regional factors (for example, the profound economic crisis since the 1970s, militarization of the region since 1979, and now the "peace process"). This is the framework, as I shall indicate below, for the Guatemala-Nicaragua comparison.

5. The construction of democracy is analyzed here as a historically evolving process. In this regard, I agree with John Booth's approach in chapter 1 of this volume. Further, it is neither methodologically sound nor fruitful to apply a "democracy checklist," using the most common features of advanced Western

democracies, to construct a Platonic-"universal" ideal-type against which to measure Central American politics.[2]

6. Democracy is examined here both from the perspective of pluralism and representational democracy (the classical Western conception) and from the perspective of participatory or popular revolutionary democracy. Hence, we are concerned with the possibilities for autonomous mass movements to operate freely, as well as for individuals to exercise their civil and human rights. Both of the above are to be distinguished from the geopolitical, counterinsurgent conception, which in effect equates democracy with anti-Communism.

7. It follows from the above that elections are an important expression of legitimation, but by no means the only one, nor even (by themselves) definitive or constitutive of a democratic political order. They can be (and frequently have been in Central American history) used to legitimate military dictatorships or foreign interventions or to consolidate military rule behind a civilian facade. Therefore, we seek to avoid fetishizing elections by analyzing recent electoral processes in Central America within the historical and structural framework indicated above.

In the same vein, elections by themselves do not tend to initiate major political transitions, although they can be part of such transitions. Elections are more likely to *reflect* the level of participation and representativity in a given situation than to determine it.

The above considerations lead me to agree with Booth on a number of methodological and substantive premises about elections: first, elections cannot be understood outside the framework of larger questions about democracy; second, democracy must include some conception of "participation" in the rule of a society by its general populace; third, democracy is not an absolute which "exists" or "doesn't exist," but a variable which depends on the amount and quality of popular participation in decision making, the degree of support for participatory norms, and so forth.

I would add the following emphases: (a) political democracy cannot be divorced from the socioeconomic structure of society and socioeconomic advances for the majority of the population (see above, note 1); (b) meaningful democracy requires, beyond an interelite consensus or "pact," active involvement by the majority classes; and (c) popular participation should be understood as emerging from a popular base ("from below") and as *autonomous* from control by the state or official parties ("at the top"). Inherent here is the notion that democracy in the full sense cannot be reduced simply to elections, but also includes the construction of autonomous popular organizations; to put it another way, we are concerned not only with issues of state power but also with social movements both organized and spontaneous.

State and Counterinsurgency State

My starting point is a structural analysis of the state—structural in reflecting both the level of capital accumulation and economic development and the relations between different forces in the class struggle. The state functions to maintain and reproduce a mode of production in which a specific class is dominant (Hamilton, 1982:4–5). Even where it does not act directly as the instrument of the dominant classes, the state is always "in the last instance the guardian of the order established by these classes" (Lowy and Sader, 1985:11). While linking particular political regimes to underlying socioeconomic structures, this conception does not view the state as monolithic or unitary, nor as a "thing-in-itself."

Within this framework, a central concept for our purposes is the counterinsurgency state, as elaborated by Ruy Mauro Marini (1980) and other Latin American scholars. By "counterinsurgency state" is meant a particular form of the counterrevolutionary state, a variant of the bourgeois state in Latin America that combines the traditional authoritarian-oligarchical state with the institutionalized apparatus created and imposed by the United States in the 1960s to prevent "another Cuba" (Torres Rivas, 1986:6). As such, it is a historically specific response to the challenge from revolutionary movements since the 1960s. Although the counterinsurgency state has been elaborated with increasing sophistication since the 1960s, its essential structure and goals still fit the general description offered by Ruy Mauro Marini (1980:4 ff.).

First, it is a class-based corporate state of the monopoly bourgeoisie and the armed forces, designed to defend the interests of that bourgeoisie (including transnational capital as well as local capitalists) with the support of the armed forces, which in many cases has become part of the bourgeoisie.

Second, its objective is not merely to defeat but to annihilate "the enemy," that is, revolutionary movements that challenge the bourgeois order, and to destroy their social base among the population. It is characterized by a recourse to state terrorism. Based on a conception of "total war," it applies a military focus to political and social struggle during the counterinsurgency war—and subsequently, since these periods definitively alter the political life of the country.

Third, because its goal is to control the civilian population and eliminate significant opposition, it is the negation of pluralism. In this sense it excludes genuinely competitive elections with candidates from the entire political spectrum and with uncertain outcomes (Torres Rivas, 1986:22). It exists for the purpose of maintaining control and rules primarily through domination as opposed to hegemony (that is, the creation of social consensus). It denies not only the exercise of individual rights but also the autonomous functioning of mass organizations.

Finally, it does not require military government at all times; in fact, it explicitly proposes the reestablishment of formal democracy after the most intensive military phase of the counterinsurgency campaign. Thus, under certain conditions, civilian regimes can be more effective agents of pacification than military dictatorships. Within the counterinsurgent conception, "democratic" civilian regimes are restricted and controlled, preemptive of social protest movements, and unable to establish civilian hegemony over the armed forces (Petras, 1986:1).[3]

Yet, civilian counterinsurgency states are characterized by particular contradictions: they have a dual character, reflecting a dialectical balance between popular demands for democracy and the requirements of counterinsurgency, between pressures for a genuine democratic opening and constraints upon that opening. Specific factors affecting this balance in Latin America today include serious economic crisis, which creates its own social dislocations; political changes resulting from the return to civilian government; and new contradictions created by the "opening" itself, insofar as the space opened up by the lessening of repression is inevitably filled by popular, often mass, demands for change.

To put it another way, counterinsurgent democracy, or "democratization," as it is currently being called, is being challenged by demands for popular democracy, against a backdrop of profound economic crisis and aggressive U.S. interventionism (the Reagan Doctrine). Further discussion on this point is contained in the section on Guatemala below and note 4, regarding the debate over the application of the "counterinsurgency state" concept to a civilian regime such as that of Cerezo in Guatemala.[4]

Guatemala-Nicaragua Comparison

The above considerations form the context for this examination and interpretation of recent electoral experiences in Guatemala and Nicaragua. My final introductory comment concerns the Guatemala-Nicaragua comparison. Methodologically, I find it to be a useful comparison because the two countries share much historically and structurally and are affected by many of the same external and internal factors. In addition, under the particular circumstances of Central America today, a comparison of the two cases is appropriate because of the striking degree to which they have become two alternative models in Central America, each seeking viability within its own political logic (respectively, counterinsurgency and social revolution). Miguel Angel Balcarcel, a Guatemalan social scientist and intellectual adviser to his government, recently stated (perhaps overstated) this point from his perspective:

> The people of Central America have before them now two large mirrors that represent the ideological and geopolitical bipolarization of the world: Guatemala, Nicaragua. Each country represents a different experience in solving its crisis. . . . And each awaits in suspense the success or failure of the other. (*Los Angeles Times*, 29 October 1987)

Guatemala:
Counterinsurgency State and "Democratic Opening"

> "Guatemala has moved from a transitional to a post-transitional situation of democracy under Cerezo. The only question is how to expand upon the gains that have been made."—Carl Gershman, head of the U.S. government's National Endowment for Democracy (NED), 1986 speech

The "Liberal Revolution" of 1871, coinciding with the rise of the coffee oligarchy and major U.S. investments in Guatemala, established the framework for the construction of a state whose primary function was to provide police protection to the propertied classes and to apply coercion to the majority of the population in order to guarantee a cheap and docile labor force. What is significant for our purposes is that during the entire Liberal era (1871–1944), there were periodic elections. Even the Ubico dictatorship of 1930–44 came to power through an election.

The Revolution of 1944–54 (governments of Juan José Arévalo and Jacobo Arbenz) was the closest Guatemala has come to a bourgeois-democratic revolution and the only attempt to construct democracy from the bottom up. The revolution was truncated before it could be consolidated by the U.S. intervention of 1954 (the "Liberation"). Beyond overthrowing the Arbenz government—in itself, one of the most violent curtailments of democracy in Latin American history—the U.S. intervention initiated profound changes in the quality of Guatemalan political life. One of the long-range political consequences of U.S. intervention was the establishment of a counterrevolutionary state. The contradictions of the attempt to reimpose the old (pre-1944) order precipitated the rise of a revolutionary movement and sparked a political crisis beginning in the 1960s which could be contained only through a permanently institutionalized counterinsurgency campaign. This is the framework for our analysis of the 1985 Guatemalan election.

The inability of the U.S.-imposed regimes to resolve the social problems of economic modernization became clear in the early 1960s, with the rise of a guerrilla movement strong enough to challenge bourgeois-military control in some parts of the country. Although Guatemala had military governments beginning in the early 1960s, it was under the civilian government of Julio César Méndez Montenegro (1966–70) that the United States fully mounted the apparatus of the counterinsurgency state. Indeed, during the late 1960s Guatemala became a laboratory for Vietnam-style pacification techniques; and it was in the 1966–68 counterinsurgency campaign that such phenomena as death squads and disappearances became part of Guatemala's daily reality (Aguilera, 1985c and 1981; Sharckman, 1974).

From the mid-1960s through 1977 the United States played a direct and decisive role in counterinsurgency operations. The U.S. Congress suspended military aid in 1977 because of the massive human rights brutalities committed by the Guatemalan government and security forces. Even when military aid was formally banned during the late 1970s and early 1980s, however, the United States was involved in planning the counterinsurgency offensive of 1982–85. According to testimony by Elias Barahona, who served as press secretary to the minister of the interior from 1976 to 1980, this campaign was designed largely according to the United States' "Program of Pacification and Eradication of Communism" (Barahona, 1984:64 ff.).

The first stage of the campaign, from 1981 through mid-1983, was characterized by intense open brutality against the population, as the army sought literally to eradicate the guerrilla movement's civilian support base. The principal policies in the effort to "drain the sea" from which the guerrillas derived support included "scorched earth" burnings, village-wide massacres, and forced relocations of village populations. Entire sectors of the population became military targets, particularly in the indigenous areas where the guerrilla movement was strongest, leading some scholars to describe these policies as literal genocide (Falla, 1984). The statistics are staggering: over 440 villages were entirely destroyed; 100,000 civilians were killed (some estimates range up to 150,000); and there were up to one million displaced persons (500,000 internal refugees, up to 200,000 refugees in Mexico, and another 250,000–350,000 in the United States) (Americas Watch, 1987:73 ff., and church and U.N. sources).

The second stage, from mid-1983 to 1985, consolidated military control over the population through a series of coercive institutions. Among these were mandatory paramilitary-civilian "self-defense" patrols (involving one million peasants—one eighth of the entire population, one-quarter of the adult population); rural resettlement camps known as "model villages" (strategic hamlets) concentrated in "development poles"; and Inter-Institutional Coordinating Committees, which centralized administration of development projects at every level of government under military control (a striking example of the militarized state). All of these institutions were legalized in the new constitution of 1985, which provides the juridical framework for the Cerezo government.

Counterinsurgency Elections:
Politics as an Extension of War

Ever since 1954, Guatemala's counterrevolutionary state has been "legitimated" through periodic elections. In 1954 the U.S.-appointed leader of the "Liberation," Colonel Carlos Castillo Armas, was "elected" in an Ubico-style plebiscite, in which he received 99 percent of the vote. The 1957 election, following Castillo Armas's assassination by one of his own guards, was so overtly fraudulent that it was annulled. A new election in 1958 gave the presidency to Colonel Miguel Ydígoras Fuentes, a corrupt former *Ubiquista*— his opponent having been bribed by the CIA to concede. This and subsequent elections in 1959 were characterized by intimidation, bribery, and numerous irregularities. The presidential election scheduled for 1963 was preempted by a

U.S.-supported military coup, to prevent the almost certain election of progressive former president Arévalo.

The 1966 election, following three years of de facto military rule, was won by civilian "moderate" Julio César Méndez Montenegro. Although his election was a clear mandate for structural change (his campaign promised a "third government of the Revolution"), Méndez was permitted to take office only after literally signing a pact with the army, guaranteeing it a free hand in counterinsurgency and numerous other matters.

The reign of military terror under the "civilian" Méndez government set the stage for the subsequent elections, in which almost all candidates (winning and losing) were military officers. The 1970 election of Colonel Carlos Arana (who was known as the "Butcher of Zacapa" for his role in the 1966–68 pacification) institutionalized the counterrevolutionary state. The elections of 1974, 1978, and 1982 were all openly fraudulent, with the dominant faction of the military stealing office in each case from the actual winner. All of the elections after the mid-1960s, then, were counterinsurgency elections in a literal sense.

The 1985 election of civilian Christian Democrat Vinicio Cerezo was proclaimed by the U.S. embassy as the "final step in the reestablishment of democracy in Guatemala" (WOLA, 1985:65). Unlike other recent elections since 1970, it put a civilian into office; it was not fraudulent and was procedurally correct. But these factors by themselves do not constitute a basis for the sweeping claim that the election represented the culmination of a lasting transition to democracy, as a review of some interesting statistics about the election itself will reveal.

Representation. There were multiple competing parties, but a significant portion of the electorate was not represented by any of the candidates. Aside from the Socialist Democratic party (PSD), no left-of-center parties participated, the leadership of most of these parties having been exiled or eliminated in the 1960s and 1970s. Even in the case of the PSD, some of its leadership was in exile. Similarly, in regard to interest groups, participation was limited to ruling-class groups (Trudeau, 1986:18), with unions and popular organizations remaining major targets of repression.

The platforms of the participating parties, ranging from the PSD and the centrist Christian Democrats to the extreme right Movimiento de Liberación Nacional (MLN), differed very little from each other. None of the candidates proposed any serious economic reforms, any restrictions on the military, or any investigation (much less prosecution) of the crimes of the military during the previous period. Although technically civilians, all of the candidates made themselves acceptable to the military by agreeing that "the subversives must be eliminated" (Inforpress Centroamericana, 1985:38). Several of them had long histories of collaboration with the military and were actively supported by parties or factions of the army. In short, no real opposition candidate or position was represented—a point which becomes even clearer if we look at statistics on participation.

Participation. According to statistics compiled by an observers' delegation sponsored by the Washington Office on Latin America (WOLA), 55.8 percent of eligible voters did not participate, that is, either did not register, abstained from voting, or cast invalid ballots (WOLA, 1985:76–77). This occurred in a country in which voting is compulsory for citizens over eighteen, with penalties or reprisals for not voting—and overt threats during the last week (WOLA, 1985:53).

Content. The campaign was marred by continued illegal executions and disappearances (WOLA, 1985:46 ff.). More broadly, the election took place in an environment scarred by thirty years of uninterrupted terror, coercion, and the knowledge that even the slackening of human rights brutalities could be reversed from one day to the next and open military rule reinstituted.

How do we interpret the 1985 election? In interviews and written analyses, Guatemalan observers and participants have put forth various interpretations, most of them citing first the obvious limitations: the election was not broadly representative of the political forces in Guatemala; it did not involve widespread popular mobilization or participation; and it was conducted in a blatantly repressive environment. In terms of the criteria laid out by Booth, it met the formal requirements of an honest election, but participation was severely restricted in all of its dimensions.

Within these limits—despite these limits—many Guatemalans hoped that the election would initiate a change and regarded it as an opportunity to express their rejection of military dictatorship and their desire for democracy and reform. Those who voted gave a 70 percent mandate in the runoff election to Cerezo, who was the most progressive of the major candidates. From this perspective, moreover, the election was an opportunity for some political parties (those acceptable to the army) to reorganize on a more normal basis and to revitalize political activity for some sectors of the population.

Some Guatemalan analysts refer ironically to the contradictory experience of the election and rejection of military government as being perhaps Guatemala's "best hope" to begin a democratic transition. Others have referred to it as a "consulta pública," a controlled attempt at legitimation within the context of the ongoing counterinsurgency war. And more popularly, these lines of interpretation are sometimes expressed in the context of Guatemala's history of "facade democracy," which combines formal legality with illegal violence. (For the above see: Torres Rivas, 1987:171 ff., and 1986:23–26; Aguilera, 1985a and 1981; Rosada, 1986:57; Solórzano,1987).

Whatever the shades of interpretation, there is broad agreement on one fundamental point: even taking into account the democratic aspirations of a majority of Guatemalans, the dominant reality about the election is that it took place as part of a counterinsurgency war and it did not involve a real transfer of power from military to civilians. Once the army had completed the genocidal phase of its counterinsurgency campaign—and once the apparatus of the counterinsurgency state was in place and its institutions (civilian defense patrols, "model villages," and so forth) legalized in the 1985 constitution—elections and civilian government could proceed without requiring a fundamental change. And in practice, although the balance between civilians and military has changed in some respects since 1986, much of the power has remained in the hands of the military, which emerged from the counterinsurgency campaigns of the early 1980s immensely fortified, politically as well as militarily.

For these and other reasons, I do not view the 1985 election as constituting a fundamental break from the counterinsurgency state—although I recognize that a civilian counterinsurgency state has its own particularities and that this conceptualization is open to extensive and significant debate.[5] The 1985 election was part and parcel of the counterinsurgency planning of the early 1980s—a third stage of the campaign, so to speak. In fact, it was viewed in this way by important sectors of the Guatemalan military, as reflected in their 1982 National Plan for Security and Development: "With only military and police operations, it is not possible to definitively annihilate subversive activity, because, independent of the aid they get from abroad, the causes of the subversion are based in the existing contradictions [of Guatemala], the product of historical processes that Communism can exploit to its advantage" (Castañeda, 1986:note 20; CERG, 1985:5 ff.). In short, the Guatemalan military and their

U.S. advisers recognized the need to adjust their counterinsurgency strategy. There were several reasons why they preferred an elected civilian government.

After having been an international pariah for many years, the Guatemalan government had to establish international legitimacy, once the excesses of the counterinsurgency campaign were no longer necessary. Only thus could Guatemala obtain international aid to deal with its worst economic crisis in recent history. (This point was reinforced by the spectacular success of the Reagan administration in gaining approval for such aid to El Salvador from former critics in the U.S. Congress and Western Europe after the election of Duarte in 1984.)

Internal pressures for the election were even more intense; hence it cannot be described simply as a "demonstration election."[6] One crucial internal factor was the need for a more "open" environment in Guatemala in order to regain private-sector confidence and reactivate the economy.

It was also necessary to create a "legitimate" government as a basis for reestablishing internal stability (seriously challenged by the resistance and popular movements during the late 1970s) and for limiting social protest. Even though the army had tactically defeated the guerrillas by 1985, the experience of the massive incorporation of the Indian population into the insurgency, and the specter of future such occurrences, created a political crisis which the election was designed to address. The army, politically discredited after years of fraudulent and corrupt rule, had to redefine its relations with the civilian population, especially in the rural areas; it tried to do so in part by taking credit for returning the country to civilian rule and promising reforms. Although the redefinition of those relationships was not fundamental, it did imply a political opening of sorts and a change in the operations of the counterinsurgency state.

The above was clear not only to sectors of the Guatemalan military but also to some in the U.S. government. Perhaps this is why the United States played such an active role in the 1985 election, providing funds for the election itself, both directly and indirectly (through the U.S. government's National Endowment for Democracy, the public side of "Project Democracy," whose purpose is to channel U.S. funding to beleaguered anti-Communist movements and governments). The Reagan administration also acted as a virtual public relations firm for the Guatemalan government. In the regional context, further, its seems likely that the administration was interested in Guatemala, first, because it is the largest and most important Central American country and, second, in relation to Nicaragua, as a case in point to "prove" the Kirkpatrick thesis that authoritarian regimes pose no threat to democracy because they "inevitably" evolve toward democracy, or "liberalize" (Kirkpatrick, 1982a).

Without doubt, Guatemala in 1987 was experiencing an opening. But could it be considered in any sense the prelude to a democratic transition? In the past thirty years there had been periodic openings in Guatemala, but they were widely viewed as having accomplished little more than to generate new names for the death squad lists. More important, these openings saw the hardening of existing socioeconomic inequalities rather than any structural reform. Was the Cerezo opening doomed to follow a similar path?

This is the not the place for a full analysis of the Cerezo opening, which I have developed elsewhere (Jonas, 1988). Briefly, it is my view that this opening reflects the contradictions of an elected civilian government whose priority remains that of the army: military defeat of the guerrillas. On the one hand, this opening is real enough to have created some space and, above all, to have promoted expectations of expanded civil liberties and freer operation of unions and other popular organizations. Under these conditions, counterinsurgent democracy is, so to speak, confronted by grassroots movements for popular democracy, particularly at a time of serious economic crisis. This process generates its own contradictions, as has become evident in Guatemala in 1987.

On the other hand, there are decisive limitations to the opening. Popular movements and the institutions of Guatemalan civil society have been severely damaged during the last thirty years, particularly during the 1982–85 counterinsurgency campaign, and there is no sign that truly autonomous civil institutions will be allowed to press their own demands freely. And according to 1987 reports by Americas Watch, Amnesty International, and the Inter-American Human Rights Commission of the OAS, the human rights record under Cerezo does not offer much encouragement: there are still over 100 political murders or disappearances a month; many basic rights do not exist in practice, and those who fight for them continue to be targets of repression. (This is hardly surprising, given Cerezo's pledge not to investigate military crimes of the past.) The human rights situation deteriorated even more seriously toward the end of 1987, as the army again stepped up its counterinsurgency war.

The above is compounded by indications of reinvigorated U.S. military and police aid—needed, officials say, to defeat the insurgents and to combat the "surge of violence [that] is a result of the loosened atmosphere that democracy has brought to Guatemala" (*New York Times*, 21 May 1987).

Most important, Cerezo has given clear indications that he will not press for even minimal structural changes, much less land reform. Guatemala's experience strongly suggests that without structural reforms there can be no democracy in a country with such gross inequalities.

Nicaragua:
Revolution and Democratic Construction

A review of twentieth-century Nicaraguan history prior to 1979 reveals that elections have gone hand in hand with the oligarchic state, foreign interventions, and, since the 1930s, the Somoza dictatorship—which in its later stages became the Nicaraguan counterinsurgency state.

The U.S. Marine intervention and occupation that began in 1926 sparked the guerrilla uprising led by Augusto César Sandino, an experience which has been called the United States' "first Vietnam." Unable to definitively defeat Sandino, and in the face of great domestic and international opposition to the intervention, the United States had to withdraw its 4,600 marines in 1933, but only after having created and trained the Nicaraguan National Guard as a local constabulary force and having handpicked and installed in power Anastasio Somoza as its head.

After assassinating Sandino in 1934, the Somoza dictatorship, born as an instrument of U.S. counterinsurgency, was legitimated in a 1936 election. The subsequent forty-three years of Somoza dictatorship saw regularly staged elections (1946, 1951, 1957, 1963, 1967, and 1974). At no point did the United States ever abandon the Somozas and their cronies, nor did it seriously pressure them to hold a genuine election. During this whole period various opposition movements tried to use electoral means to unseat the Somoza dictatorship. Their efforts consistently failed, since Somoza elections were openly fraudulent or rigged and mass movements pressuring for free elections suffered outright repression.

The triumph of the revolution in 1979 brought to power for the first time in Nicaragua a political coalition committed to the principles of political pluralism (as opposed to a one-party state) and popular participation. During its first year in office the revolutionary government promised to hold elections by 1985. The FSLN views elections "not [as] a concession but rather [as] a way to strengthen the revolution" (Corragio, 1986:97). In preparation for the election the government sent delegations around the world to study other countries' electoral laws (the delegation was denied entry visas to the United States). The government also negotiated with the opposition parties the Law of Political Parties, which institutionalized basic rights for opposition parties (for the first time in Nicaragua's history) and established the role of those parties as competitive, not merely cooperative, with the government (Lobel, 1987:8; Envío, 1985:56).

The elections—both presidential and National Assembly—were held a year early. To survey rapidly some key aspects:

Participation. Of eligible voters, 93 percent registered; although voting is not mandatory, 75.4 percent of registered voters voted (24.6 percent abstention); 70.8 percent of registered voters cast valid ballots (only 6 percent of votes cast were void).

Results. The FSLN received 62.9 percent of the vote, with 13 percent of the vote going to the Conservatives and 9 percent to the Liberal Independent Party. According to members of the Electoral Council, participants on all sides were surprised by the level of support for the non-contra opposition parties (Envío, 1985:59).

Representation. In principle, no major political tendency was excluded from the electoral process. A total of six opposition parties participated in addition to the Sandinistas, and all participants were guaranteed equal resources (campaign funding, supplies, and so forth) and equal access to the mass media; no party was prevented from carrying out an active campaign or from holding rallies (LASA, 1985).

But what about the Coordinadora Democrática Ramiro Sacasa (CD), the coalition supporting Arturo Cruz's candidacy? According to the Reagan administration, this was the only real opposition party, and proponents of U.S. policy in Nicaragua maintain that the election was not genuine because the CD did not participate. But the decision not to participate was made by the CD and its U.S. backers, not by the Sandinistas. Even though the CD used its participation in the early stages of the election to legitimate the political line of the contras, the FSLN bent over backward and made significant concessions to assure the continued participation of the CD. It was the CD which pulled out, because of its own political weakness and because, according to senior U.S. officials, "the [Reagan] administration never contemplated letting Cruz stay in the race, because then the Sandinistas could justifiably claim that the elections were legitimate" (*New York Times*, 21 October 1984). The lack of good faith on the part of the CD was emphasized by the fact that it withdrew just when the rules of the election had been liberalized, to its benefit.

The openness and fairness of the Nicaraguan election was recognized with a striking degree of unanimity by the participating opposition parties and by foreign observers not directly linked to the Reagan administration. Americas Watch called it "a model of probity and fairness (Americas Watch, 1985). Based on surveys of the European and international press and interviews, observers from the Socialist International (by no means pro-Sandinista) were overall supportive of the election and critical of the opposition parties that pulled out. Reports on the election in the European press were almost uniformly favorable, as was the report by a delegation from the European Parliament (Envio, 1985: 20–21, 56). Even American observers outside of the U.S. government—for example, the ideologically diverse delegation from the Latin American Studies Association, former American diplomats, and congressmen—judged the elections most favorably (LASA, 1985; Smith, 1987:93).

Aside from being honest and procedurally fair, the election was marked by a genuine pluralism: "a high degree of 'open-endedness,' taking the form of continuous bargaining between the FSLN and opposition groups . . ." (LASA, 1985). Although there were incidents of press censorship, a high level of freedom of the press and free speech prevailed overall (Booth, 1986:58), and most of the wartime emergency restrictions were lifted. As reported by the broad spectrum of observers from LASA, the FSLN could not be charged with abusing its incumbency or its relationship to mass organizations.

Two weeks before the election the seven participating parties signed a series of accords delineating the major elements of pluralism to be institutionalized in the yet-to-be-written constitution (Reding, 1985:556). The election itself produced an Assembly based on proportional representation, hence maximizing representation of minority opposition parties in the legislature (LASA, 1985). The new legislature was "exactly the same as any other Western style Assembly," according to the chairman of the Democratic Conservative party, and generally reflected the great ideological diversity of Nicaraguan political life—a fact that is obscured by the Reagan administration's focus only on the CD (Reding, 1985:557; Envio, 1985:56). The results of the election, and particularly the fact that over a third of the vote was won by opposition parties, surprised both the FSLN and the opposition (Envio, 1985:59). The wide variation in the level of support for the FSLN (Envio, 1985:45) also contradicts the charges of a "managed election."

Pluralism and Revolution

If there is general agreement that the election was exemplary in form, there is more debate about how to interpret its significance. In chapter 1 of this volume, Booth argues that despite its fairness the election cannot be considered "democratizing," given the absence of political consensus as a result of the U.S.-imposed war and intervention, as well as internal ideological differences. He goes on to state that, without peace, "Nicaragua seems unlikely to move forward" toward democracy. I shall briefly offer a somewhat different interpretation of the broader meaning of the election based on my interviews, experiences, and research in Nicaragua.

Political pluralism is expressed in the Nicaraguan Revolution through a multiparty system and the existence of competing political forces in government institutions, the mass media, and voluntary associations. In Nicaragua, as in every social system, there are structural limits on pluralism: although "no social group or class as such is excluded from the political system," Somocistas and the contras (because they are willing to surrender national sovereignty) are explicitly excluded (Corragio, 1986:27). "The structural limits set on pluralism in Nicaragua are quite consistent with norms observed in advanced Western democracies . . . " (Corragio and Irvin, 1985:254 ff.). Within these limits the goal is to reconcile political pluralism with popular hegemony and profound social change, a goal which is realized to a greater or lesser extent in specific situations.

A particularly notable form of political pluralism in the election was the process of negotiations between the FSLN and opposition groups, leading to major concessions by the FSLN. This same fluidity and flexibility, this same process of compromise and negotiation with opposition forces, came to the fore during the process of ratification of the constitution in 1986. In essence, opposition forces (minority parties, the Church, private-sector organizations) exercise much greater weight than their numbers or social bases warrant because of the international attention given to them and the leverage they enjoy by their very participation in these processes. In addition, many within the FSLN leadership view the opposition as a "healthy correcting force" (Lobel, 1987:15). It is this attempt by the FSLN to reconcile popular hegemony with political pluralism that gives the Nicaraguan Revolution its originality.

But there is also another level of political pluralism in the Nicaraguan Revolution: "We have argued that the fundamental objective of the revolution is not to consolidate power in the hands of the State; rather, it is to transform civil society by creating an autonomous institutional base for the majority from which the State derives its legitimacy and political power is mandated. Within this logic, . . . the essence of pluralism is that it allows for a diversity of views that enriches political and social practice at all levels, not merely at the level of political parties . . . " (Corragio and Irvin, 1985:260).

In short, Nicaraguan pluralism can be understood only as part of the larger qualitative transformation represented by the revolution. It signifies the beginning of a real transition—a process of destruction of the counterinsurgency state dominated by the bourgeoisie and the construction of a new state based on popular and working-class hegemony. The state derives its legitimacy not only through elections but also through the mandating of political power by a base independent of the state. Hence, political participation becomes more meaningful to the extent that it occurs *autonomously* from the state apparatus (Vilas, 1986).

The above brings us to a crucial point: Nicaraguan democracy cannot be discussed exclusively in terms of Western-style representative democracy. The Nicaraguan Revolution is based on a broad conception of political pluralism which combines representative democracy with popular revolutionary democracy, and that revolution is, above all, a "new class project." It is based on overturning traditional relations of class domination; it balances the need to negotiate with the parliamentary opposition (largely middle class) with the broad principles of maintaining the basis for popular hegemony (see Lobel, 1987). Further, "elections have reinforced the government's legitimacy, but do not constitute the unique source of this legitimacy" (Envio, 1985:45). The social context for elections includes a relatively literate and politicized population, seriously concerned about education, actively participating in politics, often critical of the government and the FSLN, and committed to the democratization of social relations overall (between classes, between women and men, and so forth). These aspects of the political culture of revolutionary Nicaragua are central to the evolution of democratic politics.

This brief treatment is designed more to pose complex questions than to draw final conclusions. As Richard Fagen points out (1986:261), it is not yet entirely clear "what particular institutional forms an appropriate democratic practice might take"; there are issues of "democratic practice associated with socialism in the periphery" that will never be understood if they are evaluated from a narrow framework appropriate only to advanced nations, much less an ideological framework designed to delegitimate and provide arguments for overthrowing the Nicaraguan Revolution.

Democracy is by no means a settled question in Nicaragua. The construction of democracy is an ongoing process, one that raises many issues of principle and practice. What legacies of the Somocista state affect revolutionary practice? How can the needs of the majority be reconciled with the demands of property owners in a mixed economy? How autonomous can mass organizations be in a wartime mobilization? How far is it possible—to return to Booth's concern—to advance toward democracy amid a U.S.-sponsored contra war and economic war (creating a massive economic crisis) and political disruption which exacerbates internal political divisions? And finally, independent of the war, what are the effects of Sandinista mistakes (for example, in economic planning, in policies toward the Miskito Indians in the early years of the revolution)? These are serious problems, requiring constant reassessment, but in my view none precludes the evolution of democracy in Nicaragua—and this has been reinforced in recent months through close observation of Nicaragua's implementation of the Central American peace accords. Rather, they are the political problems and contradictions of Nicaragua's process of democratic construction.

U.S. Policy and the Real Threat
to Democracy in Central America

Since the United States sees elections as absolutely essential in legitimating and delegitimating governments, it was central to the Reagan administration policy of gaining support for the contras to show that the 1984 Nicaraguan election was not valid. For this reason, facts (as established by virtually all other observers of the 1984 election) made no difference to officials in the Reagan administration; they had to stick to their preestablished conclusions, even though the evidence demonstrated the opposite. The United States viewed the election as a threat, I would suggest, not because it was insufficiently democratic, but because it was too democratic.

The United States did not limit itself to denouncing the Nicaraguan election, but sought to sabotage it and use it as a justification for further hostilities against Nicaragua. For example, as became clear in the National Security

Council document leaked to the press and reported on 6 November 1984, it was a deliberate U.S. strategy to denounce the Nicaraguan election as a "Soviet-style sham." This campaign was kicked off by Secretary of State Shultz and the State Department in early 1984, only days after elections were announced, and the administration pronouncements continued in this vein before, during, and after the election.

Furthermore, as noted above, the United States pressured candidates Arturo Cruz of the Coordinadora Democrática and Virgilio Godoy of the Liberal Independent Party to pull out of the election and "never contemplated letting Cruz stay in the race. . . ." The U.S. goal was "to isolate the Sandinistas and discredit the regime" (John Oakes, *New York Times*, 5 November 1984) rather than to let Cruz run and accept the result of a free vote.

Finally, under U.S. guidance, the contras carried out numerous activities to sabotage the election militarily (USOCA, 1985:3). Afterward, Washington explicitly threatened Nicaragua that the election constituted a "setback for peace talks" in the region and would "heighten tensions" with the United States and warned that it intended to pressure Nicaragua to hold a "real election" as a condition for future peace talks (*New York Times*, 5 November 1984).

The above were not isolated actions, but part of a comprehensive U.S. policy in Central America. I suggest it can be shown that U.S. policy is in some respects incompatible with representational democracy and with broader goals of socioeconomic democracy and peace in the region. Why incompatible? Because in several important respects democratic processes in Third World countries conflict with a fundamental U.S. objective in the postwar era: maintaining U.S. economic and political control over the Third World. Here is a brief sketch of the arguments.

The imperative for economic and political control has restricted the United States from supporting truly democratic political processes in the Third World—and in many situations has led the United States to undermine them—because such processes presuppose a level of uncertainty about the outcome which the United States cannot tolerate (or has not tolerated in practice). Fully competitive elections necessarily include the full spectrum of political players, leftist as well as rightist. But it has been characteristic of U.S.-sponsored elections, such as the Guatemalan election of 1985, to exclude the left, even (or especially) when it has significant support. Conversely, when a government perceived as challenging U.S. interests (for example, Nicaragua) holds a pluralistic election, the United States responds by sabotaging it. In this regard, the United States has undermined representational democracy or pluralism.

More broadly, the imperative for control explains the consistency of U.S. policy in the Third World over time (for example, the inability to "let go" in Central America today, even in the aftermath of Vietnam). It reveals also the lack of flexibility in that policy, with each revolution (Guatemala, Cuba, Vietnam, Nicaragua, El Salvador) being turned into a test case for drawing the line or teaching a lesson to the Third World about the price to be paid for challenging U.S. interests.

This explains the dual thrust of the Reagan administration policy of "promoting democratic revolution." The key is the obfuscation of the relationship between representative democracy and anti-Communist or counterinsurgent democracy, promoting the latter under the guise of the former. One pillar of this policy is the punishment of independent revolutionary governments (labeled "Communist"): "restoring democracy" in this sense means rollback or elimination of those governments. In Nicaragua today the deliberate U.S. goal is to overthrow the Sandinista government or, failing that, to cause as much physical and human destruction as possible, in order to make Nicaragua a negative rather than a positive example to the Third World. Sowing destruction in the name of "promoting democracy" is incompatible with democratic goals, except when "democratic" is equated with "anti-Communist."

The other pillar of U.S. policy is counterinsurgency. The goal is to establish democratic (anti-Communist, pro–United States) governments, either military or civilian, authoritarian or liberal, depending on the circumstances, as bulwarks against nationalist or socialist revolutionary movements. At the present time there is a preference for elected civilian governments in some situations— for example, Guatemala—but that is not a commitment of principle. Rather, it is seen as the most effective way (within a counterinsurgency framework) to resolve economic and political crisis and avoid another Nicaragua-type debacle (that is, the debacle of having supported Somoza until he was overthrown). The United States has also used the election of civilian governments in Guatemala and El Salvador to justify action against Nicaragua (the "rotten apple" argument), going so far as to imply that the present Nicaraguan government was not really elected at all.

The two aspects of U.S. policy are integrally related. It is virtually impossible to speak of "democratization" as a U.S. policy without at the same time understanding the regional implications of rollback. First, rollback is designed not only to destroy the Nicaraguan Revolution but also forcibly to prevent "another Nicaragua" (that is, another independent government) in El Salvador or Guatemala. Second, the bottom line of the rollback policy is that the United States cannot tolerate any genuinely independent Third World government; hence, "democracy" is pitted against Third World sovereignty.

Finally, for Central America and for Latin America as a whole, current U.S. policy is ultimately militarizing, destabilizing, and polarizing, and it seriously threatens regional peace. Unlike the counterinsurgency policies of the 1960s, which nominally purported to stabilize the existing balance (the status quo), the rollback policy of the 1980s is designed to upset the existing balance. Further, the current destabilization campaign has proven to undermine civilian governments or forces not only in Central America but also in neighboring countries in Latin America. It is precisely for these reasons that the Contadora governments are so vehemently opposed to U.S. policy. And, in a final irony, it is precisely for these reasons that even the pro–United States "democratic" governments in Central America eventually had to abandon the Reagan Doctrine (at least the contra policy). That is the real message of the Central American peace process.

Conclusion:
Elections and Transitions

This chapter began from the premise that the significance of an election lies less in its mere occurrence than in the broader political process of which it is a part. In this broader context, I have argued, the Nicaraguan election came closer than the Guatemalan to meeting Western standards with respect to representation and participation. I have also argued that the Nicaraguan election was part of a process of democratic transition, which was not the case in Guatemala.

Although the 1985 election was part of a transition to civilian rule in Guatemala (which may or may not last), it is not the kind of fundamental shift that a real democratic transition implies. Evidence to date suggests that it comes closer to repeating the pattern of "circular transitions" (Torres Rivas, 1986:20) that has prevailed in past decades—in other formulations, an "interlude" more than a transition, or a recomposition of the counterinsurgency state

(Jonas, 1988; Torres Rivas, 1986:25; Aguilera, 1985b). Among the ruling forces, both civilian and military, are some who understand the need for adjustments within the existing structure in order to deal with the economic crisis and to accommodate real pressures from the lower classes. There is a political opening of sorts, though one that is extremely constrained and that does not meet the minimum standards of representative democracy and pluralism, much less of social reform.

In Nicaragua, by contrast, the election was part of a new social project that opened up, for the first time in Central American history since the Guatemalan Revolution of 1944 (setting aside Costa Rica), the possibility of meaningful representative democracy.

Looking beyond the two countries, this study leads me to suggest that in areas of the world where resource distribution is marked by gross inequalities, it makes little sense to speak of democracy without structural change. In this sense, meaningful democratic transition (on the scale of bourgeois-democratic or socialist revolution, as opposed to temporary liberalizations or openings) requires a profound social change of one kind or another. Classical representational democracy cannot be achieved on a lasting basis in the polarized countries of Central America today in the absence of mass popular movements fighting for structural socioeconomic reforms and a transformation of class relations. Even in situations of counterinsurgent democracy, as in Guatemala today, mass popular movements fighting for structural socioeconomic reforms are the main source of strong pressures for political democracy. A further implication is that, under these conditions, meaningful democratic transitions are the product, not primarily (and certainly not solely) of elections or interelite pacts, but of struggles waged by popular and working-class movements.

Finally, one of the particular lessons of the Central American experience concerns the relation between internal structural factors and external, or international, factors. I have argued that internal structural factors are the primary ones in the long term. But at this particular historical moment, the violent U.S. response to revolutionary movements in Central America has taken on unusual significance. At the risk of restating the obvious, without peace there can be no democracy.

Notes

I wish to acknowledge with gratitude the invaluable contribution of Guatemalan and Nicaraguan colleagues who read and commented on the first draft of this chapter during the summer of 1987.

1. To be clear, I am distinguishing my analysis from (a) that of the Neo-Conservative U.S. policy theorists like Jeane Kirkpatrick, for whom "democratic" is synonymous with "pro–United States" and "anti-Communist"; and (b) that of a broad array of political scientists who have been analyzing the "transition to democracy from authoritarian regimes." The former is best exemplified by Jeane Kirkpatrick, whose famous article, "Dictatorships and Double Standards" (1979) argues that the United States should support the military in countries like Guatemala and El Salvador in their evolution from a (right-wing) "authoritarian dictatorship" into a democracy—while the Sandinista government in Nicaragua must be overthrown, since a (left-wing) "totalitarian dictatorship" cannot evolve into a democracy. Additionally, the United States must be willing to intervene militarily to reverse the tide of Marxist revolution; hence, overthrow of revolutionary governments is the specific meaning of the policy of "promoting the democratic revolution," as another proponent of this theory, Michael Ledeen (1985), put it. It is in relation to the counterinsurgent conception of democracy as anti-Communism that we can understand the defense made by these policy analysts of the Nicaraguan contras as model democrats and "freedom fighters." While they speak in the name of representative democracy, elevating elections as the central criterion, in fact their policy recommendations have proven consistently antithetical to democracy in any of its traditional forms.

Starting from very different concerns, a number of scholars in the United States and Latin America focus on political democracy and contemporary transitions to democracy. A major portion of the current scholarship regarding democracy in Latin America is being carried out within the framework of the "bureaucratic-authoritarianism" analysis, which has been developed particularly for the Southern Cone (O'Donnell, Schmitter, and Whitehead, 1986; Collier, 1979).

This study, however, concerns two cases in Central America, a region that differs from the Southern Cone in several basic respects. The internal dynamic is different, since Central America did not undergo a period of semiautonomous, import-substituting industrialization in the 1930s. Nor did the region experience a prolonged period of populism during the 1930s and 1940s. Equally important, historically the United States has played a particularly preponderant role in Central America and continues to do so today with its violent response to revolutionary movements there. Given these differences, I believe that the analysis advanced in the "bureaucratic-authoritarianism" literature cannot be adopted wholesale in regard to Central America—and indeed, O'Donnell et al. do not attempt to apply the model of the "non-revolutionary transition" to Central America.

Other scholars more particularly concerned with Central America, however, have taken an approach that shares the same basic assumption: that political (representative) democracy can be analyzed apart from a broader conception of democracy which includes social-economic equality and popular or mass participation in fighting for such equality. (See, for example, Karl, 1986.) In contrast, I believe that while the two conceptions can be definitionally separated, in a case like Central America it is necessary from the very outset to examine political democracy *in relation to* social-economic issues and political participation by the majority classes. Therefore, I do not agree with the view that a democracy can be formed primarily by an interelite consensus or pact (see Karl, 1985a and 1985b). Based on historical and current experience in Central America, I would argue for a broader view that meaningful "transitions to democracy" there involve more sweeping social change (on the scale of the major bourgeois and socialist revolutions). In the conclusion of this chapter, I shall make a more specific argument about the relationship between representative and participatory democracy, and between political and socioeconomic conceptions.

2. In this regard, Richard Fagen's distinction between "instrumental" or "operational" aspects of democracy—"necessary conditions or institutions"—and "definitional" aspects is useful. On this basis he offers a working definition (guidelines) of democracy as involving "effective participation by individuals and groups, a system of accountability, and political equality," but cautions that no definition can fully encompass the realities of actual situations (Fagen, 1986:258).

3. Another characterization of the above phenomena is Lowy and Sader's "militarization of the state," which is "not simply the transition from the purely military to the political [in the role of the armed forces] but the overwhelming of the state apparatus as a whole by the armed forces—in essence the 'colonization' of the majority of state and state-related structures . . . by the military and the partial or total fusion of the repressive apparatuses with other apparatuses of the system of political domination" (1985: 9). (See also Aguilera, 1981 and 1985c.) Other characterizations refer to the "national security state" and the "militarized state" (see Torres Rivas, 1987).

4. From the mid-1960s until 1985, Guatemala was recognized as the archetypical counterinsurgency state. More controversial is the application of this concept to the civilian Cerezo regime—a topic that I discussed from many different perspectives with a wide variety of Guatemalan political analysts and actors.

Questions are raised on the following grounds: (a) it is the regime, rather than the state, that is counterinsurgent and is affected by elections; (b) the concept of a *civilian* counterinsurgency state forces the category and renders it meaningless by being used to explain both military and civilian governments; (c) it overdetermines one aspect of the Cerezo period (the military-counterinsurgent), sacrificing other aspects; (d) for the same reason, this focus tends to liquidate a class analysis; (e) counterinsurgency is "instrumental" rather than "definitional" as an aspect of the counterrevolutionary state.

Although I greatly appreciate and even agree with some of these concerns, nevertheless, I am among the interpreters of Guatemala who have chosen to maintain the concept in regard to the present period. There are several reasons for concluding that the concept, flexibly viewed, remains useful.

First, historically, it describes important elements of continuity between different regimes since the early 1960s; variations have been more in the form taken by different regimes than in the essential character of the state. One of the most important aspects is continuity in the class basis of state power, that is, domination by the monopolistic factions of the bourgeoisie (which include transnational capital and top officials of the army, as well as sectors of the Guatemalan financial, industrial, and agricultural bourgeoisie) (Aguilera, 1981:33, 40).

Second, to refer to the Cerezo regime as a civilian continuation of the counterinsurgency state describes better than any other conception I have found the origins *and the priority concerns* of this regime, with all its contradictions and nuances.

Third, the concept expresses the fact that the army's project has failed in its attempt to become "legitimate" in the eyes of the people; hence, the political system, even after the election, is still based primarily on coercion rather than consensus.

Fourth, it is a cogent formulation of a response to the thesis underlying U.S. policy that the 1985 election constituted almost automatically and ipso facto a "transition to democracy," and the Cerezo regime has "consolidated" that democracy.

Finally, even recognizing that elections per se cannot be expected to change the nature of the state, it still makes sense to assess a given election in relation to whether it opens up a process that could lead to such change.

While using the concept of "counterinsurgency state" for the above reasons, I view it more as a heuristic category than as a "thing" which exists or does not exist. Additionally, it describes a dominant aspect of the counterrevolutionary state at this time rather than its totality. Perhaps it would be more accurate to think of "counterinsurgency state" as shorthand for the counterinsurgent character of the counterrevolutionary state, which has been its dominant characteristic in this historical period of the Central American revolution.

5. See note 4.

6. The widely used conceptualization of "demonstration elections" (Herman and Brodhead, 1984)—elections staged primarily for the purpose of international legitimation—is particularly applicable to situations in which there is strong dependency on an external power that is "calling the shots" (e.g., the Salvadoran elections of 1982 and 1984). However, there are other situations (among them the Guatemalan election of 1985) in which the internal structural factors requiring elections are equally important. For these latter situations, it is important not to reduce elections analytically to simply a sham or by-product of the U.S. government's hidden agenda. The concept of counterinsurgency elections, which can include, but is not limited to, demonstration elections and which incorporates foreign influences on the election, is conceptually more adequate.

References Cited

In addition to the references listed below, this chapter is based on interviews during the summer of 1987 with a wide range of participants and observers of the electoral process and politics generally in both Guatemala and Nicaragua.

Adams, Richard. 1970. *Crucifixion by Power*. Austin: University of Texas Press.

Aguilera Peralta, Gabriel. 1981. El proceso de militarización en el estado Guatemalteco. *Polémica* no. 1 (September–October).

———. 1985a. Centroamérica: Elecciones, Negociación, Guerra. *Polémica* no. 16 (January–March).

———. 1985b. Las fases del conflicto bélico en Guatemala (1951–1985). Typescript. ICADIS, Costa Rica.

———. 1985c. *Militarismo y lucha social en Guatemala*. Cuadernos de CITGUA, no. 3. Mexico City: CITGUA.

Aguilera Peralta, Gabriel, et al. 1981. *Dialéctica del terror en Guatemala*. San José: EDUCA.

Americas Watch. 1985. *Human Rights in Nicaragua: Reagan, Rhetoric and Reality*. New York: Americas Watch.

———. 1987. *Human Rights in Nicaragua, 1986*. New York: Americas Watch.

Americas Watch and British Parliamentary Human Rights Group. 1987. *Human Rights in Guatemala during President Cerezo's First Year*. New York: Americas Watch.

Barahona, Elías. 1984. Testimony. In *Guatemala: Tyranny on Trial*, edited by Susanne Jonas, Ed McCaughan, and Elizabeth Martínez. San Francisco: Synthesis Publications.

Black, George, with Jamail, Milton, and Stoltz Chinchilla, Norma. 1984. *Garrison Guatemala*. New York: Monthly Review Press.

Booth, John. 1986. Election amid War and Revolution: Toward Evaluating the 1984 Nicaraguan National Elections. In *Elections and Democratization in Latin America, 1980–1985*, edited by Paul Drake and Eduardo Silva. San Diego: University of California, Center for Iberian and Latin American Studies.

Carnoy, Martin. 1984. *The State and Political Theory*. Princeton: Princeton University Press.

Castañeda, Gilberto. 1986. El estado Guatemalteco contemporáneo. Paper presented at Congress of the Asociación Centroamericana de Sociología.

Centro de Estudios de la Realidad Guatemalteca (CERG). 1985. Contrainsurgencia y Régimen Constitucional. *Temas de la Realidad Guatemalteca*, no. 1 (Mexico).

———. 1986. El estado Guatemalteco contemporáneo. Notas para una investigación necesaria. *Temas de la Realidad Guatemalteca*, no. 3 (Mexico).

Collier, David, ed. 1979. *The New Authoritarianism in Latin America*. Princeton: Princeton University Press.

Cornelius, Wayne. 1986. The 1984 Nicaraguan Elections Revisited. *LASA Forum* (Winter).

Corragio, José Luis. 1986. *Nicaragua: Revolution and Democracy.* Boston: Allen and Unwin.

Corragio, José Luis, and Irvin, George. 1985. Revolution and Pluralism in Nicaragua. In *Towards an Alternative for Central America and the Caribbean,* edited by George Irvin and Xabier Gorostiaga. London: Allen and Unwin.

Drake, Paul, and Silva, Eduardo, eds. 1986. *Elections and Democratization in Latin America.* San Diego: University of California, Center for Iberian and Latin American Studies.

Envio. 1985. Monográfico: The Final Stretch of the Electoral Process, Analysis of Electoral Results (I–II), and Interview: An Inside View of the Elections. Managua: Instituto Histórico Centroamericano.

Fagen, Richard. 1986. The Politics of Transition. In *Transition and Development,* edited by Richard Fagen, Carmen Diana Deere, and José Luis Corragio. New York: Monthly Review Press.

Falla, Ricardo. 1984. We Charge Genocide. In *Guatemala: Tyranny on Trial,* edited by Susanne Jonas, Ed McCaughan, and Elizabeth Martinez. San Francisco: Synthesis Publications.

Gleijeses, Piero. 1985. The Guatemalan Silence. *New Republic,* 10 June.

Hamilton, Nora. 1982. *The Limits of State Autonomy: Post-Revolutionary Mexico.* Princeton: Princeton University Press.

Herman, Edward, and Brodhead, Frank. 1984. *Demonstration Elections: U.S.-Staged Elections in the Dominican Republic, Vietnam, and El Salvador.* Boston: South End Press.

Huntington, Samuel. 1984. Will More Countries Become Democratic? *Political Science Quarterly* (Summer).

Inforpress Centroamericana. 1985. *Guatemala: Elections, 1985.* Guatemala: Inforpress Centroamericana.

Jonas, Susanne. 1974. Guatemala: Land of Eternal Struggle. In *Latin America: The Struggle with Dependency and Beyond,* edited by Ronald Chilcote and Joel Edelstein. Cambridge: Schenkman.

———. 1976. Nicaragua. *NACLA's Latin America and Empire Report* (February).

———. 1987–88. Whose Transition? Whose Guatemala? *World Policy Journal* (Winter).

———. 1988. Contradictions of Guatemala's Political Opening. *Latin American Perspectives* (Summer).

Jonas, Susanne, and Tobis, David, eds. 1974. *Guatemala.* Berkeley: NACLA.

Jonas, Susanne; McCaughan, Ed; and Martinez, Elizabeth, eds. 1984. *Guatemala: Tyranny on Trial.* San Francisco: Synthesis Publications.

Karl, Terry. 1985a. After La Palma: The Prospects for Democratization in El Salvador. *World Policy Journal* (Spring).

———. 1985b. Debate. *World Policy Journal* (Summer).

———. 1986. Imposing Consent? Electoralism vs. Democratization in El Salvador. In *Elections and Democratization in Latin America, 1980–1985,* edited by Paul Drake and

Eduardo Silva. San Diego: University of California, Center for Iberian and Latin American Studies.

Kirkpatrick, Jeane. 1979. Dictatorships and Double Standards. *Commentary* (November).

———. 1982a. *Dictatorships and Double Standards: Rationalism and Reason in Politics.* New York: American Enterprise Institute, Simon & Schuster.

———. 1982b. Statement before the Conference on Free Elections, 4 November 1982. In *Promoting Free Elections.* Washington: Department of State, Bureau of Public Affairs, Current Policy no. 433 (November).

Latin American Studies Association (LASA). 1985. Report of the LASA Delegation to Observe the Nicaraguan General Election of 4 November 1984. *LASA Forum* (Winter).

Ledeen, Michael. 1985. How to Support the Democratic Revolution. *Commentary* (March).

Lobel, Jules. 1987. The New Nicaraguan Consitution: Uniting Participatory and Representative Democracy. *Monthly Review* (December).

Lowy, Michel, and Sader, Eder. 1985. The Militarization of the State in Latin America. *Latin American Perspectives* 12, State and Military in Latin America (Fall).

Malloy, James M., and Seligson, Mitchell A., eds. 1987. *Authoritarians and Democrats: Regime Transition in Latin America.* Pittsburgh: University of Pittsburgh Press.

Marini, Ruy Mauro. 1980. The Question of the State in the Latin American Struggle. *Contemporary Marxism* no. 1, Strategies for the Class Struggle in Latin America (Spring).

O'Donnell, Guillermo; Schmitter, Philippe; and Whitehead, Laurence, eds. 1986. *Transitions from Authoritarian Rule.* Baltimore: Johns Hopkins University Press.

Petras, James. 1986. The Redemocratization Process. *Contemporary Marxism* no. 14, Dialectics of Democracy in Latin America (Fall).

Przeworski, Adam. 1986. Some Problems in the Study of the Transition to Democracy. In *Transitions from Authoritarian Rule: Comparative Perspectives,* edited by Guillermo O'Donnell, Philippe Schmitter, and Laurence Whitehead. Baltimore: Johns Hopkins University Press.

Reding, Andrew. 1985. On Nicaraguan Democracy. *World Policy Journal* (Summer).

Rosada Granados, Héctor. 1986. Guatemala, 1944–1985: Práctica política y conducta electoral. Guatemala: ASIES (typescript).

Sharckman, Howard. 1974. The Vietnamization of Guatemala. In *Guatemala,* edited by Susanne Jonas and David Tobis. Berkeley: NACLA.

Smith, Wayne. 1987. Lies about Nicaragua. *Foreign Policy* no. 67 (Summer).

Solórzano Martínez, Mario. 1987. *Guatemala: Autoritarismo y democracia.* San José: EDUCA/FLACSO.

Stephens, Evelyne Huber, and Stephens, John. 1987. Democracy and Authoritarianism in the Caribbean Basin. Paper presented at the conference of the Caribbean Studies Association, 27–29 May, Belize City.

Thomas, Clive. 1984. *The Rise of the Authoritarian State in Peripheral Societies*. New York: Monthly Review Press.

Torres Rivas, Edelberto. 1984. Problemas de la contrarevolución y la democracia en Guatemala. *Estudios Sociales Centroamericanos* (May–August).

———. 1986. Centroamérica: guerra, transición y democracia. Paper presented at Congress of the Asociación Centroamericana de Sociología.

———. 1987. *Centroamérica: La democracia posible*. San José: EDUCA.

Trudeau, Robert. 1986. Democracy in Guatemala: Present Status, Future Prospects. Paper presented at the XIII International Congress of the Latin American Studies Association, 23–25 October, Boston.

United States Out of Central America (USOCA). 1985. *Democracy in Nicaragua*. San Francisco: USOCA.

Vilas, Carlos. 1986. *The Sandinista Revolution*. New York: Monthly Review Press.

Washington Office on Latin America (WOLA) and International Human Rights Law Group. 1985. *The 1985 Guatemalan Elections: Will the Military Relinquish Power?* Washington: WOLA.

6 Ordinary Elections in Extraordinary Times

The Political Economy of Voting in Costa Rica

Mitchell A. Seligson and Miguel Gómez B.

Almost all discussions of Central American politics begin with the caveat that generalizations do not apply to Costa Rica. Costa Rican "exceptionalism" emerges in many aspects of its political life; for the purposes of this volume, the differences between Costa Rica and its Central American neighbors can be summarized with reference to the questions John Booth raises in chapter 1. Booth seeks to determine the role of elections in the institutionalization of democracy in Central America. Specifically, he views elections as a potential instrument for democracy building.

In that context, it is legitimate for him to inquire of the impact of elections on the range, breadth, and depth of participation in Guatemala, El Salvador, Honduras, and Nicaragua. But in Costa Rica, for at least the last four decades, participation has been as wide, broad, and deep as it has been among the most highly developed and institutionalized democracies in Western Europe and North America. Similarly, it is appropriate for Booth to inquire about the fairness of elections in the other countries, whereas Costa Rican elections have been a model of fairness matched by few other systems in the world. Consolidation of stable democracy, so central a question elsewhere in the region, has not been of concern since the 1960s in Costa Rica. In short, whereas recent elections in Central America can be viewed as instruments of democracy building, recent elections in Costa Rica were more of a reaffirmation of the stability and strength of a system that previously had been consolidated.

Recent elections in Costa Rica take on a very different meaning from those held elsewhere in the region. In Costa Rica very few observers would question the achievements of democratization over the past four decades. Recent elections there were not an independent variable to be viewed as an exercise in building democracy. Rather, an appropriate view of the recent elections is that they were a test of the survivability of consolidated democratic rule in a ministate under conditions of extreme economic stress. This is a relevant, indeed immediate, question to be answered in the case of Costa Rica, as will be shown in this chapter.

From a regional perspective the analysis presented here would become relevant to questions of the long-term stability of democracy if and when it was consolidated in other Central American nations. As will be shown by the data collected for this paper, consolidated democratic systems are very resistant to economic crisis, especially when a political culture supportive of democracy (Booth's sixth question) has been established.

Economic Crisis and Elections

Electoral results depend heavily upon economic results. This seemingly simple assertion, first systematically tested a little over fifteen years ago (Kramer, 1971), has become a fundamental axiom of modern research on voting behavior. We now have scores of major books and articles that demonstrate with great consistency that economic downturns, inflation, and rising unemployment all have major influences on elections in Western Europe and the United States.[1] Recent research has found the impact of economics on electoral politics to be equally or more important than class, religion, and party identification, the variables that traditionally have been regarded as the principal explanatory factors of electoral choice (Lewis-Beck, 1986). Although the specific form of the equations utilized to model the impact of economics on politics varies, recent studies are consistently able to explain a large proportion of the variance in electoral outcomes as a result of including economic factors.

The success of these efforts to formulate a political economy of elections, as it were, has led some to conclude that this is one area in which the discipline can boast with pride of the cumulative nature of its research; we appear to be approaching a "bottom line." Such pride may be justified, however, only if one's interest in generalizing is narrowly limited to the countries of Western Europe and North America. And even for those countries, one needs to further restrict the generalizability of the findings to those elections that occur in economies experiencing only comparatively small upswings or downswings; the bulk of research on the political economy of elections has been based upon those of the past decade or two when the economies of the nations studied have been relatively stable.[2] The case of Britain, which is experiencing protracted economic decline, is a partial exception, and not surprisingly studies on that system have uncovered important changes in the structure of the British electorate as a result of that decline.[3] But even in the British case the decline has been a gradual one, occurring over several decades, rather than one reflecting a dramatic shift and break with the past.

Notwithstanding the limited attention given them by the scholarly community, regular, competitive elections do occur in a wide range of countries outside of Europe and North America, in countries as populous as India or as tiny as Trinidad, as oil-rich as Venezuela or as poor as Sri Lanka (see Weiner and Ozbudun, 1987). As a group, these and other Third World nations differ in many ways from the cases that have been the central focus of attention; but in terms of the development of a science of the political economy of voting behavior, their most salient characteristic is their greater vulnerability to far deeper, more protracted, and more frequent economic crises than have been experienced in post–World War II Western Europe and North America.

By way of contrast, in their discussion of the British case, Hibbs, Jr., and Vasilatos (1981:32) argue that in the 1970s, "both inflation and unemployment stood at *disastrously* high rates. Inflation actually *soared* to more than 20 percent per annum in 1975" (emphasis added). It is true that unemployment increased—by over 50 percent between 1973 and 1975. But these dramatic increases need to be compared to the rates of inflation and unemployment experienced in the Third World. While the increase in unemployment in Britain may have been "disastrous," it had only increased from 2.6 percent to 4.1 percent.[4] In developing countries it is not uncommon for inflation to run at over five times the British rate and unemployment to remain at three to four times the British rate, for decades at a time. Indeed, in many Third World countries, achieving unemployment and inflation rates matching the worst performance in Britain would be considered a major victory. In 1986, according to the International Monetary Fund, inflation rates in poor countries averaged thirty-two times the rate in the United States.[5]

There are many reasons why the Third World suffers from more acute economic fluctuations than the West, but this is not the place to discuss them. Suffice it to say that one major factor is that most of these countries are heavily dependent financially and economically on the industrialized countries and that minor perturbations in the economies of the latter usually have greatly magnified effects on the former. In addition, economic policies that have been forged in much of the Third World are designed to achieve major spurts of growth over short time periods in an effort rapidly to overcome underdevelopment. These policies have, however, turned out to be particularly vulnerable to failure.[6]

How do the generalizations regarding the impact of economic performance on electoral behavior hold up under conditions of far greater variability in the independent variables? According to Fiorina (1981b:74), if relatively small ups and downs of the economy can be shown to substantially influence voting behavior, there is no question of the effects of large shifts: "Who doubts that some part of the electoral outcome reflects voter reaction to economic conditions? The question becomes trivial when one considers extreme cases like the Great Depression, from which the American Republican Party has yet to recover." Applying Fiorina's logic to the Third World, one would anticipate that the linkage between economics and electoral behavior should be readily apparent.

Unfortunately, we cannot make that assertion, since virtually no research on the political economy of elections has been conducted in other areas of the world.[7] An investigator interested in broadening our knowledge of the impact of economic performance on electoral behavior to include the Third World might hope to find some guidance in the literature on violence and revolution, a literature that is quite extensive. That literature specifically considers the impact of economic crises on system stability, but largely ignores questions of electoral politics per se. Currently, for example, a wide-ranging debate has emerged over the explanation for coups d'état in Africa.[8] Unfortunately, elections are largely ignored in that debate, and thus it is of little help. Moreover, the key variables in the political economy of elections research, especially inflation and unemployment, are ignored entirely in this African research.[9] Similarly, the older literature on the role of crises in development, a literature which was explicitly cross-national and heavily emphasized the Third World, largely ignored economic crises and focused instead on crises of national identity, legitimacy, participation, distribution, and penetration (Binder et al., 1971).

Broad generalizations linking economic crises to political crises emerge from some studies. One such general explanation is embedded in Mancur Olson's well-known analysis of the impact of economic growth on political stability. Olson (1963:543) states that "a severe depression, or a sudden decrease in the level of income, could, of course, also be destabilizing—and for many of the same reasons that rapid economic growth itself can be destabilizing. A rapid economic decline, like rapid economic growth, will bring about important movements in the relative economic positions of people and will therefore set up contradictions between the structures of economic power and the distribution of social and political power." Olson does not explain, however, how these "movements" manifest themselves in particular political forms.

But Olson is not alone in failing to specify the explicit linkages of economic crisis to political crisis. A review of the literature on the impact of economic crises on electoral behavior, the subject of this essay, offers precious little guidance for hypothesis formulation. Nevertheless, some hypotheses have emerged. The first of these is that economic crises lead to the strengthening of extremist parties (be they of left or right).

In Zimmermann's (1983:189–90) review of the crisis literature he notes that a serious economic downturn during 1966–67 in West Germany "led to a political crisis, one indicator being the simultaneous gaining in strength of the National Democratic Party (NPD, the right extremist party)." A similar relationship between economic crisis and the rise of extremism was apparent during the Weimar Republic in Germany. According to Lepsius (1978:50–51), "The impact of the economic depression on the rise of Nazism and the breakdown of democracy in Germany cannot be overestimated. It has often been stated, and the assumption is very plausible, that without the disruption of the economic situation, the political system would not have entered a prolonged crisis, nor would a large segment of the population have been mobilized by the Nazi movement. The rise of the Nazi movement and the unemployment curve show a close similarity. Germany was hit particularly hard by the world depression. Next to the United States, she suffered most, much more than France, Great Britain, the Scandinavian countries, Holland and Belgium."

But not all economic crises are of the same magnitude. According to Kornhauser's classic study, the more severe the crisis, the greater the likelihood that extremist parties will receive increased support. Kornhauser draws his evidence directly from a study of nine European nations in which elections were held shortly before and after the onset of the Great Depression. In six of those cases the Communist vote increased, but in the other three it declined. Kornhauser (1959:161) concludes that "when the crisis is less severe, the electorate is more inclined to support pragmatic programs of amelioration within the established order. The orientation is less one of destruction and more one of improvement."

Perhaps these milder crises give rise to milder voter reactions. One such political manifestation of economic crisis, presenting the second hypothesis to be tested by the Costa Rican case, may be that of electoral realignment (Burnham, 1970). Voters need not necessarily abandon traditional parties in times of crisis, but as happened in the United States during the Roosevelt years, class-based voting is altered in form but the party system per se remains intact.

A third hypothesis of the possible reaction of a polity to protracted economic crisis is voter disaffection with the electoral system and the consequent abstention from voting. A variant of this thesis is argued and tested by Coleman (1976) and found to hold in the case of Mexico. In the Mexican case abstention as a form of protest resulted from the exclusion of some sectors from the overall benefits of several decades of growth enjoyed by the society as a whole.

A fourth hypothesis is that under conditions of economic crisis, politics should become increasingly characterized by violence. While the connection between violence and regime change is not at all clear (Zimmermann, 1983: 192–93), severe economic crises have frequently been associated with escalating political violence. One recent illustration is that of Jamaica, a country which is experiencing a protracted economic downturn and in which recent elections have been dominated by violent acts, including widespread murder (Seligson, 1987). An explanation of the link between violence and economic crisis may be found in the impact of economic crisis on increasing income inequality that in turn is linked to violence (Muller and Seligson, 1987).

Our purpose here is to extend understanding of the political economy of elections both generally and with reference to Central America in particular. First, the focus on a Central American case allows us to see if the patterns that emerge there parallel those uncovered in the industrialized nations. Second, given the extraordinary volatility of the economies of Central America (because of their extreme dependence on export agriculture), data from this region allow us to study an economy undergoing a severe economic crisis rather than one experiencing the small shifts characteristic of the European and North American cases studied to date. The goal is to determine if, under Central American crisis conditions, democratic rule in the form of elections can be expected to survive.

To initiate this explorative research we have selected Costa Rica, the one Central American country that has held free, open, and competitive elections uninterruptedly since 1953, and is frequently held up as a model Latin American democracy (Peeler, 1985). Indeed for most of the twentieth century Costa Rica has held regular elections, but a civil war in 1948, largely fought over an attempted violation of the integrity of the electoral system, interrupted the series (Seligson, 1987).

The Costa Rican Election of 1986

On 2 February 1986 Costa Rica held national elections for president, vice-president, the legislative assembly, and municipal councilmen.[10] The election took place while Costa Rica was undergoing its most severe and protracted economic crisis of the century. As a result of seriously misguided economic policies, coupled with an unfavorable international environment during the administration of President Rodrigo Carazo (1978–82), the Costa Rican economy went into a tailspin. Details of the causes and manifestations of the economic crisis have been recounted elsewhere and will not be repeated here.[11] The 1982 elections, not surprisingly, saw the defeat of the incumbent party and a definitive victory for the challengers, led by Luis Alberto Monge and his Partido Liberación Nacional (PLN). During the administration of President Monge the decline of the economy was stabilized and inflation and unemployment were reduced markedly, but the damage done to the economy was not repaired and the underlying problems seemed worse than ever. As President Monge left office, interest payments on the foreign debt were suspended and the country went into technical default.

The most notable manifestation of the economic crisis has been the foreign debt: standing at $1.1 billion in 1978, it had more than tripled to $3.8 billion by 1984, exceeding the GDP (which hovered around $3.1 billion). But individuals do not directly experience the weight of these debts and could have safely excluded them from their voting calculus if it had not been for the wide variety of other factors that did directly affect the Costa Rican voter. In concrete terms, between 1979 and 1984 the GNP per capita declined 13 percent, open unemployment increased by 69.5 percent, consumption of basic food items declined by 37.4 percent,[12] the currency was devalued by some 550 percent, and imports declined by 48.3 percent and exports, by 11.6 percent (Céspedes et al., 1985:80).

Perhaps more important than the impact of the crisis on current economic conditions was the widespread consensus among economists that the crisis, which had already lasted for six years, was not going to be resolved for the foreseeable future. Costa Rica relies upon agricultural exports for the bulk of its foreign exchange earnings. World commodity markets are depressed and will probably remain so for some years to come. Moreover, even if those markets were to take a dramatic upswing, the magnitude of the foreign debt and the cost of servicing it are so large that it would take years of unprecedented high prices for Costa Rica's commodity exports to generate sufficient funds to pay off the bulk of the debt. Other sources of income traditionally have included trade within the Central American Common Market, but conditions in the region, especially the protracted conflicts in El Salvador and Nicaragua, have been and continue to be very unfavorable for a significant turnaround in what have been, since the beginning of the decade, severely depressed levels of intraregional commerce. The crisis is a long-term phenomenon, not subject to a "quick fix."

Costa Rican voters have not escaped the economic hardships implied by these figures. Yet an examination of the overall voting figures would not have revealed that such a severe crisis was underway. Indeed, none of the expectations regarding the impact of an economic crisis that were hypothesized above has been realized.

Let us look first at voting for extremist parties. Since the 1930s parties of the left have presented the main challenges to the traditional parties.[13] For many years the Communist party, known as Vanguardia Popular, led the left but was frequently banned from running candidates for office.[14] Since 1970, however, leftist parties have been continually allowed to compete for office and have consistently won at least two seats in the legislative assembly.[15] Votes for the left are summarized in table 6.1.

Voting for the left peaked in 1982, as a reflection of voter dissatisfaction with the administration that was held responsible for the crisis. At its high point, however, the left received only a tiny proportion of the vote; and even though the economic crisis continued through the 1986 elections, votes for the left declined to their lowest point since 1970. Dissatisfaction with economic conditions, at least at the macro level, is not in evidence from these figures.

If voters did not cast their votes for extremist parties, perhaps an electoral realignment occurred among the major parties. Evidence of that at the macro level likely would be revealed in a sudden major shift of voters away from one traditional party and toward another. In fact, as the data in table 6.2 show,

Table 6.1. Votes for the Left, 1962–1986

Year	Votes for Deputies (percent)	Votes for President/V.P. (percent)
1962	2.4	0.9
1966	Communists excluded from election	
1970	5.5	1.3
1974	4.4	2.9
1978	7.7	2.9
1982	7.2	3.3
1986	5.1	1.3

Source: Tribunal Supremo de Elecciones.

Table 6.2. Votes by Party, 1953–1986

Year	National Liberation Party	Opposition
1953	64.7	35.3
1958	42.8	58.3
1962	50.3	48.8
1966	49.5	50.5
1970	54.8	43.9
1974	43.4	53.7
1978	43.8	53.3
1982	58.8	37.9
1986	53.4	45.1

Sources: 1986, Tribunal Supremo de Elecciones, and Jiménez (1977).

Table 6.3. Abstentions, 1953–1986

Year	Percent Abstention
1953	32.8
1958	35.3
1962	19.1[a]
1970	16.7
1974	20.1
1978	18.7
1982	21.4
1986	18.1

a. Voting made mandatory beginning with this election. Another factor producing a decline in abstention since 1962 is that in that year the losing side in the 1948 civil war initiated a complete return to electoral politics. Dr. Calderón Guardia, who had lost the civil war, ran again for president in 1962.
Source: 1986, Tribunal Supremo de Elecciones, and Jiménez (1977).

although the party elected to office in 1978 lost much ground in 1982, the election of 1986 was relatively close, with the incumbent party losing a good share of the lead it had accumulated in 1982.

According to the theory we have reviewed, another mechanism for manifesting discontent with the political system is abstention. This would be a particularly viable alternative for those voters who perceive no real choices among the parties. The abstention rates, however, reveal no evidence of rising discontent among Costa Rican voters.[16] As is shown in table 6.3, abstention in the 1986 elections was at it lowest level in over thirty years.

Finally, the election campaign in Costa Rica was conducted almost without violence. There were a few reported incidents of shoving at some campaign rallies, but nothing of any serious nature occurred.

In sum, the 1986 elections appeared to be merely another in the long series of normal elections that Costa Rica has experienced since 1953. There has been no rise in voting for extremist parties, no evidence of major party realignment, and no increase in abstention. None of the expected impacts of the economic crisis on the electoral system seems to have occurred.

An examination of these results might suggest that we may need to revise our theory of the political economy of elections. One possibility is that Costa Rican election results imply that the voters in a developing country are immune to the economic "facts of life." Perhaps their view of the culpability of elected public officials in determining economic outcomes differs from the views of voters in industrialized nations. Certainly not all voters are equally sensitive to economic conditions. In Europe, as Lewis-Beck (1986:340) notes, the link between economics and politics is not the same for each of the nations he studied: in Britain they were far more "tightly joined" than in Italy. Lewis-Beck points to the work by Putnam (1973:9) that suggests that the British view their government as more effective and responsive than do the Italians. If Costa Ricans hold similar or more unfavorable views of their government than do the Italians, then the apparent absence of a linkage between politics and economics would help explain the results presented above. Another possibility is that, contrary to Fiorina's assertion that under extreme economic conditions voting decisions must obviously reflect economic conditions, voters in crisis conditions respond to other stimuli more familiar to them, such as traditional partisan appeals.

Further examination of the macro data is unlikely to prove fruitful because in order to understand voting behavior under the conditions described here, one needs to look into the mind of the voter, a procedure perhaps best accomplished with survey data. Survey data gathered during the period of the crisis alone, however, will not help unravel the puzzles posed above. For example, if we were to find that voters in Costa Rica during the crisis did not hold their elected officials responsible for economic conditions, we would not know if they had held them responsible *prior* to the onset of the crisis. Survey data for the crisis period alone, therefore, do not allow us to attribute to the extreme economic conditions themselves the alteration of the well-established linkage of voting to economic conditions. What is needed is survey data of a sample of Costa Rican voters interviewed prior to the onset of the crisis and later during the crisis, as described below.

The 1978 and 1985 Surveys

The two surveys analyzed in this study are drawn from an ongoing comparative investigation of public opinion in which the authors have been engaged since the early 1970s.[17] One was drawn in 1978, the high point of Costa Rica's prosperity prior to the onset of the economic crisis, and a second in 1985, some months prior to the February 1986 elections.

Both surveys are multistage, stratified probability samples covering the Metropolitan Region of greater San José and its surrounding suburbs and towns. This is the principal urban area of the country, incorporating 80 percent of the nation's urban population and 40 percent of the population of the country as a whole. The minimum voting age in Costa Rica is eighteen; hence the surveys cover only those eighteen years of age and older. Both question-naires were administered in the homes of the respondents.

The 1978 survey included 201 respondents. In the 1985 survey an effort was made to reinterview those who had responded to the earlier interview, thereby establishing a panel design. However, since the initial study was not conducted with a panel design in mind, relocating the respondents was a difficult task, one that met with only partial success. Of the 201 respondents from 1978, a total of 75 were relocated and reinterviewed. In terms of basic socioeconomic characteristics, the panel differs little from the cross-section survey of 1985 except that it does not contain anyone who was younger than eighteen years of age in 1978. Hence, the reinterviewed panel comprises respondents twenty-five years of age and older. An examination of the cross-section data did not reveal any significant age-related associations among the variables analyzed in this study. Reference will be made to this panel at several points in the discussion.

The 1985 sample was not limited to the reinterviews. Rather, it was also designed to form a cross-section of the 1985 population and hence be directly comparable with the entire 1978 cross-section. In total, the 1985 sample contains 506 valid cases, including the 75 reinterviews from 1978.

Voter Evaluation of Government Performance

At the level of the individual, nearly all research on the linkage between the economy and voting behavior adheres to some form of a theory of retrospective voting first postulated by Key (1966) and refined by Fiorina (1981b), among others. At its most basic level, this theory simply says that before casting a ballot the voter considers the incumbent's success in dealing with the economy, and if that evaluation is positive, the incumbent (or his party) is rewarded with a vote.[18] On the other hand, if the evaluation of the economy's performance is negative, the voter punishes the incumbent and casts his ballot for the opposition. A more general elaboration of this theory is suggested by Linz and Stepan (1978), who argue that beyond the narrower question of voting is the larger question of democratic stability itself, and that the stability of democracy rests heavily upon the efficacy of the government in dealing with the problems of the day. After all, as Gurr (1974) has found in studying his sample of 336 polities in the 170 years between 1800 to 1970, the average life expectancy of historical polities has been only thirty-two years. Ineffectual governments may not only lose the next election but they may also be responsible for insurrection, revolution, and a total collapse of the system of government.

Advances in formulating instruments for measuring voter retrospection on economic issues have been occurring for several years. Comparative research by Lewis-Beck (1986) has found that there is little predictive power in asking voters how the economy has fared in recent months. Rather, the use of a "mediated retrospective" set of questions, ones that focus on the impact of the government on the economy, is far more powerful.[19] We used a battery of items similar to, but more specific and more finely graduated than, the mediated retrospective items utilized by Lewis-Beck in his European research.

In both our 1978 and 1985 surveys we asked the respondents to evaluate the performance of the incumbent administration on six specific dimensions, three of which were explicitly related to the performance of the economy, while the others dealt with various aspects of the administration's performance.[20] In each case we asked the respondent to evaluate the impact of the government on the basis of a seven-point scale. According to the studies conducted by Rosenstone, Hansen, and Kinder (1986), the three-option wording ("better, worse or about the same") used in much of the research on economic voting is inferior to scales that offer a wide range of options.[21] We do not claim our measure is necessarily better than the others, but we do believe it is sensitive enough to register the expected decline in evaluation of administration performance resulting from the economic crisis. Indeed, this is precisely what we found. Table 6.4 compares the mean scores on each of the six administration performance items for the 1978 and 1985 cross-sections.

Examination of table 6.4 shows quite clearly that Costa Ricans are not insensitive to the performance of their incumbents. On every one of the six

Table 6.4. Evaluation of Administration Performance, 1978 and 1985 Cross-Section Samples

Item	1978 Mean[a]	1985 Mean	Sig. of t
On a scale of 1 to 7, to what degree would you say that the administration[b] of President _____:			
1. Controlled the problem of the cost of living.	4.7	3.8	<.001
2. Helped the needy classes.	5.5	4.0	<.001
3. Increased national production.	5.5	4.7	<.001
4. Guaranteed the protection and security of individuals.	5.6	4.9	<.001
5. Demonstrated strong, capable leadership.	5.8	4.6	<.001
6. Combated crime.	4.9	4.2	<.001
(Maximum N: 1978 = 201; 1985 = 506)			

Note: The 1978 survey was conducted shortly after the new government had taken power, and hence the respondents were asked to evaluate the performance of the prior government.
a. A score of 1 indicates the poorest level of performance while a score of 7 indicates the highest.
b. It should be noted that in Spanish the word used in this item is "el gobierno," which some have incorrectly translated directly into English to mean "the government." The correct meaning of the term in Spanish, however, is equivalent to the English "the administration."

items respondents rated the precrisis administration as more effective than the administration in power during the crisis. One might suspect, however, that this finding may be merely an artifact of the partisan preferences of the respondents. This suspicion can be laid to rest in two ways. First, the administration's performance being evaluated in the precrisis survey was controlled by the same party as that evaluated during the second survey.[22] Second, an analysis of individual opinions through an examination of the data from the panel sample reveals that the lowered opinion of administration performance is not produced by sampling error in the cross-section design. As shown in table 6.5, those reinterviewed in 1985 had a lower opinion of the administration's performance than they did in 1978. Indeed, close comparison of the panel results on these items with the cross-section reveals that they are remarkably similar.

A final doubt about the interpretation of these data is that they may not directly reflect an evaluation of the effectiveness of a given administration but rather may reflect the personal popularity of the incumbent president. An examination of presidential popularity shows that President Monge in 1985 was actually more popular than was President Daniel Oduber in 1978. In December 1977, three months prior to the election of 1978, President Oduber's administration was evaluated favorably by 53 percent of the electorate. In January 1986, a month before the 1986 election, President Monge's administration was evaluated favorably by exactly the same proportion of the electorate. The proportion of those evaluating Oduber negatively, however, was higher than for Monge (18 versus 11 percent). The percentage difference score (positive support minus negative support) of Monge was + 44, compared to + 33 for Oduber.[23]

Further evidence is contained in a recent Gallup International poll of 1,215 adult Costa Ricans, which found President Monge to be more popular than any living president and more popular than any other living political figure in Costa Rica. Former president Oduber was rated favorably by 69.1 percent of the respondents, compared to 83.9 percent for Monge.[24] Therefore, if presidential popularity had contaminated the items on the administration's effectiveness, the effect would be to further widen the gap in the evaluation of the effectiveness of the two administrations. That is, one would expect that the somewhat lower popularity of Oduber may have been responsible for a lowering of the effectiveness scores for 1978, whereas the greater popularity of Monge may have helped raise the effectiveness scores for 1985. This expectation is confirmed by the strong correlation between presidential popularity and the evaluation of administration performance, as shown in table 6.6.[25] In sum, there is ample evidence that presidential popularity is not responsible for the perceived higher effectiveness of the precrisis government; therefore the lower perceived effectiveness of the 1985 government is a response to the conditions of the day and not the personal popularity of the president.

Table 6.5. Evaluation of Administration Performance, 1978/1985 Panel

Item	1978 Mean[a]	1985 Mean	Sig. of t
On a scale of 1 to 7, to what degree would you say that the administration of President _____:			
1. Controlled the problem of the cost of living.	5.1	3.6	<.001
2. Helped the needy classes.	5.7	4.2	<.001
3. Increased national production.	5.9	5.0	.003
4. Guaranteed the protection and security of individuals.	5.9	4.8	<.001
5. Demonstrated strong, capable leadership.	6.2	4.5	<.001
6. Combated crime.	5.0	4.1	<.001
(Maximum N = 75)			

a. A score of 1 indicates the poorest level of performance while a score of 7 indicates the highest.

To this point in the analysis, a comparison of the macro and micro data presents an unexpected disjuncture. The brief review we presented of the 1986 election suggested by its normalcy (lowered voting for extremist parties, lowered rate of abstentions, absence of realignment, and absence of violence) that Costa Rican voters were somehow immune to the political effects of an economic crisis. If this had indeed been the case, then we would need to begin to reexamine the assumed universality of the theory of the political economy of voting behavior because either it might not apply to developing countries or it might not apply under conditions of crisis. The survey data, however, reveal quite clearly that the Costa Rican voters are sensitive to the economic crisis and that they hold their elected officials responsible for it. That is, their mediated retrospective evaluation of administration effectiveness seems to clearly reflect their awareness of the economic crisis and the government's inability to resolve it. The disjuncture lies in the fact that this awareness was not translated into

Table 6.6. Correlation of Evaluation of Administration Performance (1985) and Presidential Popularity

Item	r
On a scale of 1 to 7, to what degree would you say that the administration of President Monge:	
1. Controlled the problem of the cost of living.	.52[a]
2. Helped the needy classes.	.47[a]
3. Increased national production.	.39[a]
4. Guaranteed the protection and security of individuals.	.30[b]
5. Demonstrated strong, capable leadership.	.40[a]
6. Combated crime.	.47[a]
(Maximum N = 506)	

a. = sig. at < .001.
b. = sig. at < .01.

behaviors consistent with the theory. In extraordinary times Costa Rican voters have acted in ordinary ways. We need to know why this has been so.

The "Deep Structure" of the
Political Economy of Voting Behavior

Research on the political economy of voting behavior has focused heavily upon short-term forces. At the macro level, economic cycles are correlated with election results. At the micro level, individual perceptions of national and personal economic situations, sometimes coupled with overall measures of incumbent popularity, are used to predict individual votes. But probably because the studies that have been conducted to date have not examined elections during crisis conditions, they have not generally probed deeper factors underlying voting decisions. In other words, the research on the political economy of voting behavior has largely been content to make successful predictions of individual election outcomes. It has not concerned itself with

Table 6.7. Approval of Violent Political Protest, 1978 and 1985 Cross-Section Samples

I am going to read you a list of some actions that people can take to achieve their goals and political objectives. I would like you to tell me (on a scale of 1 to 7) how firmly you approve or disapprove of people taking these actions:

Action[a]	Mean 1978	Mean 1985	Sig. of t
Taking over factories, offices, and other buildings.	2.12	1.50	<.001
Participating in a group that wants to overthrow the government by violent means.	1.63	1.29	.003
Participating in demonstrations that damage buildings, vehicles, or other property.	1.29	1.27	NS
Participating in fights with the police or with other demonstrators.	1.62	1.41	.015

a. Scale position 1 indicates lowest support while 7 indicates highest support.

voters who decide not to vote, who abandon traditional politics and move on to support extremist parties, or who engage in political violence.

The crisis conditions facing the Costa Rican voter have not (at least not yet) been translated into extraordinary behavior. An examination of the survey data we have collected gives us two very clear indications why this is so.

First, Costa Ricans, in spite of the economic crisis, reject violent behavior as a means to achieve their political goals. In both 1978 and 1985 we asked our respondents a series of five questions on the extent to which different forms of violent actions would be justified as a means to achieving a political objective (see tables 6.7 and 6.8).

Table 6.8. Approval of Violent Political Protest, 1978/1985 Panel Sample

I am going to read you a list of some actions that people can take to achieve their goals and political objectives. I would like you to tell me (on a scale of 1 to 7) how firmly you approve or disapprove of people taking these actions:

Action[a]	Mean 1978	Mean 1985	Sig. of t
Taking over factories, offices, and other buildings.	2.06	1.45	.017
Participating in a group that wants to overthrow the government by violent means.	1.56	1.28	NS
Participating in demonstrations that damage buildings, vehicles, or other property.	1.27	1.41	NS
Participating in fights with the police or with other demonstrators.	1.70	1.45	NS

a. Scale position 1 indicates lowest support while 7 indicates highest support.

The level of support for violent protest activity is very low in both 1978 and 1985. On the seven-point scale used for this study, the means hover close to the lowest scale point (i.e., 1). Equally important, the level of support for violent activities has not increased between 1978 and 1985. Indeed, the cross-section samples show some significant decreases, but that pattern is not repeated in the panel sample.

Second, high levels of support for the basic institutions of government seem to protect the system from extreme reactions to economic crisis. In both 1978 and 1985 we asked our respondents about their support for the basic institutions of government.[26] We asked them seven questions, each rated by a seven-point scale, as shown in tables 6.9 and 6.10. What we found is that there was

Table 6.9. Support for Institutions, 1978 and 1985 Cross-Section Samples

Item[a]	Mean 1978	Mean 1985	Sig. of t
To what degree . . .			
1. do you believe that the courts in Costa Rica guarantee a fair trial?	5.3	5.1	NS
2. do you have respect for the political institutions of Costa Rica?	5.9	6.1	NS
3. do you believe that the basic rights of citizens are well protected under the Costa Rican political system?	5.2	5.7	<.001
4. are you proud to live under the Costa Rican political system?	6.3	6.5	NS
5. do you believe that the Costa Rican political system is the best possible system?	5.7	6.2	<.001
6. do you believe that one ought to support the Costa Rican political system?	5.9	6.5	<.001
7. do you believe that you and your friends are well represented in the Costa Rican political system?	5.0	5.3	.007
(Maximum N: 1978 = 189; 1985 = 505)			

a. A scale of 1 to 7 was used, with 1 indicating lowest support and 7 highest support.

no decline in support for the basic institutions of government in spite of the crisis. In the cross-section sample, four of the seven items did show significant differences between 1978 and 1985, but in each case the 1985 means were slightly higher (i.e., more supportive) than in 1978. The panel results were even more consistent, with only three of the seven items showing significant differences, but again the direction was in terms of slightly *higher* support in 1985. Hence, the survey data show that despite the crisis, levels of system support remained high in Costa Rica.

Table 6.10. Support for Institutions, 1978/1985 Panel Sample

Item[a]	Mean 1978	Mean 1985	Sig. of t
To what degree . . .			
1. do you believe that the courts in Costa Rica guarantee a fair trial?	4.9	5.4	.015
2. do you have respect for the political institutions of Costa Rica?	6.2	6.2	NS
3. do you believe that the basic rights of citizens are well protected under the Costa Rican political system?	5.4	5.4	NS
4. are you proud to live under the Costa Rican political system?	6.6	6.3	NS
5. do you believe that the Costa Rican political system is the best possible system?	6.2	5.9	<.001
6. do you believe that one ought to support the Costa Rican political system?	6.6	6.1	.005
7. do you believe that you and your friends are well represented in the Costa Rican political system? (Maximum N = 69)	5.3	5.3	NS

a. A scale of 1 to 7 was used, with 1 indicating lowest support and 7 highest support.

Conclusions

In marked contrast to the other Central American nations, Costa Rica has a deeply entrenched system of democratic rule. No other nation in the region has a history of widespread participation, regular free and competitive elections, institutionalized parties, and respect for civil and human rights. The economic crisis of the 1980s has shaken the economic foundations of the system, however, leading some to question the resilience of its democracy. This chapter has shown that although Costa Ricans are keenly aware of the economic crisis and hold their leaders accountable for it, those feelings have not spilled over into a more generalized dissatisfaction with the basic system of government. Hence, in spite of the economic crisis, Costa Ricans still express a degree of pride in and support for their political system undiminished from the precrisis period. In addition, they continue to express strong opposition to violent political actions. In short, Costa Ricans have developed a political culture supportive of democracy, a culture that, according to the other chapters of this book, is embryonic at best in the other nations of the Central American region.

There are, of course, limits of tolerance for poor economic performance even in systems as deeply democratic as Costa Rica's. Like all new administrations, the administration elected in February 1986 was given a "honeymoon" of immunity from criticism, but never in recent Costa Rican history has that honeymoon period lasted for such a brief period. Indeed, in the weeks *prior* to the installation of the new president in May 1986, critical voices were already being heard in the press as rumors surfaced regarding acceptance of new "structural adjustment packages" imposed by the International Monetary Fund. Labor groups were particularly sensitive to potential threats from reduction of public-sector jobs.

But perhaps the most serious concern was the potential reduction of U.S. foreign assistance. The closing of *contra* bases near the Costa Rican border with Nicaragua, along with the leadership role Costa Rica has taken in promoting the "Arias Plan" for peace in the region, has caused friction between the U.S. State Department and Costa Rica. Foreign assistance in the period 1981–84 totaled slightly more than $3 billion (Céspedes et al., 1985:124). A sharp decline in that assistance would probably precipitate a collapse of the Costa Rican economy.

Under those conditions, Costa Rican voter reaction might well follow the more extreme formulas described earlier in this essay. The first months of the Arias administration were punctuated by a dramatic increase in strikes. One sign that Costa Ricans are clearly linking economics and politics is that the most recent demonstrations for the first time have shifted from their traditional locus, the Legislative Assembly, to the front door of the Central Bank. Farmers were protesting the reduction of price supports for several agricultural products and apparently saw the direct connection between the externally imposed financial adjustments and domestic economic policy. If a massive economic collapse were to occur, one could predict that a far larger proportion of the electorate would move toward lower support for the political system as they seek new alternatives to rescue them from the pain induced by economic collapse. As the illustration of the collapse of the Weimar Republic discussed earlier demonstrates, not all alternatives chosen under circumstances such as these are necessarily democratic ones.

Notes

An earlier version of this essay was presented at the Thirteenth International Congress of the Latin American Studies Association in Boston, 23–25 October 1986. The study has been supported by grants from the Social and Behavioral Sciences Research Institute of the University of Arizona and by a Senior Research Fulbright grant to Seligson. We wish to thank Pedro Valenzuela for his help in preparing the bibliography and John Peeler for his helpful comments on the earlier version.

1. Initially there appeared to be a contradiction between macro- and micro-level studies. Those studies found that the economy had a strong effect on the outcome of elections, but did not uniformly find that the economy had similar effects on the individual voter (Hibbs, Jr., and Vasilatos, 1981). However, the use of more refined survey questions has found that individuals are indeed sensitive to economic conditions when deciding for whom to cast their ballots. Currently the debate centers on which factor, the general state of the economy or personal economic well-being, is more important (Rosenstone, Hansen, and Kinder, 1986).

2. Important historical voting behavior research has been conducted, especially on the United States, but much of that work (and debate) has focused on the causes of partisan realignment and low voter turnout (see Burnham, 1970, 1982; Rusk, 1978).

3. Some of the key work on the impact of economic decline on voting behavior is found in Crewe, Särlvik, and Alt (1977), Franklin and Maugham (1978) and Finer (1980). Hibbs, Jr., and Vasilatos (1981:34) have modeled the impact of economic performance on party popularity over the period 1960–79, but they avoid dealing with the Depression because of their assertion that a single model ought not to hold in both the "pre- and post-Keynesian eras."

4. For unemployment data for Britain, see Hughes and Perlman (1984:12).

5. As reported in the New York Times, 5 August 1986, p. 34.

6. Beginning in the 1930s many Latin American governments embarked upon programs of massive state investments in order to spur industrialization (Hirschman, 1963). In the 1970s neoconservative policies were attempted (Foxley, 1983; Ramos, 1986). Although much was achieved in some of these countries, especially in the improvement of infrastructure, triple-digit inflation, double-digit unemployment, and massive foreign debts have remained an almost constant feature throughout the region.

7. But readers should note Joel D. Barkin's paper (1987) in a new book on African elections.

8. See the extended exchange of views in the March 1986 (vol. 80) issue of the *American Political Science Review*, pp. 225–49.

9. The economic variables included by Johnson, Slater, and McGowan (1984) include growth in GNP, growth in industrial jobs, the ratio of exports-imports to GNP, and changes in commodity concentration. It should be noted that reliable measurements of inflation and, especially, unemployment are particularly hard to come by for many of the African countries under study.

10. Costa Rica has a unicameral legislature, with representatives (*diputados*) elected from each of the nation's seven provinces. Provinces are further subdivided into cantons, each canton electing its municipal government officials.

11. See Seligson (1983a) and Céspedes, DiMare, and Jiménez (1985).

12. This is based upon per capita consumption of the "canasta básica," or basic food basket.

13. The right has been organized into the Movimiento de Costa Rica Libre, but has not had any significant electoral presence.

14. Article 98 of the Constitution of 1949 prohibited participation in elections by parties that were linked to international movements and viewed as being antidemocratic. This provision was applied to the Communist party of Costa Rica.

15. In 1982 they won four seats, the highest number since the 1940s.

16. In Costa Rica registered voters are given a "cédula," or identification card, which serves not only to allow them to vote but is also required identification for a wide variety of formal transactions, such as cashing a check, obtaining a passport, or applying for a job. Abstention rates are calculated as the proportion of registered voters who do not actually vote. Small fines may be levied against nonvoters, but are rarely collected.

17. In 1978 Edward N. Muller began participating in this collaborative effort as well.

18. Key's theory is broader than a focus on the economy, but much of the empirical testing of the theory has been concerned primarily with the economic dimension. Other factors, such as foreign policy during the Vietnam War, have influenced the voter, but such issues are not often very salient when compared to economic issues. Edward Tufte's (1978) seminal (and prize-winning) volume, *The Political Control of the Economy*, makes only one passing reference to the Vietnam War.

19. In a multiple regression equation, Lewis-Beck found that the simple retrospective evaluation of the economy tended to shrink to insignificance when mediated retrospective items were introduced. He also found that mediated prospective evaluations (i.e., the opinion of the voter as to the government's probable future success in dealing with the economy) played a key role in determining the vote.

20. The questionnaires contained additional items in this battery that were not identical in both surveys and therefore are not analyzed here. Specifically, in 1985 respondents were asked to evaluate how well the government was doing in promoting "democratic principles" generally speaking, whereas in 1978 that item was broken

down into three separate questions, one focusing on business, another on unions, and a third on universities.

21. But note that Lewis-Beck (1986:325) used a five-point scale in his measurement of the impact of the economy upon the individual and found no improvement over previous studies. In both his mediated retrospective and mediated prospective items he uses a three-point coding scheme.

22. That is, the 1978 survey respondents evaluated the performance of the government in power from 1974 to 1978, whereas the 1985 respondents evaluated the government in power from 1982 to 1986. In both cases the Partido Liberación Nacional (PLN) was in power.

23. These data come from surveys conducted by Gómez in the Metropolitan Area, the same area covered by the 1978 and 1985 surveys of public opinion analyzed in this paper. The 1986 survey, however, was limited to the Alajuela region.

24. This poll was conducted by Consultoría Interdisciplinaria en Desarrollo (CID), the Gallup affiliate in Costa Rica. The results were reported in *La Nación*, 13 April 1986, p. 8a. These data, however, are retrospective with regard to Oduber and hence do not reflect popular views toward Oduber near the end of his period in office. The survey conducted in 1977 reported above, therefore, is a more accurate guide. In any event, both studies show the greater popularity of Monge.

25. No correlation is presented for the 1978 data since the popularity question asked in that survey focused on the newly elected president, whereas the evaluation data focused on the previous administration.

26. The development and cross-national validation of the items used to make up this scale have been discussed in Muller, Jukam, and Seligson (1982), Seligson (1983b), and Booth and Seligson (1984).

References

Barkin, Joel D. 1987. The Electoral Process and Peasant-State Relations in Kenya. In *Elections in Independent Africa*, edited by Fred M. Hayward. Boulder: Westview Press.

Binder, Leonard, et al. 1971. *Crises and Sequences of Political Development*. Princeton: Princeton University Press.

Booth, John A., and Seligson, Mitchell A. 1984. The Political Culture of Authoritarianism in Mexico: A Reexamination. *Latin American Research Review* 19 (January): 106–24.

Burnham, Walter Dean. 1970. *Critical Elections and the Mainsprings of American Politics*. New York: Norton.

———. 1982. *The Current Crisis in American Politics*. New York: Oxford University Press.

Céspedes, Víctor Hugo; DiMare, Alberto; and Jiménez, Ronulfo. 1985. *Costa Rica: Recuperación sin reactivación*. San José, Costa Rica: Academia de Centroamérica.

Coleman, Kenneth M. 1976. *Diffuse Support in Mexico: The Potential for Crisis*. Beverly

Hills: Sage Publications, Professional Papers in Comparative Politics.

Crewe, Ivor; Särlvik, Bo; and Alt, James. 1977. Partisan Realignment in Britain, 1964–1974. *British Journal of Political Science* 7 (April): 129–90.

Duncan, Otis Dudley. 1975. Measuring Social Change via Replication of Surveys. In *Social Indicator Models*, edited by K. C. Land and S. Spilerman. New York: Russell Sage Foundation.

Finer, S. E. 1980. *The Changing British Party System, 1945–1979.* Washington, D.C.: American Enterprise Institute.

Fiorina, Morris P. 1981a. *Retrospective Voting in American National Elections.* New Haven: Yale University Press.

————. 1981b. Short- and Long-Term Effects of Economic Conditions on Individual Voting Decisions. In *Contemporary Political Economy*, edited by D. A. Hibbs, Jr., and H. Fassbender. Amsterdam: North-Holland.

Foxley, Alejandro. 1983. *Latin American Experiments in Neoconservative Economics.* Berkeley: University of California Press.

Franklin, Mark, and Maugham, Anthony. 1978. The Decline of Class Voting in Britain: Problems of Analysis and Interpretation. *American Political Science Review* 72 (June): 523–34.

Gurr, Ted Robert. 1974. Persistence and Change in Political Systems, 1800–1971. *American Political Science Review* 68 (December): 1482–1504.

Hibbs, Douglas, Jr., and Vasilatos, Nicholas. 1981. Macroeconomic Performance and Mass Political Support in the United States and Great Britain. In *Contemporary Political Economy*, edited by D. A. Hibbs, Jr., and H. Fassbender. Amsterdam: North-Holland.

Hirschman, Albert O. 1963. *Journeys Toward Progress: Studies in Economic Policy-Making in Latin America.* New York: Twentieth Century Fund.

Hughes, James J., and Perlman, Richard. 1984. *The Economics of Unemployment: A Comparative Analysis of Britain and the United States.* New York: Cambridge University Press.

Jiménez, Wilburg. 1977. *Análisis electoral de una democracia, 1953–1974.* San José, Costa Rica: Editorial Costa Rica.

Johnson, Thomas H.; Slater, Robert O.; and McGowan, Pat. 1984. Explaining African Military Coups d'Etat, 1960–1982. *American Political Science Review* 78 (September): 622–40.

Key, V. O. 1966. *The Responsible Electorate.* New York: Vintage.

Kornhauser, William. 1959. *The Politics of Mass Society.* Glencoe: Free Press.

Kramer, G. H. 1971. Short-term Fluctuations in U. S. Voting Behavior, 1896–1964. *American Political Science Review* 65 (March): 131–43.

Lepsius, M. Rainer. 1978. From Fragmented Party Democracy to Government by Emergency Decree and National Socialist Takeover: Germany. In *The Breakdown of Democratic Regimes*, edited by Juan J. Linz and Alfred Stepan. Baltimore: Johns Hopkins University Press.

Lewis-Beck, Michael S. 1986. Comparative Economic Voting: Britain, France, Germany and Italy. *American Journal of Political Science* 30 (May): 315–46.

Linz, Juan, and Stepan, Alfred, eds. 1978. *The Breakdown of Democratic Regimes: Crisis, Breakdown and Reequilibrium.* Baltimore: Johns Hopkins University Press.

Malloy, James M., and Seligson, Mitchell A., eds. 1987. *Authoritarians and Democrats: Regime Transition in Latin America.* Pittsburgh: University of Pittsburgh Press.

Muller, Edward N., and Seligson, Mitchell A. 1987. Inequality and Insurgency. *American Political Science Review* 81 (June): 427–51.

Muller, Edward N.; Jukam, Thomas O.; and Seligson, Mitchell A. 1982. Diffuse Political Support and Antisystem Political Behavior: A Comparative Analysis. *American Journal of Political Science* 26 (May): 240–64.

Olson, Mancur, Jr. 1963. Rapid Growth as a Destabilizing Force. *Journal of Economic History* 23 (December): 529–52.

Peeler, John. 1985. *Latin American Democracies: Colombia, Costa Rica, Venezuela.* Chapel Hill: University of North Carolina Press.

Putnam, Robert D. 1973. *The Beliefs of Politicians: Ideology, Conflict and Democracy in Britain and Italy.* New Haven: Yale University Press.

Ramos, Joseph. 1986. *Neoconservative Economics in the Southern Cone of Latin America, 1973–1983.* Baltimore: Johns Hopkins University Press, 1986.

Rosenstone, Steven J.; Hansen, John Mark; and Kinder, Donald R. 1986. Measuring Change in Personal Economic Well-Being. *Public Opinion Quarterly* 50 (Spring): 176–92.

Rusk, Jerrold G. 1978. The Effect of the Australian Ballot Reform on Split Ticket Voting: 1876–1908. *American Political Science Review* 64 (December): 1220–38.

Seligson, Mitchell A. 1983a. Costa Rica. In *Latin America and Caribbean Contemporary Record, Volume I: 1981–82*, pp. 399–408, edited by Jack W. Hopkins. New York and London: Holmes and Meier Publishers.

———. 1983b. On the Measurement of Diffuse Support: Some Evidence from Mexico. *Social Indicators Research* 12 (January): 1–24.

———. 1987. Costa Rica and Jamaica. In *Competitive Elections in Developing Countries*, edited by Myron Weiner and Ergun Ozbudun. Durham: Duke University Press.

Seligson, Mitchell A., and Carroll, William. 1982. The Costa Rican Role in the Sandinista Victory. In *Nicaragua in Revolution*, edited by Thomas W. Walker. New York: Praeger.

Seligson, Mitchell A., and Muller, Edward N. 1987. Democratic Stability and Economic Crisis: Costa Rica, 1978–1983, *International Studies Quarterly*, 31 (September): 301–26.

Tufte, Edward R. 1978. *Political Control of the Economy.* Princeton: Princeton University Press.

Weiner, Myron, and Ozbudun, Ergun, eds. 1987. *Competitive Elections in Developing Countries.* Durham: Duke University Press.

Zimmermann, Ekkart. 1983. *Political Violence, Crises and Revolution: Theories and Research.* Boston: G. K. Hall, Schenkmann Pub. Co.

7 Democracy and Elections in Central America

Autumn of the Oligarchs?

John A. Peeler

Everything had come to an end before he did, we had even extinguished the last breath of the hopeless hope that someday the repeated and always denied rumor that he had finally succumbed to some one of his many regal illnesses would be true, and yet we didn't believe it now that it was, and not because we really didn't believe it but because we no longer wanted it to be true, we had ended up not understanding what would become of us without him, what would become of our lives after him. . . .—Gabriel García Márquez, *The Autumn of the Patriarch*

The Reagan administration, like many before it, has proudly claimed credit for the emergence of democracy in Central America, as well as elsewhere in Latin America.[1] The contributors to this volume have demonstrated that such a claim is unfounded: Central American political evolution has indeed been decisively shaped by the United States, but the regimes established and the elections held under strong U.S. pressure cannot by any reasonable standard be called democratic, and their prospects for long-term stability are minimal. This chapter attempts to synthesize the arguments and evidence presented in the preceding chapters by investigating the political and economic constraints on democracy in Central America and by examining the nature of electoral experiences in the region. It concludes with a discussion of prospects and problems in Nicaragua's revolutionary approach to democracy.

International Constraints: The Impact of the United States and the World Economy

As small countries deeply embedded in the U.S. sphere of influence, the Central American nations cannot be adequately understood without reference to the policies of the United States and to the effects of world economic conditions. The very emergence of political crisis and change in Central America over the last decade owes much to petroleum price increases and worldwide recession in the late 1970s and early 1980s, which culminated in the massive indebtedness currently afflicting many Third World countries, including most of Central America. It is scarcely surprising that the stability of most of the region's governments was undermined by this prolonged economic crisis. In 1978 only Costa Rica was ruled by an elected civilian government; thus what now appears as a wave of democratization could turn out to be a normal response of the political cycle to a downturn in the economic cycle.[2]

Nicaragua, El Salvador, and Costa Rica provide considerable support for this economic hypothesis. In Costa Rica the primary impetus for political crisis after 1979 was clearly a prolonged and serious economic crisis touched off by the deterioration of world economic conditions and exacerbated by government mismanagement of the economy under President Carazo. The liberal democratic regime proved able to contain the political crisis within the normal constitutional cycle of competitive elections, with the opposition Partido Liberación Nacional winning the 1982 elections and retaining power in 1986.

Although the deterioration of economic conditions in El Salvador and Nicaragua in the late 1970s certainly contributed to their political crises, longer-term trends in the economies, class structures, and polities of those countries must be considered carefully. The evolution of the Somoza regime into an ever more obviously corrupt family hegemony drove increasing numbers of Nicaraguans, including the bourgeoisie, into open opposition by the late 1970s. In El Salvador the long-standing political dominance of the armed forces deteriorated into a tawdry and savage dictatorship that was stopped from perpetuating itself only by the civilian-military coup of 1979. Thus, in these two cases perhaps the best analysis would be that short-term international economic conditions helped undermine the viability of the regimes, but other circumstances led to their overthrow.

It is clear that the conditions in the international economy negatively affected Guatemala and Honduras, but there is little evidence that those conditions contributed substantially to their political crises.

United States policies have constituted a second major international constraint, with significant impact on all five countries. The nature of that impact, though, has varied a great deal from country to country. The United States has been critical to sustaining Costa Rica during its economic difficulties, while simultaneously putting intense pressure on three successive Costa Rican presidents to actively support the Nicaraguan contras and to depart from Costa Rica's long-standing policy of demilitarization. Although these pressures have placed great stress on the Costa Rican political system, it has so far endured.[3]

The Carter administration made strenuous, if belated and unsuccessful, efforts to influence the course of the insurrection in Nicaragua. After 19 July 1979, the day Somoza fell, the administration pursued an ambivalent policy of accommodation toward the Sandinista regime. The Reagan administration, of course, implacably sought the destruction of that regime by all means short of direct U.S. invasion. In turn, many of the restrictions imposed by the Sandinistas on opposition groups must be viewed as efforts to enhance security in the face of this overwhelming external threat. Finally, the election of 1984 and the constitution approved in 1987 were probably significantly shaped by the need to retain the support of the U.S. Congress and of Social Democrats in Latin America and Western Europe, as a counterpoise to Reagan administration hostility.

United States influence was not highly visible and may not have been decisive in the Salvadoran coup of October 1979, but the minds of U.S. policymakers had been remarkably focused by the Nicaraguan Revolution earlier that year. The Carter administration sought to prevent a repetition of the Nicaragua experience in El Salvador by putting itself firmly on the side of reforms that would eliminate the worst abuses of the old regime. However, the United States either could not or would not prevent military conservatives from staging a creeping countercoup over the next several months of 1979 and 1980, until all civilian and military reformers were removed from positions of power. Once conservative Christian Democrat José Napoleón Duarte joined the Junta in 1980, the United States backed him firmly against rightist opposition. With the election of a constituent assembly under extreme rightist control in 1982, Duarte left the Junta. He returned as president in 1984, after elections organized under pervasive U.S. guidance.[4] Since then the United States has continued to give Duarte strong backing, actively discouraging a military coup against him. José García has rightly emphasized in this volume that the transition to democracy in El Salvador should be seen as a stratagem of the United States and dominant groups in El Salvador to exclude the FMLN from power. But if the United States has been able to keep Duarte in power, it has not provided enough clout to assure passage of his modest reform program, which has been bitterly resisted by extreme rightist forces. Thus, the issues that feed the insurgency have not been resolved.

There probably would not have been a transition to elected civilian government in Honduras if the United States had not insisted on it. What is much more likely, given past patterns, is that the military regime of General Policarpo Paz García would have attempted to perpetuate itself, been overthrown in a bloodless coup, and been replaced by another military regime allied with the Conservative party. Instead, the United States induced Paz to hold reasonably open elections in which Liberal Roberto Suazo Córdoba won the presidency. Subsequently, the United States has insisted on the maintenance of the civilian regime and the formal integrity of the constitutional order (by, for example, actively discouraging Suazo from succeeding himself in office), while the policy of building up Honduras militarily has provided a massive windfall for the armed forces, which in return must cooperate with the United States in supporting the contras and in maintaining the image of democracy in Honduras.

Guatemala, paradoxically, in view of its history, provides the most complex and subtle case of U.S. influence. Direct U.S. influence was minimized during the Carter administration because the Guatemalan military regime chose to reject all U.S. military aid rather than bow to pressure to improve its human rights performance. Even after resumption of aid well into the Reagan administration, Guatemala has received only limited amounts. Yet few close observers would dispute that the successive coups that put generals Ríos Montt and Mejía Víctores in power, as well as the election that ended the military regime and placed Christian Democrat Vinicio Cerezo in the presidency, were all heavily influenced by Guatemalan perceptions of U.S. policy.

Elections and the Transition to Democracy

Even in the middle of the many dark nights of Central American despotism, elections have occurred with astonishing regularity.[5] However, elections in Central America have not normally decided who will govern, but rather have served to legitimate those currently in power. Prior to 1979, Costa Rica was the only Central American country in which elections were the principal means of changing the government. Costa Rica made the transition to stable democracy in the early 1950s, in the wake of a profound political crisis that divided the country between 1940 and 1948, culminating in a brief but bloody civil war (Peeler, 1985). The victors in that war were the Social Democratic party of José Figueres (later to evolve into the National Liberation party) and the conservative National Union of Otilio Ulate. In spite of significant policy divergences and political rivalries, the two parties forged an explicit pact that committed each to conduct honest elections, respect the results, and refrain from policies that would directly damage the vital interests of the other. Figueres demonstrated his respect for the pact when he yielded the presidency to Ulate, as he had agreed to do in 1949, even though he held a virtual monopoly of armed force. For his part, Ulate held honest elections in 1953 that were won by Figueres; Ulate, too, gave up power.

Thus, by 1953 a viable electoral democracy had taken shape, founded on mutual trust between center-right and center-left political forces. The Costa Rican election of 1953 did contribute to the formation of a political culture of support for participation and for democratic rules along the lines suggested by Booth's sixth question in the first chapter of this volume, although the environment of the election did restrict participatory rights and was not entirely fair to the losers of the 1948 civil war (see Booth's fourth question). Within a few years the backers of Calderón had accepted the new political order and reentered the political process as allies of Ulate and opponents of the National Liberation party. Later, in the 1970s, the Communists and other leftist parties sought and gained acceptance as legitimate participants in the liberal democratic electoral process. Thus, the initial accommodation between Ulate and Figueres was built upon and consolidated to include all significant political sectors. That original pact permitted Costa Rica to move from a naked struggle for political hegemony in the 1940s to the present shared hegemony of the centrist parties, in which struggle occurs within the electoral and political institutions of liberal democracy.[6]

It is striking that in none of the newly established democracies in the rest of Central America has such an elite pact or accommodation occurred. In El Salvador the rightist ARENA and PCN have never accepted the legitimacy of the Christian Democratic government of José Napoleón Duarte and have done all they could to frustrate his policies and undermine his government. The armed forces have supported Duarte, not out of commitment to democracy, but because of their need for U.S. aid. And there certainly is no spirit of accommodation between the FMLN and the government. Indeed, as noted by

José García, recent elections in El Salvador can best be seen as part of a strategy to defeat the FMLN.

Similarly in Honduras, the rival Liberal and National party elites show no sign of mutual trust or of working together to maintain the newly established democracy. Each has a long history of seeking to forge an alliance with the armed forces that would permit it to monopolize control of the government and exclude the rival party. The Nationals were junior partners in such an alliance under General Paz García, but since the election of Suazo Córdoba in 1981, the Liberals have been on the inside. Suazo's leadership was of such caliber that Mark Rosenberg felt called upon to ask, "Can democracy survive the democrats?" In the absence of accommodation, the Nationals might still win an election under current circumstances if the armed forces decide to switch allies again, or if the U.S. government has reason to desire such an outcome.

Either contingency is conceivable because there are few major differences between the parties; thus, neither the armed forces nor the United States is likely to veto either party. It is surely evident, though, that the regime of elected civilians in Honduras is exceedingly fragile, built on the shifting sands of U.S. policy. Booth asks in chapter 1 (his question 5), "Did the election(s) consolidate or help consolidate a stable regime under democratic rules?" It is quite clear that the Honduran elections of the 1980s did nothing of the sort.

The Guatemalan case resembles that of El Salvador, except that the Guatemalan leftist insurgency is weaker than the FMLN and the Guatemalan armed forces are neither as dependent on the United States nor as responsive to it. Like El Salvador, Guatemala was ruled for decades by a succession of military presidents, most elected fraudulently, in close alliance with the majority of the economic elite. The Guatemalan response to the regional crisis and its local manifestations closely resembles that of El Salvador: the embarrassingly repressive and corrupt Lucas García was replaced initially by Ríos Montt and a year later by the more orthodox Mejía Victores; the latter presided over elections won by the Christian Democrat Cerezo.

But Cerezo, like Duarte, has been utterly unable to control his armed forces or to bring human rights violators to trial. Human rights violations indeed continue in both countries, though apparently at rates much below the worst levels of a few years ago. Like Duarte, Cerezo has been unable to carry out even modest agrarian reform or other policies for structural reform, encountering tenacious rightist opposition to every such initiative. Cerezo has indicated that he hopes to serve democracy in Guatemala by completing his term and passing on the sash to an elected successor, but clearly his ability to do even that is entirely in the hands of the armed forces. In Guatemala, as in El Salvador and Honduras, democracy is thus extremely fragile despite recent elections.

The Nicaraguan Revolution's approach to the issue of elections and democracy has been unique, as recognized by Susanne Jonas in her comparison of Guatemala and Nicaragua. When the Sandinistas came to power in 1979, they did not follow conventional advice to hold immediate elections (which they would certainly have won overwhelmingly). The reason given was that after decades of large-scale electoral abuses before and during the Somoza regime, and with half the population illiterate, Nicaraguans were simply not prepared for a meaningful exercise in electoral democracy. They chose instead to begin a long process of revolutionary education and mobilization, highlighted by a literacy campaign and the expansion of mass organizations. An unelected provisional regime was established, with an executive junta exercising extensive decree powers and a legislative Council of State that included representatives from a wide range of parties and organizations but held a clear pro-Sandinista majority. The provisional regime lasted until the inauguration of the elected president and assembly in January 1985.

The elections held in November 1984 (two days before the U.S. national elections) were carefully prepared and organized, taking advantage of experience and advice from Latin America, Europe, and the United States. The electoral law and the independent mechanism for administering it were quite similar to successful models in Venezuela and Costa Rica. A president and a unicameral assembly were elected—the latter by proportional representation. Diverse international observers praised the honesty and fairness of the process; only the United States and its clients refused to accept the legitimacy of the elections. The results, not surprisingly, gave the FSLN nearly two-thirds of the vote; Daniel Ortega easily won the presidency and the Front attained over 60 percent of the assembly seats. But numerous other parties, to the left as well as the right of the Sandinistas, also won seats.[7]

This first election of the revolutionary regime in Nicaragua illustrates an important pattern that occurs elsewhere in Central America (again, with the recent exception of Costa Rica): not every significant political force participated in the election or accepted the legitimacy of its outcome. In Nicaragua various rightist parties, with the overt encouragement of the United States, refused to participate in the elections, alleging that Sandinista control of the

communications media and harassment of opposition groups made a meaningful election impossible. Other parties participated, but echoed many of the
same complaints. Those not participating accused the Sandinistas of willfully
refusing to create the conditions for a fair election, in effect forcing their
opponents not to participate. They argued, in fact, that instead of holding an
election the Sandinistas should negotiate a political settlement with the
contras. For their part, the Sandinistas flatly refused to negotiate with those
they believed to be traitors and U.S. puppets and accused their opponents of
seeking reasons not to participate in order to cast doubt on the legitimacy of
the election.

There is a distinct symmetry between these arguments and those about the
Salvadoran elections. In that case the center-right (U.S.-supported) government was holding an election in which it sought broad participation in order to
support its claim to democratic legitimacy. The leftist FMLN-FDR coalition
refused to participate, on the grounds that the government was unable or
unwilling to assure the security of their candidates and members; instead, the
coalition demanded a place in a provisional government which would then
hold elections. The government rejected that demand and accused the FMLN-
FDR of "trying to shoot their way into power."

This sort of argument about the status of elections also prevails, but less
distinctly, in the cases of Guatemala and Honduras. And it should be remembered that charges like these were the staple of Costa Rican politics in the
1940s. What such arguments demonstrate, quite simply, is the persistence of a
predemocratic attitude toward elections. Central American elections have traditionally served to legitimate those in power; so the main task of the opposition must be to undermine the legitimacy of the elections by any means
possible, for an opposition electoral victory would be inconceivable. The
government, seeking to remain in power, tries to structure the process to the
disadvantage of the opposition, while avoiding at all costs cancellation of the
elections and subsequent measures to perpetuate itself in power nakedly. As
long as rival political elites feel they cannot trust each other to hold political
power, elections will be no more than another means of war.

These parallels having been drawn, we must also emphasize the uniqueness
of the Nicaraguan case. When the government fell into the hands of revolutionaries in 1979, the effective political spectrum was radically expanded and the
center moved to the left. Instead of a mere struggle over which elite would
control the government, politics became an epic battle over fundamental

values. Revolution thus intensified the either/or quality of traditional politics by drastically widening the divergence between the alternatives.

The exclusion or self-exclusion of important political sectors from early elections in a democratic regime need not doom the democratic experiment. The first election in post–civil war Costa Rica saw the self-exclusion of the Calderonistas and the proscription of the Communists, but as previously noted, the regime later incorporated wider participation. Similarly, in both Colombia and Venezuela leftist forces were long nonparticipants in electoral politics, but finally were allowed to incorporate themselves. This progressive expansion of participation is a key component of the consolidation of democracy.

The questions Booth raises in chapter 1 may help us to consider the extent to which these initial elections following military regimes have contributed to the consolidation of democracy. All have certainly expanded the range and breadth of participation as compared with what prevailed under the military regimes (Booth's first and second questions), but it is not clear that the depth of participation (question 3) has been much enhanced, save in Nicaragua. The most extreme opponents of each government certainly did not accept that the elections were conducted fairly or in an environment conducive to the free exercise of participatory rights (Booth's question 4). Given that the legitimacy of the elections was widely controverted in each of the four countries, they could not have contributed much toward a "political culture of support for participation and for democratic rules" (Booth's question 6). Unlike the 1953 Costa Rica election cited earlier in this chapter, it is thus highly doubtful that recent elections in the other four Central American countries helped much to consolidate a stable regime under democratic rules (Booth's question 5).

The Consolidation of Democracy

Two contributions to this volume emphasize different aspects of the problem of democratic consolidation. Robert Trudeau makes the point that if democracy is to be established in Guatemala, the basic structure of economic and political power needs to be changed; it is not enough simply to hold honest elections. This point applies equally well to El Salvador and Honduras, and of course to Nicaragua. As long as income and property are distributed extremely unequally, and as long as power is concentrated in the hands of the military elite and its economic allies, no democratic transition can be consolidated. Democracy as an idea posits the political equality of citizens, and political equality is only an illusion in the face of extreme economic inequality. The idea of democracy presupposes a government broadly responsible and responsive to the popular will, an impossible goal as long as real power lies in the hands of the armed forces. Substantive democracy, in short, requires more equality and less military domination than currently prevails in most of Central America.

This requirement is of course relative. All existing democracies, whether in advanced industrial countries, in Latin America, or elsewhere in the Third World, are characterized by substantial economic inequality and less than complete governmental responsiveness to the popular will. But the Central American cases illustrate the limits of inequality and unresponsiveness beyond which no meaningful democracy can be established. Most of the elections considered in this book have done almost nothing to enhance the depth of democracy (the efficacy and autonomy of popular participation noted in Booth's question 3). Jonas's comparison of the Guatemalan and Nicaraguan elections makes a good case that the Nicaraguan election did in fact enhance the depth of participation. Recent Costa Rican elections may not have much enhanced depth, but at least they did not diminish Costa Rica's already respectable performance on this dimension.

The contribution of Miguel Gómez B. and Mitchell Seligson emphasizes another point about the consolidation of democracy. The public opinion data they report from Costa Rica show that even in times of extraordinary economic and political crisis, the response of Costa Rican voters to economic adversity is conditioned and moderated by an appreciation of democracy and a strong desire to maintain it. My own research indicates that the Costa Rican elites generally share this concern, and few are willing to pursue political agendas to the point of undermining the democratic regime (Peeler, 1985).

A consolidated democracy such as Costa Rica's has reached that point through a combination of cultural, structural, and political developments. Culturally, in addition to the appreciation of democracy as a value in itself (cf. Booth's question 6), a significant consensus on other politically salient issues is important insofar as it reduces the stakes of competition for power. A key development in political structure is the emergence of the competitive election process as a self-stabilizing, pressure-releasing mechanism that focuses public discontent on the opportunity to vote against the incumbents and obviates the need for opposition elites to conspire against the government; they stand a good chance to win the next elections anyway. Politically, a consolidated democracy is normally characterized by substantial accommodation among rival elites, who have confidence that those in power will not seek to exclude others (for example, through fraudulent elections) and will not assault the vital interests of the main opposition forces. The Costa Rican case illustrates that these cultural, structural, and political factors interact to create a regime with frequent alternation in control of the government but minimal policy changes from one government to the next, as policy oscillates in a narrow range between the two main alternative governing parties.

Democracy, as defined in the everyday sense, is clearly a good thing relative to the usual alternatives in Central America. Few Central Americans would hesitate if given the opportunity to live in a political system like Costa Rica's, and the Costa Ricans surely know the value of their system. Yet even Costa Rica is not a full democracy in the sense of real equality and effective accountability (cf. Booth's question 3). The advent of democratic institutions in El Salvador, Guatemala, and Honduras has at best mitigated the violation of human rights and the abuse of power, serving mainly to mask and legitimate unchanged structures of domination. Elections in these cases have contributed to what Booth has called, in chapter 1, the liberalization of authoritarian regimes, rather than to an authentic democratization. We ought not to be deceived about the extent or significance of the changes, but neither should we denigrate the value of whatever liberalization has occurred. For however long it lasts, there will be less repression. And there is the possibility that a more authentic democracy could evolve over time out of this initial liberalization. Several competitive elections successfully conducted, with some opposition victories, could begin to build confidence over time that did not exist initially (Booth's questions 4 and 6). The odds are against such an evolution in Central America, but it could happen under favorable circumstances, including, notably, an unambiguous and persistent U.S. policy supporting such democratization.

Nicaragua:
Toward a Model of Revolutionary Democracy

Nicaragua is attempting to carry out revolutionary changes in society while retaining a pluralistic political system, with independently organized political interests and with opposition parties competing in elections and represented in the National Assembly.[8] This is a unique effort, and, as Susanne Jonas argues, it may well prove impossible. The main thrust of the Sandinista political program has been the organization of peasants, workers, and the poor for effective participation within the revolutionary political process. This thrust is intimately related to the larger purpose that Joseph Collins (1984) has called "the logic of the majority," the evaluation of all decisions in terms of what will be most beneficial to the poor majority of the population. The revolution has thus defined itself as fundamentally democratic in aspiration (cf. Booth's questions 1, 2, and 3).

There are two key difficulties with conventional liberal democracy from the standpoint of democratic aspirations: first, inequality of political resources vitiates the formal equality of citizenship; second, pluralistic political processes diminish the effective accountability of the government to the popular majority. On the other hand, liberal democracy permits greater individual liberty and restricts abuses of authority more effectively than any other existing type of political system. Nicaragua's revolutionary model appears to hold the potential for retaining the strengths of liberal democracy while reducing its difficulties.

The apparent commitment of the Sandinista revolutionary leadership to the establishment of political pluralism within the revolution, and of effective restraints on governmental abuse of power, suggests that they are trying to create a revolutionary regime that retains the best of liberal democracy. Until now this commitment has not presented serious difficulties for the Sandinistas, because they remain by far the most popular political force. They won fair elections in 1984, and they would doubtless win again at the present time.

Nevertheless, there is ambivalence or division among the Sandinistas over the fundamental issue of revolutionary legitimacy. Are only Sandinistas and their supporters fully revolutionary, or is it possible for opponents of the Sandinistas to be fully incorporated in the revolutionary fold? If the Sandinistas see themselves as the exclusive custodians of the revolution, they will scarcely permit any of their opponents the ultimate political right, the possibility of winning an election and taking control of the government. It is undeniably true that under current conditions in Nicaragua, a loss of power by the Sandinistas would lead to a dismantling of their most fundamental initiatives for the transformation of Nicaraguan society. And if the Sandinistas were to yield power after an honest election, there is nothing in Nicaraguan history to suggest (democratic protestations of the internal and external opposition notwithstanding) that any successor government would permit the Sandinistas an honest chance to win the next election. In short, concrete historical conditions do not permit the Sandinistas to be completely liberal in their policy toward the opposition without risking the integrity of the revolution itself, not to mention their own destruction at the hands of vengeful and distrustful opponents.

Thus, the election of 1984, seen as part of the ongoing development of the Nicaraguan Revolution, has not unambiguously worked toward democratization in the sense of Booth's questions 4, 5, and 6. The election was fairly conducted, and the political environment of the campaign promoted the free exercise of participatory rights for the majority of Nicaraguans, but not for those whose support for the revolution was suspect. Suspicion between Sandinistas and their most militant opponents prevented the consolidation of a political culture fully supporting participation and democratic rules. The Nicaraguan Revolution raises pointedly—and poignantly—the issue of how wide a chasm of principle can be bridged by tolerance and the liberal civility of an election in which the opposition is actually allowed to win.

The emerging political model is neither liberal democratic nor Stalinist. The Sandinistas will permit their opponents to organize politically, to criticize and make demands of the government, and to compete in elections, so long as the basic legitimacy of the revolution and its Sandinista leadership is not questioned. They are not likely to permit an election victory by any existing opposition party or coalition. They are evolving not toward a Cuban-style single revolutionary party but rather toward a Mexican-style system tolerating substantial freedom of opposition without permitting the displacement of the ruling party.

Assuming an eventual decision by the U.S. government to cease its active attempts to destroy the revolutionary regime, an evolution in the indicated direction would permit the Sandinistas to continue with programs directed toward equalizing resources in society (for example, agrarian reform, health care, education). This is important from the point of view of democracy because it will permit the less well-off to increase their relative weight in the political process, increasing the range, breadth, and depth of popular participation. The equalization of resources is thus an important element in the empowerment of the majority, without which meaningful democracy is inconceivable.

Nevertheless, even a radically egalitarian society may not be democratic in the sense of popular participation in rule. That aspect of empowerment assumes the effective accountability of the government to the people. Liberal democracy in general has done poorly in assuring equality of resources, but its mechanism of competitive elections, with more or less frequent alternation of governing parties, is the best means yet devised to secure government accountability. Moreover, from the point of view of regime maintenance, competitive elections and party alternation are an unsurpassed mechanism for releasing the pressure of popular discontent. The relative unresponsiveness and corruption of the Mexican regime suggests the consequences of having no such effective mechanism.

Nicaragua, and even Cuba, with revolutionary leadership still in the first generation, can minimize corruption and unresponsiveness insofar as their leaders are morally committed to the ideals of the revolution, but as generational succession occurs, it will be increasingly difficult to avoid the sorts of abuses so evident in Mexico. Alternation with the existing opposition, on the other hand, even if there were sufficient popular support to make it conceivable, would pose unacceptable risks to the integrity of the revolution.[9] The path to establishing a revolutionary democracy thus lies open to the Nicaraguans, but it is a path full of hazards.

Notes

1. Literally, of course, democracy means rule by the people. Contemporary everyday usage, associated with pluralist theory, abandons the literal definition and interprets democracy as a regime with near-universal adult suffrage, periodic competitive elections in which opposition parties have a reasonable chance to win, and widely respected freedoms of speech and political organization. I have elsewhere called such a polity "a liberal political system legitimized by the appearance of democracy" (Peeler, 1985:6). John Booth in chapter 1 of this volume partially reaffirms the classical focus on popular rule, defining democracy as "popular participation in rule." In this chapter we will use the everyday definition descriptively, while Booth's definition will be taken to embody the aspiration for a more authentic democracy.

2. With the recent exception of Costa Rica, Central American countries have been characterized by a cyclical alternation of periods of authoritarian rule (frequently military) and transitional periods of constitutional government (usually short) terminated by the imposition of a new authoritarian regime. I have elsewhere called this the hegemonic cycle (Peeler, 1985).

3. It should not be forgotten that the establishment of the Costa Rican democracy as the outcome of the crisis of the 1940s was substantially influenced by shifting U.S. policy toward Communists in Latin American governments. The reformist President

Calderón Guardia had Communist backing with the blessing of the United States during World War II, but in the context of the emerging cold war Calderón's hand-picked successor, Teodoro Picado (1944–48), was much more vulnerable to opposition attacks on his Communist support (Peeler, 1985:chap. 2).

4. The role of elections in supporting U.S. foreign policy is explored provocatively in Herman and Brodhead (1984).

5. On the general subject of transitions to democracy, see O'Donnell, Schmitter, and Whitehead (1986), Malloy and Seligson (1987), and Linz, Lipset, and Diamond (forthcoming).

6. For a provocative comparative analysis of the significance of such elite pacts, see Higley and Burton (1986).

7. For a fine overview of the campaign and election, see Latin American Studies Association (1984).

8. For a provocative perspective on this theme, see the chapter by Coraggio and Irvin in Irvin and Gorostiaga (1985) and Coraggio (1985).

9. It might be possible, in the absence of current external threats, for the Sandinistas to engineer the establishment of a new political center within the revolution, in which voters would have a real choice between two or three revolutionary tendencies, each committed to maintaining the foundations of the revolution but differing in emphasis. For example, there might be a Sandinista party committed to pushing revolutionary change more rapidly and another emphasizing consolidation. This would have the potential of establishing a self-stabilizing centrist dynamic within the revolution, marginalizing the nonrevolutionary political forces in the same way the left is typically marginalized in most existing liberal democracies: people don't vote for it because it can't win; it can't win because people don't vote for it.

References

Collins, Joseph. 1984. *What Difference Could a Revolution Make?* Rev. ed. San Francisco: Institute for Food and Development Policy.

Coraggio, José Luis. 1985. *Nicaragua: Revolution and Democracy*. Boston: Allen and Unwin.

García Márquez, Gabriel. 1975. *The Autumn of the Patriarch*. New York: Harper and Row.

Herman, Edward, and Brodhead, Frank. 1984. *Demonstration Elections: U.S.-Staged Elections in the Dominican Republic, Vietnam, and El Salvador*. Boston: South End Press.

Higley, John, and Burton, Michael. 1986. Elite Settlements. Revision of a paper presented to the American Sociological Association, 30 August–3 September, New York.

Irvin, George, and Gorostiaga, Xabier, eds. 1985. *Towards an Alternative for Central America and the Caribbean.* London: Allen and Unwin.

Latin American Studies Association. 1984. *The Electoral Process in Nicaragua: Domestic and International Influences.* Report of the Latin American Studies Association Delegation to Observe the Nicaraguan General Election of 4 November 1984. Austin: Latin American Studies Association.

Linz, Juan; Lipset, Seymour Martin; and Diamond, Larry, eds. Forthcoming. *Democracy in Developing Nations.* Stanford: Hoover Institution.

Malloy, James M., and Seligson, Mitchell A., eds. 1987. *Authoritarians and Democrats: Regime Transition in Latin America.* Pittsburgh: University of Pittsburgh Press.

O'Donnell, Guillermo; Schmitter, Philippe; and Whitehead, Laurence, eds. 1986. *Transitions from Authoritarian Rule.* Baltimore: Johns Hopkins University Press.

Peeler, John. 1985. *Latin American Democracies: Colombia, Costa Rica, Venezuela.* Chapel Hill: University of North Carolina Press.

Contributors

John A. Booth, Professor and Chairperson of Political Science at the University of North Texas, has researched and published widely on political participation, elections, political violence and revolution in Nicaragua, Costa Rica, and Guatemala. He is the author of *The End and the Beginning: The Nicaraguan Revolution* (Westview Press, 1985).

José Z. García is Associate Professor of Government at New Mexico State University. He has traveled widely in Central America and is presently completing a book on El Salvador.

Miguel Gómez B. is Professor of Statistics at the University of Costa Rica. Receiving his graduate education at the University of Michigan, he has conducted extensive survey research on Costa Rican social and political phenomena for governmental and international agencies for many years. He has published over fifty books and articles, many of them in the field of demography.

Susanne Jonas has published extensively during the last twenty years on Central American politics and political economy. Among the books she has written and edited are *Guatemala (NACLA), Guatemala: Tyranny on Trial, Nicaragua under Siege,* and *Revolution and Intervention in Central America.* She is currently teaching Latin American Studies at the University of California, Santa Cruz, and is on the staff of Global Options, a research and advocacy center in San Francisco.

John A. Peeler, Professor of Political Science at Bucknell University, has conducted extensive research on the origins of democratic rule in Latin America. He is the author of *Latin American Democracies: Colombia, Costa Rica, Venezuela* (University of North Carolina Press, 1985).

Mark B. Rosenberg is Professor of Political Science and Director of the Latin American and Caribbean Center, Florida International University. He has published on social policy and politics in Central America, including Costa Rica and Honduras. He is cooeditor with Philip L. Shepard of *Honduras Confronts Its Future: Contending Perspectives on Critical Issues* (Lynne Reiner Publications, 1986).

Mitchell A. Seligson is Professor of Political Science and Director of the Center for Latin American Studies, University of Pittsburgh. He has conducted research on peasants, agrarian development, political participation, and democratization in Costa Rica, Guatemala, Honduras, Ecuador, and Jamaica. His most recent books include a co-edited volume with James M. Malloy, *Authoritarians and Democrats: Regime Transition in Latin America* (University of Pittsburgh Press, 1987) and *The Gap Between Rich and Poor: Contending Perspectives on the Political Economy of Development* (Westview Press, 1984).

Robert H. Trudeau, Associate Professor of Political Science at Providence College, has published widely on Guatemalan politics. He recently spent a year in Guatemala as a Fulbright lecturer.

Index